ANARCHISM:

Its Philosophy and Scientific Basis

As Defined by Some of Its Apostles.

"If the people are silent under oppression, it is lethargy,—the forerunner of Death to Public Liberty." *Thomas Jefferson.*

BY

A. R. PARSONS.

CHICAGO:
MRS. A. R. PARSONS, PUBLISHER,
785 MILWAUKEE AVE.

COPYRIGHT 1887,

BY

MRS. A. R. PARSONS.

*THE REFORMER.

All grim and soiled and brown with tan,
   I saw a Strong One, in his wrath,
Smiting the godless shrines of man
   Along his path.

The Church beneath her trembling dome
   Essayed in vain her ghostly charm;
Wealth shook within his gilded home
   With strange alarm.

Fraud from his secret chambers fled
   Before the sunlight bursting in;
Sloth drew her pillow o'er her head
   To drown the din.

"Spare," Art implored, "yon holy pile;
   That grand, old time-worn turret, spare;"
Meek Reverence kneeling in the aisle
   Cried out "Forbear!"

Gray-bearded Use, who, deaf and blind,
   Groped for his old accustomed stone,
Leaned on his staff, and wept to find
   His seat o'erthrown.

Young Romance raised his dreamy eyes,
   O'erhung with paly locks of gold,—
"Why smite," he asked in sad surprise,
   "The fair, the old?"

Yet louder rang the Strong One's stroke,
   Yet nearer flashed the axe's gleam;
Shuddering and sick of heart I woke
   As from a dream.

I looked: Aside the cloud-dust rolled—
   The Waster seemed the Builder too;
Up springing from the ruined Old
   I saw the New.

'Twas but the ruin of the bad,—
   The wasting of the wrong and ill;
Whate'er of good the old time had
   Was living still.

Calm grew the brows of him I feared;
   The frown which awed me passed away,
And left behind a smile which cheered
   Like breaking day.

The grain grew green on battle plains,
   O'er swarded war-mounds grazed the cow,
The slave stood forging from his chains
   The spade and plow.

Where frowned the fort, pavillions gay,
   And cottage windows, flower-entwined,
Looked out upon the peaceful bay
   And hills behind.

Through vine-wreathed cups with wine once red,
   The lights on brimming crystal fell,
Drawn, sparkling, from the rivulet head
   And mossy well.

Through prison walls, like heaven-sent hope,
   Fresh breezes blew, and sunbeams strayed,
And with the idle gallows rope
   The young child played.

Where the doomed victim in his cell
   Had counted o'er the weary hours,
The school girls, answering to the bells
   Came crowned with flowers.

Grown wiser for the lessons given,
   I fear no longer, for I know
That, where the share is deepest driven,
   The best fruits grow.

The out-worn rite, the old abuse,
   The pious fraud transparent grown,
The good held captive in the use
   Of wrong alone,—

These wait their doom, from that great law
   Which makes the past time serve to-day;
And fresher life the world shall draw
   From their decay.

Oh backward-looking son of time!
   The new is old, the old is new,
The cycle of a change sublime
   Still sweeping through.

So wisely taught the Indian seer;
   Destroying Seva, forming Brahm,
Who wake by turns, earth's love and fear
   Are one, the same.

Idly, as thou, in that old day
   Thou mournest, did thy sire repine;
So in his time, thy child grown gray
   Shall sigh for thine.

But life shall on and upward go;
   Th' eternal step of Progress beats
To that great anthem, calm and slow,
   Which God repeats.

Take heart!—The Waster builds again—
   A charmed life old Goodness hath;
The tares may perish, but the grain
   Is not for death.

God works in all things; all obey
   His first propulsion from the night;
Wake thou and watch!—the world is gray
   With morning light!
           —WHITTIER

---

* This poem had long been a favorite with Mr. Parsons, and was recited by him to the jailers and the reporters but a short time before his death.

DEDICATED

To the toiling masses in every land, striving for their Economic Emancipation. not the least of whom is my beloved wife,
LUCY E. PARSONS.

"Let the voice of the people be heard! O—"

CONTENTS.

PART I.

		PAGE
CHAPTER I.	CAPITALISM—ITS DEVELOPMENT IN THE UNITED STATES	11
II.	" " " " " (continued)	15
III.	" " " " " "	19
IV.	" —ITS ORIGIN AND DEVELOPMENT IN EUROPE	21

PART II.

CHAPTER I.	ANARCHY ON TRIAL	51
II.	VIEWS OF THE PRISONERS	53
	AUGUST SPIES ON ANARCHY	53
	ADDRESS OF MICHAEL SCHWAB	66
	OSCAR NEEBE'S REMARKS	72
	ADOLPH FISCHER	74
	ADDRESS OF LOUIS LINGG	83
	GEORGE ENGEL ON ANARCHISM	86
	SAMUEL FIELDEN ON SOCIALISM AND ANARCHISM	89
	ALBERT R. PARSONS ON ANARCHISM	92
	PARSONS' PLEA FOR ANARCHY	107
	LUCY E. PARSONS ON ANARCHY	109
III.	THE SCIENTIFIC BASIS OF ANARCHY	111
IV.	THE COMING ANARCHY	123
V.	AN ANARCHIST ON ANARCHY	136
VI.	DYER D. LUM ON ANARCHY	149
	1. What is Anarchy?	
	2. What Anarchy Offers.	
	3. Who should be Anarchists.	
	4. Co-operation.	
VII.	ANARCHY—C. L. James	159
VIII.	THE SOCIAL REVOLUTION	164

APPENDIX.

PHILOSOPHIC ANARCHISM	171
A. R. PARSONS' APPEAL	178
OPEN LETTER TO GOVERNOR OGLESBY	185
LAW VS. LIBERTY	186
VIEWS OF GENERAL PARSONS	188
LETTER TO GEORGE FRANCIS TRAIN	193
ARREST OF MRS. PARSONS AND CHILDREN	194
LAST HOURS OF LIFE	197
LAST LETTER TO AN OLD COMRADE	200

PUBLISHER'S NOTE

To my Friends and the Public:

With the aid of friends, I am enabled to present for your perusal and consideration, the last efforts of my dear deceased husband, to enlighten the seekers after truth and information upon the great and burning questions of the age: the relations of the wage-earner to the wage-absorber in society.

This book, as the reader is doubtless aware, was prepared near the close of an eighteen months' incarceration in a lonely, narrow, prison-cell. If it should at times lack any of the old-time vigor which characterized his former writings, please remember that the author was debarred from all the advantages and elements that go to making up a full and complete life; that from the day on which he voluntarily came forward and gave himself into the hands of the State, (the "Law and Order" people,) he had never breathed a breath of pure, fresh air, never looked upon a growing sprig of grass, never beheld either earth or sky; that nothing met his eye but frowning bare stone walls relieved only by bolts, bars and chains; that in his 6x8 inner tomb he was confined twenty one hours six days in the week, and forty hours on "the Lord's day"—from Saturday afternoon until Monday morning; and that he was denied the company of friends excepting the few moments when granted the privilege of conversing with them through a close wire netting, and having never touched the hand of even his wife, save twice, through all the long period of his imprisonment.

Should there be a tinge of sadness in these last words of a noble and courageous soul, remember they were written beneath the shadow of that coming tragedy, whose gloom fell athwart all true and loving hearts.

With these few remarks—meaning no apology where none is needed—I present to you these last efforts of one who lived in the world with the one purpose of making it better and happier for his having lived.

And now, I speak as one who knows and has the right to speak: No nobler, purer truer, more unselfish man ever lived, than Albert R. Parsons, and when he and his comrades were sacrificed on the altar of class hatred, the people of the nineteenth century committed the hideous crime of strangling their best friends.

Fraternally yours,

LUCY E. PARSONS.

TO THE READER.

To trace the origin and growth of the Wage-Labor system, known as modern Capitalism, to delineate the Philosophy and Scientific Basis of the modern Labor movement, known as Anarchism, is the purport of this little book.

The first part of this work gives a historical outline of the period prior to the Revolution of 1776 up to the present time in the United States; it also traces the origin and development of the wage system in Europe from the fourteenth century, and contains copious extracts from Karl Marx's "Capital" on the economic law of wages.

The second part is devoted to extracts from the speeches of the eight condemned Anarchists, Samuel Fielden, August Spies, Oscar Neebe, Adolph Fischer, Louis Lingg, George Engle, A. R. Parsons and Michel Schwab on the subject of "Anarchy," which were delivered before the court in reply to the question why sentence should not be pronounced; also articles defining Anarchy, by Peter Krapotkin, Elisee Reclus, C. L. James and other well-known Anarchists.

This book has been written and compiled in response to the public demand for information upon the subjects treated of. The circumstances under which the work has been performed, in my dungeon, beneath the shadow of the gallows, should. if aught could, lend additional interest and importance to the matters presented therein. If the public is furnished information, or assisted in reaching a clearer understanding of the great question of *Capital and Labor* by a perusal of these pages, I shall deem that a sufficient reward for my humble effort to supply it.

THE AUTHOR.

Cell 29, Cook Co., Jail.
Chicago, Illinois, Oct. 27th, 1887.

HOLLY LODGE, KENSINGTON,
LONDON, May 23, 1857.

As long as you (Americans) have a boundless extent of fertile and unoccupied land, your laboring population will be far more at ease than the laboring population of the old world, and while that is the case the Jeffersonian politics may continue to exist without causing any fatal calamity. But the time will come when New England will be as thickly peopled as old England. Wages will be low, and will fluctuate with you as well as with us. You will have your Manchesters and Birminghams, and in those Manchesters and Birminghams hundreds of thousands of artisans will assuredly be sometimes out of work. Then your institutions will be fairly brought to the test. Distress everywhere makes the laborer mutinous and discontented.

* * * The day will come when in the state of New York there will be a multitude of people, none of whom has had more than half a breakfast, or expects to have more than half a dinner. On one side is a statesman preaching patience, respect for vested rights, strict observance of public faith. On the other is a demagogue ranting about the tyranny of capitalists and usurers, and asking why anybody should be permitted to drink champagne and ride in a carriage, while thousands of honest folks are in want of necessaries. What is the workingman likely to do when he hears his children cry for bread?—LORD MACAULEY.

PART I.

CHAPTER I.

CAPITALISM—ITS DEVELOPMENT IN THE UNITED STATES.

Among all nations, the United States of America has alone possessed the opportunity for developing representative or Republican government to its utmost. Separated by two oceans, isolated and comparatively secure from sudden invasion or the diplomatic embroglios of imperialistic Europe and Asia, the united capacity of Republican government to minister to the peace and welfare of its citizens and the experience—history—of one hundred years has formed the record from which the living present learns its lesson of the past.

Free government, a free people, was the talismanic charm which caused the emigrant to abandon the old world and hasten to the new.

The population of the colonies in 1776 was 3,500,000. Today the population of the United States is estimated at 65,000,000. The controlling influence which impelled the emigrant to the United States was the belief in the inducement held out that a home for his loved ones could be acquired. It is, therefore, a fact, that the United States has been developed and populated because of economic rather than political influences. It has been and is still the belief of many that the comparative economic freedom which the poor have enjoyed in this country was owing to its political institutions, its republican form of government. Lord Macauley, whose prognostication is quoted at the opening of this chapter, foresaw what experience has since demonstrated, to-wit: That the Republic itself was the result and the cause of the comparative economic liberty which prevailed in America.

The revolution of 1776 was precipitated when the British government sought to impose "taxation without representation" upon the colonies, but there was a long antecedent train of offenses which the colonists had endured. The British nobility, aristocrats and landlords had been for years past engaged in seizing upon the wild lands of America and subjecting its inhabitants to the servitude prevailing in the old world. A few noblemen held "patents" from George III, which covered vast regions of territory and embraced millions of acres. The revolution of 1776 was inspired by determination to escape the tyranny of British rule, from the oppressions of which most of the American colonists had fled. The authors of the Declaration of Independence gave the key-note of that struggle when they proclaimed the inalienable Rights of Man as the issue involved. During the seven years' war which followed, and for five years afterward (1787) the inhabitants of the colonies were practically without government or law. Thomas Paine, of whom it has been said he did as much with his pen as Washington had done with his sword for American liberty, describes in his writings the motives and purposes of the men engaged in that conflict. Paine's work, entitled "Rights of Man," embodied the "American Idea" of liberty as then contended for. He says:

> It is therefore a perversion of terms to say that a charter (government) gives rights. It operates by a contrary effect,—that of taking rights away. Rights are inherently in all the inhabitants, but charters, by annulling those rights in the majority, leave the right by exclusion in the hands of a few. If charters were constructed so as to express in direct terms "that every inhabitant who is not a member of a corporation shall not exercise the right of voting," such charters would, in the face, be charters, not of rights, but of exclusion. The effect is the same under the form in which they now stand; the only persons on whom they now operate are the persons whom they exclude.

The period following the war, when the colonies or states were engaged in framing the national constitution, is most instructive, as it was now that the fruits of that struggle were to be garnered. Some of the states were slow to enter the compact and some for a time refused to do so, such was the fear of the people for centralized government. Finally, a reconciliation was brought about mainly by those whose property rights gave them influence and power, and delegates from all the states were chosen to the national convention to form the Federal Constitution. Here were assembled men of varying ideas, instincts and interests. But the predominating influence was the property interest, property in land, etc., but especially in slaves. The people having struggled and suffered for seven long and bloody years, were alive to the importance of the work of the convention and its possible effects upon their welfare. But there were those who reverenced human rights only so far as these did not intrude upon their property rights. Thus began the game of Politics. The convention found it necessary to conduct their proceedings with closed doors, excluding from its sessions all who were not members. Here, for four months the "Star Chamber" (secret) sessions were held in an endeavor to bring about a compromise of divergent interests and ideas upon the property question. The debates were long and heated. At times the convention was threatened with disruption. There were those who believed in a landed aristocracy and restricted suffrage, led by Alexander Hamilton; others wanted free land and manhood suffrage; and still others contended the liberation of the chattel slave was included in the meaning of the Declaration of Independence,— and vice versa. A compromise was finally reached which left the rights of property in slaves, land and money intact. The assertion of the Declaration of Independence that "all men were created free and equal, and possessed with certain inalienable rights, among which were life, liberty and the pursuit of happiness" was defended by those who favored a constitution framed in accordance with the intent and spirit of that document. The slave holding interest objected and held that the blacks—the chattel slaves— were not included in the meaning or intent of the Declaration. John

Adams, the aristocrat, who also favored a limited monarchy as against Jefferson, Franklin, Paine, Henry, Washington and others, in the memorable debate upon this question said: "What matters it whether you give the food and clothes to the slaves direct, or whether you just give him enough in wages to purchase the same?" This view of the question finally prevailed and was accepted as the basis of compromise. The rights of property triumphed. The wage-worker was categorical with the chattel slave. Indeed the difference was recognized among the wealthy class as existing not only in form but identical in effect. The Constitution as agreed upon by the convention was submitted to the states—the people for ratification or rejection. Though dissatisfied, the people were induced to accept it, on the ground that universal suffrage, vesting all law—making power in the people; guaranteeing free speech, free press, and unmolested assemblage, the right to keep and bear arms; speedy trial by an impartial jury; and protection against unreasonable and unlawful search or seizure of persons or property—were constitutional safeguards deemed ample protection for their rights.

The United States formed a vast, unsettled, inexhaustible region. A comparatively small strip of country from Maine to Florida was sparsely inhabited. All who desired could acquire a competency. The wage-class felt no apprehension on that score. The doors of the nation were thrown open and the poor and miserable and despoiled of every clime were invited to come to the "land of the free and home of the brave" as the "harbor and refuge of the oppressed." That invitation was eagerly heard and quickly accepted, and to this fact alone is due the rapid development and growth of the Republic. For years after the adoption of the Constitution the slave trade flourished and thousands upon thousands of ignorant helpless Africans were kidnapped and brought in chains to the United States. The treatment of the great populous tribes of Indians was of a similar character. Those who could not be subdued and enslaved were killed, and as America was the native heath of the Indian they chose death rather than slavery, until there remains scarcely a remnant of this once powerful race upon the continent. About 1830, when population had greatly increased, in common with land values and other property, the special advantages of chattel-slave labor which was so apparent in a new, unsettled country began to diminish. With a growth of population came an augmentation of wage-laborers, and the modes of industry, such as manufacture, etc., where not very well adapted to chattel labor. *It began to appear that wage labor was cheaper and therefore more remunerative to capital than was chattel-slave labor.* There arose in consequence conflicting interests upon this subject, which by degrees—as population increased—developed into sectional conflicts, which were geographically designated "north" and "south."

For certain forms of labor—agriculture for instance—chattel-slave labor was considered to be more profitable than wage labor. But in manufacture and all departments of skilled industry the labor of wage-workers was preferred because more remunerative. The supply of chattel-slaves was cut off by a law enacted prohibiting the slave trade, and this fact was alone sufficient to cause the death-blow to that form of labor. But the simple, primitive forms of production for which the labor of chattel-slaves was adopted caused the owners of that form of capital to invest it where it would bring the greatest returns. Therefore the slave-holding interests gravitated to the southern portion of the United States, where a mild climate, lengthened seasons and consequently cheaper clothes, fuel and shelter was to be obtained. The propertied class—capitalists—were intent only on profits and losses. Out of these two forms of labor—chattel and wage—arose the "irrepressible conflict" and the political shibboleth, "America must be all slave or all free." The slave-holding interests became alarmed at the increasing power of the wage-labor system. They perceived their "vested right" to lawfully, constitutionally hold property in slaves to be threatened. Their power had until now been supreme in national affairs and they were blinded with arrogance. They refused all overtures to peaceably manumit their slaves by means of gradual emancipation, to be recompensed out of the public treasury, but, on the contrary, indignantly rejected all such proposals and insisted upon their constitutional right to extend slavery into the Territories. Their attitude sharpened the contest between the wage-labor capitalists and the chattel slave-owners. Upon the election of Abraham Lincoln to the Presidency of the United States in 1860 "the South" seceeded from "the North" and set up a Confederacy which recognized chattle-slave labor as its corner-stone. Mr. Lincoln, though in sentiment an "Abolitionist," an ardent defender of man's abstract right to life and liberty, was also, for the time being, the representative of the wage-labor system. The exigencies of the war of the rebellion afforded the sought-for opportunity, the Emancipation Proclamation was issued as "a military necessity." Chattel-slave labor was abolished and the system of wage-labor established in its stead. While upon its surface this struggle between the "North" and the "South" was waged ostensibly in behalf of "free" against "slave" labor, and was apparently a political question waged for the preservation of the Union, it was, in fact, an economic question growing out of the two diverse and conflicting systems of labor, viz.: chattel and wage. The owners of capital in the form of chattel-slaves were compelled by armed revolution to relinquish that form of property. They threw themselves as a barrier across the pathway of societary evolution, of historic development and were swept aside by its irresistable force.

The Rebellion of 1861 was a failure. The Rebellion of 1776 was a success. The former was a struggle against the evolutionary development of modern capitalism; the latter was fought on the line with and for progress. Both contests are generally regarded as political; but the underlying, moving cause in each was economic. The apparently political character of these two revolutionary struggles arises from the fact the contest in both instances was waged by one portion of the propertied class against the other upon questions of property.

Ever since the organization of the Government of the United States there has existed among the people a small, but earnest minority, known as "Abolitionists," because they advanced the abstract right of "all men" to "life, liberty and the pursuit of happiness." But the Abolitionists were an insignificant minority. Their demands were never heeded until the requirements of modern capitalism began to require an extension of the system of wage labor in preference to the system of chattel-slave labor. Capital invested in wage labor and capital invested in chattel-slave labor were hostile in their interests. The slave-holding interests were more sensitive and apprehensive of injury and were in consequence easily mobilized on the political battle-field. From the organization of the Government up to the slave-holders' rebellion in 1861 the propertied interests in chattel-slaves had practical control and direction of the affairs of Government.

CHAPTER II.

CAPITALISM—ITS DEVELOPMENT IN THE UNITED STATES.—CONTINUED.

With the termination of the war of 1861 began the second epoch of capitalism in the United States. The ex-chattel slave was enfranchised, —made a political sovereign. He was now a "freeman" without an inch of soil, a cent of money, a stitch of clothes or a morsel of food. He was free to compete with his fellow wage-worker for an opportunity to serve capital. The conditions of his freedom consisted in the right to work on the terms dictated by his employer, or—starve. There no longer existed any sectional conflicts or other conflicts of a disturbing political nature. All men were now "free and equal before the law." A period of unprecedented activity in capitalistic circles set in. Steam and electricity applied to machinery was employed in almost every department of industry, and compared with former times fabulous wealth was created.

Political parties, no longer divided in interest upon property questions, all legislation was centered upon a development of the resources of the country. To this end vast tracts of goverment land, amounting to many million acres, equalling in extent seven states the size of Illinois were donated as subsidies to the projectors of railways. The national debt, incurred to prosecute the rebellion, and amounting to three billion dollars was capitalized, by creating interest upon the bonds. Hundreds of millions were given as bonuses to proposed railways, steamship lines, etc. A protective tariff law was enacted which for the past twenty years has imposed a tax upon the people amounting to one billion dollars annually. A National Banking system was established which gave control of finance to a banking monopoly. By means of these and other laws capitalist combinations, monopolies, syndicates, and trusts were created and fostered, until they obtained absolute control of the principle avenues of industry, commerce and trade. Arbitrary prices are fixed by these combinations and the consumers—mainly the poor—are compelled by their necessities to pay whatever price is exacted. Thus during the past twenty-five years,—since the abolition of the chattel-slave labor system—twenty-five thousand millionaires have been created, who by their combinations control and virtually own the fifty billion dollars estimate wealth of the United States, while on the other hand twenty million wage workers have been created whose poverty forces them into a ceaseless competition with each other for opportunity to earn the bare necessities of existence. What had, therefore, required generations to accomplish in Great Britain and the continent, was achieved during the past twenty-five years in the United States, to wit: The practical destruction of the middle-class (small dealers, farmers, manufacturers, etc.), and the division of society into two classes—the wage worker and capitalist. While the fabulous fortunes resulting from legislation enacted in the name of the people were being acquired, the people were not conscious of the evil effects which would flow from those laws. Not until the evil effects were felt were they aware of the slavery to which they had been lawfully reduced. The first great pinch of the laws was felt throughout the whole country in the financial panic of 1873-77, resulting in the latter year in wide-spread strikes of the unemployed and poorly paid wage class. In response to the demand for information upon economic matters, Bureaus of Labor were established in many States, as also for the general government at Washington. These statistics related to operations and effects of capitalism in the chief departments of industry and trade. The absorption of the smaller industries etc., etc., into the great corporations, syndicates, etc., was very rapid. The National commercial agency (Bradstreet's) furnished statistics showing unprecedented bankruptcies. The Agricultural Bureaus of the various States gave accounts of simular depressions in agriculture. Illinois, the richest agricultural State in the United States and for that reason a criterion for the others, is shown by the statistics of the State Board of Agriculture for 1886 to have over three-fourths of its farms mortgaged, and that the crops for the last five years have not paid the cost of production! Illinois is the greatest corn producing State in the Union and the statistics given by the State Board of Agriculture on that crop is as follows:

> For the year 1882 at a loss of.................$1,273,571.00
> For the year 1883 at a loss of................. 8,621,440.00
> For the year 1884 at a loss of.................11,780,554.00
> For the year 1885 at a loss of.................10,831,701.00
> For the year 1886 at a loss of.................19,070,209.00
>
> Total loss in five years...................$51,577,475.00

The Bureau also states that more than two-thirds of the farms which have suffered these losses are mortgaged. Investigation shows the same condition exists in every State. Statistics show that the condition of the farming class, as a class, is far worse than it was twenty or thirty years ago. The American farmer as a class is enslaved by mortgages, and rapidily drifting into peasantry and serfdom agriculture. Meanwhile the stupendously increasing aggregation of wealth into the hands of a few is going on.

In manufacture statistics it is shown that while the number of manufacturers are diminishing from 10 to 30 per cent every year the remainder are increasing their wealth enormously, and that while the wages of labor have been diminishing yearly the number of workers wanting work and unable to procure it have rapidly increased. The United States census for 1880, gives in Census Bulletin 302 elaborate details of capital invested, number of persons employed, the amount of wages paid, value of materials used, the value of all the establishments of manufacturing industry, gas excepted, in each of the States and Territories as follows:

The number of industrial establishments is 253,840, having a capital of $2,790,223,506. Of this number New York has 42,739, with a capital of $514,246,575, employing 364,551 males above sixteen years of age, and 137,393 females above the age of fifteen years. The total amount paid in wages during that year aggregated $298,634,029, and the value of the products was $1,080,638,696.

Pennsylvania follows the Empire state with 31,225 workshops, 387,112 employes, and a capital of $447,499,993. The value of its products is $744,748,045, or $335,890,651 less than that of New York. In the northern states, including Maine, New Hampshire, Vermont, Massachusetts, Connecticut, Rhode Island, New York, New Jersey, Pennsylvania, Ohio, Indiana and Michigan, there are 153,453 places of industry, or 8,982 more than in the states of Delaware, Maryland, Virginia, West Virginia, North Carolina, South Carolina, Kentucky, Tennessee, Georgia, Alabama, Mississippi, Florida, Arkansas and Texas.

Rhode Island, the smallest State in the Union, has 2,205 workshops, which is 1,459 more than Delaware, the next smallest, and only 791 less than Texas, the largest State in the Union. In amount of capital involved, however, Rhode Island is $66,330,382 ahead of Texas, and the value of her products is $104,163,621, while that of Texas is only $20,719,128.

The District of Columbia, with 971 establishments and $5,552,526 capital, is ahead of Florida and Colorado in the value of its products and in the number of workshops. The District employs 5,495 males above sixteen years of age, and 1,389 females above fifteen years of age, and 1,389 children and youths. The establishments pay to these hands $33,924,612 in wages yearly, and the products manufactured aggregate $11,882,316, the value of materials used being $3,365,400.

Colorado, the youngest State, which was admitted into the Union in 1876, can show but very little increase in the value of its products over that of the District of Columbia. This State has 599 establishments and a capital of $4,311,714. It employs 4,625 males, 266 females, 156 children, and pays in wages $2,314,427, or $1,610,185 less than is paid for wages in this District.

Forming the rear of this long line of States and Territories comes Arizona with 66 workshops and an invested capital of $272,600. There are 216 men employed in the Territory, which, added to the two females and the two children, make a total of 220 persons actively engaged in industrial occupations. The total amount of wages is $111,180, while the value of the products from these establishments is $615,655.

In the 253,840 workshops throughout the country, the average number of hands employed is 2,738,950. Of this number 2,025,279 are males, 531,753 females, and 181,918 children. The total amount of wages paid out during the year is $947,919,674, and the value of the products is $5,369,667,706.

The list quotes the value of the materials used in manufacturing as aggregating $3,394,340,029, which leaves a profit on products of $1,975,327,677. When the amount paid for wages is deducted from this, there remains a clear margin on the figures quoted of $1,027,408,003.

From the statistics given above we learn that the average wages of each wage worker amounts to $304 per annum, and the average annual net profit on the labor product of each wage worker is $374. The United States census for the year 1880 contains tables which show that the daily average product of each wage worker in manufacturing industry is valued at $10, and the daily average wage at $1.15. The increase in the quantity of wealth which a wage laborer can now produce as compared to 1880 is ascribed to the increased application of machinery and the increased sub-division and consequent simplification of the process of production. To this fact is also due the diminution of the share (wages) of their product, which the workers now receive, as well as the increase of the number of enforced idle since 1880.

The United States Census for 1880 gives the annual average wages of each laborer engaged in manufacture at $304, and the annual average net profit on capital invested at $374. In other words, each laborer produced values amounting to $678, for which they received $304 in wages, the remaining $374 being the amount which the owners of capital charged them for its use.

The wage system is the foundation upon which the United States Government, in common with all other governments, rests. This foundation was laid in the Constitutional Convention of 1787, as described by John Adams when he said: "What matters it whether you give the food and clothes to the slave direct, or whether you just give him enough in wages to purchase the same?" Nearly one hundred years later the citizens of the United States appealed to armed revolution; the Constitution was set aside and millions of property and nearly a million human lives were sacrificed in order to place the chattel slave upon the same industrial plane as the wage worker. Before the inauguration of the war of the rebellion offers were made to the slaveholders to pay them $1,000 a piece for their slaves, as being far cheaper and more humane than to embroil the nation in civil war. That price was indignantly rejected, as being too small; besides the slaveholders held that chattel slavery was a "divine institution," and it would, therefore, be sacrilege to attempt its abolition. In 1880, sixteen years after the close of the rebellion, the United States Census states there was invested in the woolen industries of the country capital amounting to $159,000,000, and the number of wage workers employed 100,000. The capital represented an average investment of $995 to each wage laborer. The cost of raw material was $164,000,000; the value of manufactured material was placed at $267,000,000. The increased value of the manufactured material over the raw is placed at $107,000,000. That upon $995 invested, an annual profit of $343 was obtained, while the average annual wages of each operative was $293, or fifty dollars less than the income derived from the $995.

Chattel slaves before the war were valued at $1,000 apiece. Sixteen years after the abolition of chattel slavery, wage workers employed in manufactures in John Adams' State (Massachusetts) were worth, commercially, $850, or $150 less than the former chattel slave.

These statistics prove the claim made by the supporters of the wage system of labor that wage labor is cheaper than chattel labor. They demonstrate the economic law of competition, which is the rule of the cheapest. The propertyless class—the wage workers—are by competition forced to sell their labor—themselves—to the lowest bidder, or starve.

CHAPTER III.

Capitalism.—Its Development in the United States.—Continued.

With the close of the rebellion of 1861, what is now known as the labor movement, began to assume large proportions. Not until now was there a very numerous and stationary wage class. In consequence, that state of affairs predicted by Lord Macauley, and quoted in our opening chapter, began to appear. Trades unions, labor unions, etc., composed of wage laborers had heretofore existed in small numbers, but were now rapidly formed as production in mass was increasingly developed. Strikes began to be frequently resorted to in order to prevent a reduction or to cause an increase of wages. The first national movement of organized labor was the effort made to inaugurate the eight-hour system throughout the United States in 1868. That attempt was defeated.

The effort to introduce the eight-hour system has been made repeatedly since, sometimes by isolated trades unions, at other times by national or international unions, and lastly by the Federated Trades' Unions of the United States and Canada. This latter body, representing 400,000 organized workmen, met in Chicago, in 1884, in what they styled an "International Congress of Organized Labor," and fixed upon a date, May 1, 1886, to inaugurate the eight-hour system. The organization of the Knights of Labor in 1869 had increased its membership to 400,000 in 1884. One of the principal objects of this organization was the establishment of the eight-hour system of labor. At this date, 1884, a million organized wage-workers in the United States considered the establishment of the eight-hour system one of the main objects of their organization. The agitation for a reduction of the hours of labor culminated in the strike of 360,000 men on May 1, 1886. In Chicago, the center of the eight-hour movement, over 40,000 workingmen went on a strike for the eight-hour work-day. On May 3 some of the strikers were fired on by the police, killing one and wounding several. On May 4 workingmen held an indignation meeting which was broken up by the police, when a dynamite bomb was thrown, which killed seven policemen and wounded fifty.

The effort to inaugurate the eight-hour work-day again proved a failure. The philosophy of the eight-hour movement, defined by the Boston Eight-Hour League, is as follows:

"*Resolved,* That poverty is the great fact with which the labor movement deals;

"That co-operation in labor is the final result to be obtained;

"That a reduction of the hours of labor is the first step in labor-reform; and that the emancipation of labor from the slavery and ignorance of poverty solves all the problems that now most disturb and perplex mankind.

"That eight hours do not mean less wages;

"That men are never paid, as a rule, according to what they earn, but according to the average cost of living;

"That in the long run—within certain limits—*less* hours means more *pay*—whether they work by the day or by the piece;

"That reducing the hours increases the purchasing power of wages as well as the amount of wealth produced;

"That dear men mean cheap productions, and cheap men mean dear productions;

"That six cents a day in China is dearest, and three dollars a day in America is cheapest;

"That the moral causes that have made three dollars a day cheaper than six cents a day will make higher wages still cheaper;

"That less hours mean reducing the profits and fortunes that are made on labor and its results;

"More knowledge and more capital for the laborer; the wages system gradually disappearing through *higher* wages;

"Less poor people to borrow money, and less wealthy ones to lend it, and a natural decline in the rates of interest on money;

"More idlers working, and more workers thinking; the motives to fraud reduced, and fewer calls for special legislation;

"Women's wages increased, her household labor reduced, better opportunities for thought and action, and the creation of motives strong enough to secure the ballot;

"Reaching the great causes of intemperance—extreme wealth and extreme poverty;

"And the salvation of Republican institutions;

"That whether national banks are abolished or bonds are taxed, or whether taxes or tariffs are high or low, or whether greenbacks or gold, or any system of finance proposed is adopted, or a single tax on land, or civil service, or one term for president shall prevail, are not *laborer's* questions, because they have no appreciable relation to the wage-system, through which the wage classes secure all that they can ever obtain of the world's wealth until they become sufficiently wealthy and intelligent to co-operate in its production; and whether the masses have anything to choose between a democrat, or republican, or other candidate turns entirely upon the question which one of the candidates will be most likely to secure the legislation for reduced hours of labor, as well as the enforcement upon all government works of the law already enacted.

"*Resolved*, That the factory system of our country that employs tens of thousands of women and children eleven and twelve hours a day; that owns or controls in its own selfish interest the pulpit and the press; that prevent the operative classes from making themselves felt in behalf of less hours, through a remorseless exercise of the power of discharge; that is rearing a population of children and youth whose sickly appearance and scanty or utterly neglected schooling, is proving year by year that the "lords of the loom and the lords of the lash were natural allies in the conflict between freedom and slavery."

CHAPTER IV.

CAPITALISM—ITS ORIGIN AND DEVELOPMENT IN EUROPE.

The wage system of labor is a despotism It is coercive and arbitrary. It compels the wage-worker, under a penalty of hunger, misery and distress of wife and children to obey the dictation of the employer. The individuality and personal liberty of the wage-worker, and those dependent upon him is destroyed by the wage-system. A republican form of government does not alter the class servitude of the wage-worker. While governments are necessarily despotic—they may differ in degree. But all governments based upon the wage-labor system are essentially the same. The government of the United States, based upon the wage-labor system, does not, and cannot guarantee the inalienable right of the wage-workers to "life, liberty and the pursuit of happiness." This fact is more apparent each day. Under the republic, the politician is a mere spoils-hunter. Bribery, intimidation and hypocricy is practiced upon the poor and ignorant voter, who is given a choice between capitalist candidates and measures. Halls of legislation are mere debating clubs of the rich—the propertied class—where legislation has for its sole object, the adjustment of the special, and sometimes conflicting, interest of this class.

The judicial and executive departments of a republican form of government are the officers or committees who administer the laws of the propertied class. The wage-class are by their economic dependence kept in ignorance and fear. They vote, but vote as a class only upon capitalist questions. The government itself is the instrument of capitalism to perpetuate the wage-system. Within this circle of government the votes of the workers have been unable to effect any amelioration of their condition. This is the experience of one hundred years of representative government in the United States, with the increase of population from 3,500,000 in 1776 to 65,000,000 in 1886 has also developed the wage-system upon which the government was founded. One hundred years' experience proves, that those who control the industries of the country—control its votes; that wealth votes; that poverty cannot vote; that citizens who must sell their labor or starve, will sell their votes when the same alternative is presented. The working-class of the United States have been deluded for one hundred years, with the belief that they possessed political sovereignty and law-making powers. They have believed that they could make laws in their own behalf, although they have not made or compelled the enforcement of any laws outside of capitalist interests. The wage-system of labor subjects the man of labor to the control of the monopolizers of the means of labor—the resources of life. Social misery, mental degredation and political dependence is the state of those who are deprived of the means of existence. Political liberty is possessed by those only who also possess economic liberty. The wage-system is the economic servitude of the workers. Four hundred years ago, the wage-system in Europe began to gradually supercede the surfage-system of labor. Previous to the fourteenth century, a system of vassalage existed in all nations, except a few guilds or trades in the larger cities. Under vassalage, the proprietor of an estate was owner of the men, women and children upon that estate, and when the estate was sold, these men, women and children were inventoried and sold to the purchaser. The law, defined the status of the vassal or serf as a fixture to the soil. The law was that they could not be parted from each other, or removed from the estate. In this respect vassalage differed from chattel slave labor. As at the present time, so in the past, the history of society is the history of class struggles. Freemen and slaves, patricians and plebeians, nobles and serfs, guild members and journeymen; in other words, the oppressors and oppressed have engaged each other in this class-struggle. These conflicts have sometimes been open, at other times concealed, but never ceasing. This continuous struggle has invariably terminated in a revolutionary alteration of the social system, or in the total destruction of the contending classes.

In earlier historical epochs, we find almost everywhere a minute division and subdivision of society into classes or castes—a variety of grades in social life. In ancient Rome were the partricians, knights, plebeians, slaves; in Mediæval Europe, feudal lords, vassals, burghers journeymen, serfs; and in each of these classes there were again grades and distinctions.

Modern *Bourgeois* (capitalist) society, which arose from the ruins of the feudal system has not wiped out the antagonism of classes. New classes, new conditions of oppression, new modes and forms of carrying on the struggle, have been substituted for the old ones. The characteristic of our epoch—the epoch of the *Bourgeoisie*, or middle class—is that the struggle between the various social classes has been reduced to its simplest form. Society tends more and more to be divided into two great hostile classes—to-wit: The *Bourgeoisie* and the *Proletariat*. This class struggle arises from and is inherent in the wage-system.

How that system operates in minutia, in detail; how it effects the laborer and the capitalist has been clearly and scientifically formulated by Karl Marx in his work entitled "Capital," a chapter from which is here quoted.

WAGE-LABOR AND CAPITAL.—WHAT ARE WAGES AND HOW ARE THEY DETERMINED?

" If we were to ask the laborers, ' How much wages do you get ?' one would reply, 'I get a couple of shillings a day from my employer ;' another, ' I get half-a-crown.' and so on. According to the different trades to which they belong, they would name different sums of money which they receive from their particular employers, either for working for a certain length of time, or for performing a certain piece of work ; for example, either for weaving an ell of cloth, or for setting up a certain amount of type. But in spite of this difference in their statements there is one point in which they would all agree; their wages are the amount of money which their employer pays them either for working a certain length of time, or for a certain amount of work done.

"Thus their employer buys their work for money. For money they sell their work to him. With the same sum for which the employer has bought their work, as for instance, with a couple of shillings, he might have bought four pounds of sugar, or a proportionate amount of any other wares. The two shillings with which he buys the four pounds of sugar, are the price of four pounds of sugar. The two shillings with which he buys labor for twelve hours, are the price of twelve hours' work. Work is therefore as much a commodity as sugar, neither more nor less, only they measure the former by the clock, the latter by the scales.

"The laborers exchange their own commodity with their employers'—work for money; and this exchange takes place according to a fixed proportion. So much money for so much work. For twelve hours' weaving, two shillings. And do not these two shillings represent two shillings worth of all other commodities? Thus the laborer has, in fact, exchanged his own commodity—work, with all kinds of other commodities, and that in a fixed proportion. His employer in giving him two shillings, has given him so much meat, so much clothing, so much fuel, light, and so on, in exchange for his day's work. The two shillings, therefore, express the proportion in which his work is exchanged with other commodities—the exchange-value of his work; and the exchange-value of any commodity expressed in money is called its price. Wage is, therefore, only another name for the price of work—for the price of this peculiar piece of property which can have no local habitation at all except in human flesh and blood.

"Take the case of any workman, a weaver for instance. The employer supplies him with thread and loom. The weaver sets to work, and the thread is turned into cloth. The employer takes possession of the cloth and sells it, say for twenty shillings. Does the weaver receive as wages a *share* in the cloth—in the twenty shillings—in the product of his labor? By no means. The weaver receives his wages long before the product is sold. The employer does not, therefore, pay his wages with the money he will get for the cloth, but with money previously provided. Loom and thread are not the weaver's product, since they are supplied by the employer, and no more are the commodities which he receives in exchange for his own commodity, or in other words for his work. It is possible that the employer finds no purchaser for his cloth. It may be that by its sale he does not recover even the wages he has paid. It may be that in comparison with the weaver's wages he made a great bargain by its sale. But all this has nothing whatever to do with the weaver. The employer purchases the weaver's labor with a part of his available property—of his capital—in exactly the same way as he has with another part of his property bought the raw material—the thread—and the instrument of labor —the loom. As soon as he has made these purchases—and he reckons among them the purchase of the labor necessary to the production of the cloth—he proceeds to produce it by means of the raw material and the instruments which belong to him. Among these last is, of course, reckoned our worthy weaver, who has as little share in the product, or in the price of the product, as the loom itself.

"Wages, therefore, are not the worker's share of the commodities which he has produced. Wages are the share of commodities previously produced, with which the employer purchases a certain amount of productive labor.

"Labor is, therefore, a commodity which its owner, the wage worker, sells to capital. Why does he sell it? In order to live.

"But labor is the peculiar expression of the energy of the laborer's life. And this energy he sells to another party, in order to secure for himself the means of living. For him, therefore, his energy is nothing but a means of ensuring his own existence. He works to live. He does not count the work itself as a part of his life, rather is it a sacrifice of his life. It is a commodity which he has made over to another party. Neither is its product the aim of his activity. What he produces for himself is not the silk he weaves, nor the palace that he builds, nor the gold that he digs from out the mine. What he produces for himself is his wage; and silk, gold, and palace are transformed for him into a certain quantity of means of existence—a cotton shirt, some copper coins, and a lodging in a cellar. And what of the laborer, who for twelve hours weaves, spins, bores, turns, builds, shovels, breaks stones, carries loads, and so on? Does his twelve hours' weaving, spinning, boring, turning, building, shoveling, and stone-breaking represent the active expression of his life? On the contrary. Life begins for him exactly where this activity of his ceases—at his meals, on the public-house bench, in his bed. His twelve hours' work has no meaning for him as weaving, spinning, boring, etc., but only as earnings whereby he may obtain his meals, his seat in the public-house, his bed. If the silkworm's object in spinning were to prolong its existence as a caterpillar, it would be a perfect example of a wage-worker.

"Labor was not always a commodity. Labor was not always wage-work, that is, a marketable commodity The slave does not sell his labor to the slave-owner. The slave along with his labor is sold once for all to his owner. He is a commodity which can pass from the hand of one owner to that of another. He himself is a commodity, but his labor is not *his* commodity. The serf sells only a portion of his labor. He does not receive his wages from the owner of the soil; rather the owner of the soil receives a tribute from him. The serf belongs to the soil, and to the lord of the soil he brings its fruits. The free laborer, on the other hand, sells himself, and that by fractions. From day to day he sells by auction eight, ten, twelve, fifteen hours of his life to the highest bidder—to the owner of the raw material, the instruments of work, and the means of life; that is, to the employer. The laborer himself belongs neither to an owner nor to the soil; but eight, ten, twelve, fifteen hours of his daily life belong to the man who buys them. The laborer leaves the employer to whom he has hired himself whenever he pleases; and the employer discharges him whenever he thinks fit; either as soon as he ceases to make a profit out of him, or fails to get so high a profit as he requires. But the laborer, whose only source of earnings is the sale of his labor, cannot leave the whole class of its purchasers, that is, the capitalist class, without renouncing his own existence. He does not belong to this or that particular employer, but he does belong to the *employing class;* and more than that, it is his business to find an employer; that is, among this employing class, it is his business to discover his own particular purchases.

"Before going more closely into the relations between capital and wage-work, it will be well to give a brief survey of those general relations which are taken into consideration in determining the amount of wages.

"As we have seen, wages are the price of a certain commodity—labor. Wages are thus determined by the same law which regulates the price of any other commodity.

"Thereupon the question arises, how is the price of a commodity determined?

"*By what means is the price of a commodity determined?*

"By means of competition between buyers and sellers, and the relation between supply and demand—offer and desire. And this competition by which the price of an article is fixed is three-fold.

"The same commodity is offered in the market by various sellers. Whoever offers the greatest advantage to purchasers is certain to drive the other sellers off the field, and secure for himself the greatest sale. The sellers, therefore, fight for the sale and the market among themselves. Everyone of them wants to sell, and does his best to sell much, and if possible to become the only seller. Therefore each outbids the other in cheapness, and a competition takes place among the sellers which lowers the price of the goods they offer.

"But a competition also goes on among the purchasers, which on their side raises the price of the goods offered.

"Finally there arises a competition between buyers and sellers; the one set wants to buy as cheap as possible, the other to sell as dear as possible. The result of this competition between buyers and sellers will depend upon the relations of the two previous aspects of the competition; that is, upon whether the competition in the ranks of the buyers or that in those of the sellers is the keener. Business thus leads two opposing armies into the field, and each of them again presents the aspect of a battle in its own ranks between its own soldiers. That army whose troops are least mauled by one another carries off the victory over the opposing host.

"Let us suppose that there are a hundred bales of cotton in the market, and at the same time buyers in want of a thousand bales. In this case the demand is greater than the supply. The competition between the buyers will therefore be intense; each of them will do his best to get hold of all the hundred bales of cotton. This example is no arbitrary supposition. In the history of the trade we have experienced periods of failure of the cotton plant, when particular companies of capitalists have endeavored to purchase, not only a hundred bales of cotton, but the whole stock of cotton in the world. Therefore in the case supposed each buyer will try to beat the others out of the field by offering a proportionately higher price for the cotton. The cotton-sellers, perceiving the troops of the hostile host in violent combat with one another, and being perfectly secure as to the sale of all their hundred bales, will take very good care not to begin squabbling among themselves in order to depress the price at the very moment when their adversaries are emulating each other in the process of screwing it higher up. Peace is therefore suddenly proclaimed in the army of the sellers. They present a united front to the purchaser, and fold their arms in philosophic content; and their claims would be absolutely boundless if it were not that the offers of even the most pressing and eager of the buyers must always have some definite limit.

"Thus if the supply of a commodity is not so great as the demand for it, the competition between the buyers waxes. Result: A more or less important rise in the price of goods.

"As a rule the converse case is of commoner occurrence, producing an opposite result. Large excess of supply over demand; desperate competition among the sellers; dearth of purchasers; forced sale of goods dirt cheap.

"But what is the meaning of the rise and fall in prices? What is the meaning of higher price or lower price? A grain of sand is high when examined through a microscope, and a tower is low when compared with a mountain. And if price is determined by the relation between supply and demand, how is the relation between supply and demand itself determined?

"Let us turn to the first worthy citizen we meet. He will not take an instant to consider, but like a second Alexander the Great will cut the metaphysical knot by the help of his multiplication table. 'If the production of the goods which I sell,' he will tell us, 'has cost me £100, and I get £110 by their sale—within the year, you understand—that's what I call a sound, honest, reasonable profit. But if I make £120 or £130 by the sale, that is a higher profit; and if I were to get a good £200, that would be an exceptional, an enormous profit.' What is it then that serves our citizen as the measure of his profit? The cost of production of his goods. If he receives in exchange for them an amount of other goods whose production has cost less, he has lost by his bargain. If he receives an amount whose production has cost more, he has gained. And he reckons the rise and fall of his profit by the number of degrees at which it stands with reference to his zero—the cost of production.

"We have now seen how the changing proportion between supply and demand produces the rise and fall of prices, making them at one time high, at another low. If through failure in the supply, or exceptional increase in the demand, an important rise in the price of a commodity takes place, then the price of another commodity must have fallen; for, of course, the price of a commodity only expresses in money the proportion in which other commodities can be exchanged with it. For instance, if the price of a yard of silk rises from five to six shillings, the price of silver has fallen in comparison with silk; and in the same way the price of all other commodities which remain at their old prices has fallen if compared with silk. We have to give a larger quantity of them in exchange in order to obtain the same quantity of silk. And what is the result of a rise in the price of a commodity? A mass of capital is thrown into that flourishing branch of business, and this immigration of capital into the province of the privileged business will last until the ordinary level of profits is attained; or rather, until the price of the products sinks through overproduction.

"Conversely, if the price of a commodity falls below the cost of its production, capital will be withdrawn from the production of this commodity. Except in the case of a branch of industry which has become obsolete and is therefore doomed to disappear, the result of this flight of capital will be that the production of this commodity, and therefore its supply, will continually dwindle until it corresponds to the demand; and thus its price rises again to the level of the cost of its production; or rather, until the supply has fallen below the demand; that is, until its price has again risen above its cost of production; for the price of any commodity is always either above or below its cost of production.

"We see then how it is that capital is always immigrating and emigrating, from the province of one industry into that of another. It is high prices that bring about an excessive immigration, and low prices an excess of emigration.

"We might show from another point of view how not only the supply, but also the demand is determined by the cost of production; but this would lead us too far from our present subject.

"We have just seen how the fluctuations of supply and demand always reduce the price of a commodity to its cost of production. It is true that the precise price of a commodity is always either above or below its cost of production; but the rise and fall reciprocally balance each other, so within a certain period, if the ebb and flow of the business are reckoned up together, commodities are exchanged with one another in accordance with their cost of production; and thus their cost of production determines their price.

"The determination of price by cost of production is not to be understood in the sense of the economists. The economists declare that the average price of commodities is equal to the cost of production; this, according to them, is a law. The anarchical movements in which the rise is compensated by the fall, and the fall by the rise, they ascribe to chance. With just as good a right as this, which the other economists assume, we might consider the fluctuations as the law, and ascribe the fixing of price by cost of production to chance. But if we look closely, we see that it is precisely these fluctuations, although they bring the most terrible desolation in their train and shake the fabric of bourgeois society like earthquakes, it is precisely these fluctuations which in their course determine price by cost of production. In the totality of this disorderly movement is to be found its disorder. Throughout these alternating movements, in the course of this industrial anarchy, competition, as it were, cancels one excess by means of another.

"We gather, therefore, that the price of a commodity is determined by its cost of production, in such manner that the periods in which the price of this commodity rises above its cost of production are compensated by the periods in which it sinks below this cost, and conversely. Of course this does not hold good for one single particular product of an industry, but only for that entire branch of industry. So also it does not hold good for a particular manufacturer, but only for the entire industrial class.

"The determination of price by cost of production is the same thing as its determination by the duration of the labor which is required for the manufacture of a commodity; for cost of production may be divided into (1) raw material and implements, that is, products of industry whose manufacture has cost a certain number of days' work, and which therefore represents a certain duration of labor, and (2) actual labor, which is measured by its duration.

"Now the same general laws, which universally regulate the price of commodities, regulate, of course, wages, the price of labor.

"Wages will rise and fall in accordance with the proportion between demand and supply, that is, in accordance with the conditions of the competition between capitalists as buyers, and laborers as sellers of labor. The fluctuations of wages correspond in general with the fluctuations in the price of commodities. Within these fluctuations the price of labor is regulated by its cost of production, that is, by the duration of labor which is required in order to produce this commodity, labor.

"Now what is the cost of production of labor itself?

"It is the cost required for the production of a laborer and for his maintenance as a laborer.

"The shorter the time requisite for instruction in any labor, the less is the laborer's cost of production, and the lower are his wages, the price of his work. In those branches of industries which scarcely require any period of apprenticeship, and where the mere bodily existence of the laborer is sufficient, the requisite cost of his production and maintenance are almost limited to the cost of the commodities which are requisite to keep him alive. The price of his labor is therefore determined by the price of the bare necessaries of his existence.

"Here, however, another consideration comes in. The manufacturer, who reckons up his expenses of production and determines accordingly the price of the product, takes into account the wear and tear of the machinery. If a machine costs him £100 and wears itself out in ten years, he adds £10 a year to the price of his goods, in order to replace the worn-out machine by a new one when the ten years are up. In the same way we must reckon in the cost of production of simple labor the cost of its propagation; so that the race of laborers may be put in a position to multiply and to replace the worn-out workers by new ones. Thus the wear and tear of the laborer must be taken into account just as much as the wear and tear of the machine.

"Thus the cost of production of simple labor amounts to *the cost of the laborer's subsistence and propagation*, and the price of this cost determines his wages. When we speak of wages we mean the minimum of wages. This minimum of wages holds good, just as does the determination by the cost of production of the price of commodities in general, not for the particular individual, but for the species. Individual laborers, indeed millions of them, do not receive enough to enable them to subsist and propagate; but the wages of the whole working class with all their fluctuations are nicely adjusted to this minimum.

"Now that we are grounded on these general laws which govern wages just as much as the price of any other commodity, we can examine our subject more exactly.

"Capital consists of raw material, implements of labor, and all kinds of means of subsistence, which are used for the production of new implements and new means of subsistence. All these factors of capital are created by labor, are products of labor, are stored-up labor. Stored-up labor which serves as the means of new production is capital."

"So say the economists.

"What is a negro slave? A human creature of the black race. The one definition is just as valuable as the other.

"A negro is a negro. In certain conditions he is transformed into a slave. A spinning-jenny is a machine for spinning cotton. Only in certain conditions is it transformed into capital. When torn away from these conditions, it is just as little capital as gold is money in the abstract, or sugar the price of sugar. In the work of production men do not stand in relation to nature alone. They only produce when they work together in a certain way, and mutually exchange their different kinds of energy. In order to produce, they mutually enter upon certain relations and conditions, and it is only by means of these relations and conditions that their relation to nature is defined, and production becomes possible.

"These social relations upon which the producers mutually enter, the terms upon which they exchange their energies and take their share in the collective act of production, will of course differ according to the character of the means of production. With the invention of firearms as implements of warfare the whole organization of the army was of necessity altered; and with the alteration in the relations through which individuals form an army, and are enabled to work together as an army, there was a simultaneous alteration in the relations of armies to one another.

"Thus with the change in the social relations by means of which individuals produce, that is, in the social relations of production, and with the alteration and development of the material means of production, the powers of production are also transformed. The relations of production collectively form those social relations which we call a society, and a society with definite degrees of historical development, a society with an appropriate and distinctive character. Ancient society, feudal society, bourgeois society, are instances of this collective result of the relations of production, each of which marks out an important step in the historical development of mankind.

"Now capital also is a social condition of production. It is a bourgeois condition of production, a condition of the production of a bourgeois society. Are not the means of subsistence, the implements of labor, and the raw material, of which capital consists, the results of definite social relations; were they not produced and stored up under certain social conditions? Will they not be used for further production under certain social conditions? And is it not just this definite social character which transforms into capital that product which serves for further production?

"Capital does not consist of means of subsistence, implements of labor, and raw material alone, nor only of material products; it consists just as much of exchange-values. All the products of which it consists are commodities. Thus capital is not merely the sum of material products; it is a sum of commodities, of exchange-values of social quantities.

"Capital remains unchanged if we substitute cotton for wool, rice for corn, and steamers for railways; provided only that the cotton, the rice, the steamers—the bodily form of capital—have the same exchange value, the same price, as the wool, the corn, the railways, in which it formerly embodied itself. The bodily form of capital may change continually, while the capital itself undergoes not the slightest alteration.

"But though all capital is a sum of commodities, that is, of exchange values, it is not every sum of commodities, of exchange values, that is capital.

"Every sum of exchange values is an exchange value. For instance, a house worth a thousand pounds is an exchange value of a thousand pounds. A penny-worth of paper is the sum of the exchange values of a hundred-hundredths of a penny. Products which may be mutually exchanged are commodities. The definite proportion in which they are exchangeable forms their exchange value, or, expressed in money, their price. The amount of these products can do nothing to alter their definition as being commodities, or as representing an exchange value, or as having a certain price. Whether a tree is large or small, it remains a tree. Whether we exchange iron for other wares in ounces or in hundredweights, that makes no difference in its character as a commodity possessing exchange value. According to its amount it is a commodity of more or less worth, with a higher or lower price.

"How then can a sum of commodities, of exchange values, become capital?

"By maintaining and multiplying itself as an independent social power, that is, as the power of a portion of society, by means of its exchange for direct, living labor. Capital necessarily pre-supposes the existence of a class which possesses nothing but labor-force.

"It is the lordship of past, stored-up, realized labor over actual, living labor that transforms the stored-up labor into capital.

"Capital does not consist in the fact that stored-up labor is used by living labor as a means to further production. It consists in the fact that living labor serves as the means whereby stored-up labor may maintain and multiply its own exchange-value.

"What is it that takes place in the exchange between capital and wage-work?

"The laborer receives in exchange for his labor the means of subsistence; but the capitalist receives in exchange for the means of subsistence labor, the productive energy of the laborer, the creative force whereby the laborer not only replaces what he consumes, but also gives to the stored-up labor a greater value than it had before. The laborer receives from the capitalist a share of the previously provided means of subsistence. To what use does he put these means of subsistence? He uses them for immediate consumption. But as soon as I consume my means of subsistence, they disappear and are irrecoverably lost to me; it therefore becomes necessary that I should employ the time during which these means keep me alive in order to produce new means of subsistence: so that during their consumption I may provide by my labor new value in the place of that which thus disappears. But it is just this grand productive power which the laborer has to bargain away to capital in exchange for the means of subsistence which he receives. To him therefore it is entirely lost.

"Let us take an example. A farmer gives his day-laborer two shillings a day. For this two shillings he works throughout the day on the farmer's field, and so secures him a return of four shillings. The farmer does not merely get the value which he had advanced the day-laborer replaced; he doubles it. He has thus spent or consumed the two shillings which he gave to the day-laborer in a fruitful and productive fashion. He has bought for his two shillings just that labor and force of the day-laborer which produces fruits of the earth of twice the value, and turns two shillings into four. The day-laborer on the other hand receives in place of his productive force, which he has just bargained away to the farmer, two shillings; and these he exchanges for means of subsistence; which means of subsistence he proceeds with more or less speed to consume. The two shillings have thus been consumed in double fashion: productively for capital, since they have been exchanged for the labor-force which produced the four shillings; unproductively for the laborer, since they have been exchanged for means of subsistence which have disappeared forever, and whose value he can only recover by repeating the same bargain with the farmer. Thus capital pre-supposes wage-labor, and wage-labor pre-supposes capital. They condition one another; and each bring the other into play.

"Does a laborer in a cotton factory produce merely cotton? No, he produces capital. He produces value which serves afresh to command his own labor, and to create new value by its means.

"Capital can only increase when it is exchanged for labor, when it calls wage-labor into existence. Wage-labor can only be exchanged for capital by augmenting capital and strengthening the power whose slave it is. An increase of capital is therefore an increase of the proletariat, that is, of the laboring class.

"The interests of the capitalist and the laborer are therefore identical, assert the bourgeoisie and their economists. And, in fact, so they are! The laborer perishes if capital does not employ him. Capital perishes if it does not exploit labor; and in order to exploit it, it must buy it. The faster the capital devoted to production—the productive capital—increases, and the more successfully the industry is carried on, the richer do the bourgeoisie become, the better does business go, the more laborers does the capitalist require, and the dearer does the laborer sell himself.

"Thus the indispensable condition of the laborer's securing a tolerable position is the speediest possible growth of productive capital.

"But what is the meaning of the increase of productive capital? The increase of the power of stored-up labor over living labor. The increase of the dominion of the bourgeoisie over the laboring class. As fast as wage-labor creates its own antagonist and its own master in the dominating power of capital, the means of employment, that is, of subsistence, flow back to it from its antagonist; but only on the condition that it is itself transformed afresh into a portion of capital, and becomes the lever whereby the increase of capital may be again hugely accelerated.

"Thus the statement that the interests of capital and labor are identical comes to mean merely this: capital and wage-labor are the two terms of one and the same proportion. The one conditions the other, just in the same way that the usurer and the borrower condition each other mutually.

"So long as the wage-laborer remains a wage-laborer, his lot in life is dependent upon capital. That is the exact meaning of the famous community of interests between capital and labor.

"The increase of capital is attended by an increase in the amount of wage-labor and in the number of wage-laborers; or, in other words, the dominion of capital is spread over a larger number of individuals. And, to give the most fortunate event possible, with the increase of productive capital there is an increase in the demand for labor. And thus wages, the price of labor, will rise.

"A house may be large or small; but as long as the surrounding houses are equally small, it satisfies all social expectations as a dwelling place. But let a palace arise by the side of this small house, and it shrinks from a house into a hut. The smallness of the house now gives it to be understood that its occupant has either very small pretentions or none at all; and however high it may shoot up with the progress of civilization, if the neighboring palace shoots up also in the same or in greater proportion, the occupant of the comparatively small house will always find himself more uncomfortable, more discontented, more confined within his four walls.

"A notable advance in the amount paid as wages brings about a rapid increase of productive capital. The rapid increase of productive capital calls forth just as rapid an increase in wealth, luxury, social wants, and social comforts. Therefore, although the comforts of the laborer have risen, the social satisfaction which they give has fallen in comparison with these augmented comforts of the capitalist which are unattainable for the laborer, and in comparison with the general development of comforts. Our wants and their satisfaction have their origin in society; we therefore measure them in their relation to society, and not in relation to the objects which satisfy them. Since their nature is social, it is therefore relative.

"As a rule then, wages are not determined merely by the amount of commodities for which they may be exchanged. They depend upon various relations.

"What the laborer immediately receives for his labor is a certain sum of money. Are wages determined merely by this money price?

"In the sixteenth century the gold and silver in circulation in Europe was augmented in consequence of the discovery of America. The value of gold and silver fell, therefore, in proportion to other commodities. The laborers received for their labor the same amount of silver coin as before. The money price of their labor remained the same, and yet their wages had fallen, for in exchange for the same sum of silver they obtained a smaller quantity of other commodities. This was one of the circumstances which furthered the increase of capital and the rise of the bourgeoisie in the sixteenth century.

"Let us take another case. In the winter of 1847, in consequence of a failure in the crops, there was an important increase in the indispensable means of subsistence, corn, meat, butter, cheese, and so on. We will suppose that the laborers still received the same sum of money for their labor as before. Had not their wages fallen then? Of course they had. For the same amount of money they received in exchange less bread, meat, etc.; and their wages had fallen, not because the value of silver had diminished, but because the value of the means of subsistence had increased.

"Let us finally suppose that the money price of labor remains the same, while in consequence of the employment of new machinery, or on account of a good season, or for some similar reason, there is a fall in the price of all agricultural and manufactured goods. For the same amount of money the laborers can now buy more commodities of all kinds. Their wages have therefore risen, just because their money price has not changed.

"The money price of labor, the nominal amount of wages, does not therefore fall together with the real wages, that is, with the amount of commodities that may practically be obtained in exchange for the wages. Therefore if we speak of the rise and fall of wages, the money price of labor, or the nominal wage, is not the only thing which we must keep in view.

"But neither the nominal wages, that is, the amount of money for which the laborer sells himself to the employer, nor yet the real wages, that is, the amount of commodities which he can buy for this money, exhaust the relations which are comprehended in the term wages.

"For the meaning of the word is chiefly determined by its relation to the gain or profit of the employer—it is a proportionate and relative expression.

"The real wage expresses the price of labor in relation to the price of other commodities; the relative wage, on the contrary, expresses the price of direct labor in relation to that of stored-up labor, the relative value of wage-labor and capital, the proportionate value of capitalist and laborer.

"Real wages may remain the same, or they may even rise, and yet the relative wages may none the less have fallen. Let us assume, for example, that the price of all the means of subsistence has fallen by two-thirds, while a day's wages have only fallen one-third, as for instance, from three shillings to two. Although the laborer has a larger amount of commodities at his disposal for two shillings than he had before at three, yet his wages are nevertheless diminished in proportion to the capitalist's gain. The capitalist's profit—the manufacturer's, for instance—has been augmented by a shilling, since the smaller sum of exchange-value which he pays to the laborer, the laborer has to produce a larger sum of exchange-value than he did before. The value of capital is raised in proportion to the value of labor. The division of social wealth between capital and labor has become more disproportionate. The capitalist commands a larger amount of labor with the same amount of capital. The power of the capitalist class over the laboring class is increased; the social position of the laborer has deteriorated, and is depressed another degree below that of the capitalist.

"What then is the general law which determines the rise and fall of wages and profit in their reciprocal relation?

"They stand in inverse proportion to one another. Capital's exchange-value, profit, rises in the same proportion in which the exchange-value of labor, wages, sinks; and conversely. The rise in profit is exactly measured by the fall in wages, and the fall in profit by the rise in wages.

"The objection may perhaps be made that the capitalist may have gained a profit by advantageous exchange of his products with other capitalists, or by a rise in the demand for his goods, whether in consequence of the opening of new markets, or of a greater demand in the old markets; that the profit of the capitalist may thus increase by means of over-reaching another capitalist, independently of the rise and fall of wages and the exchange-value of labor; or that the profit of the capitalist may also rise through an improvement in the implements of labor, a new application of natural forces, and so on.

"But it must nevertheless be admitted that the result remains the same, although it is brought about in a different way. The capitalist has acquired a larger amount of exchange-value with the same amount of labor, without having had to pay a higher price for the labor on that account; that is to say, a lower price has been paid for the labor in proportion to the net profit which it yields to the capitalist.

"Besides we must remember that in spite of the fluctuations in the price of commodities, the average price of each commodity—the proportion in which it exchanges for other commodities—is determined by its cost of production. The over-reaching and tricks that go on within the capitalist class therefore necessarily cancel one another. Improvements in machinery, and new applications of natural forces to the service of production, enable them to turn out in a given time with the same amount of labor and capital a larger quantity of products, but by no means a larger quantity of exchange-value. If by the application of the spinning-jenny I can turn out twice as much thread in an hour as I could before its invention, for instance, a hundred pounds instead of fifty, that is because the cost of production has been halved, or because at the same cost I can turn out double the amount of products.

"Finally in whatsoever proportion the capitalist classes—the bourgeoisie—whether of one country or of the market of the whole world—share among themselves the net profits of production, the total amount of these net profits always consists merely of the amount by which, taking all in all, direct labor has been increased by means of stored-up labor.

This sum total increases, therefore, in the proportion in which labor augments capital; that is, in the proportion in which profit rises as compared with wages.

"Thus we see that even if we confine ourselves to the relation between capital and wage-labor, the interests of capital are in direct antagonism to the interest of wage-labor.

"A rapid increase of capital is equal to a rapid increase of profits. Profits can only make a rapid increase, if the exchange-value of labor—the relative wage—makes an equally rapid decline. The relative wage may decline, although the actual wage rises along with the nominal wage, or money price of labor; if only it does not rise in the same proportion as profit. For instance, if when trade is good, wages rise five per cent., and profits on the other hand thirty per cent., then the proportional or relative wage has not increased but declined.

"Thus if the receipts of the laborer increase with the rapid advance of capital, yet at the same time there is a widening of the social gulf which separates the laborer from the capitalist, and also an increase in the power of capital over labor and in the dependence of labor upon capital.

"The meaning of the statement that the laborer has an interest in the rapid increase of capital is merely this; the faster the laborer increases his master's dominion, the richer will be the crumbs that he will get from his table; and the greater the number of laborers that can be employed and called into existence, the greater will be the number of slaves of which capital will be the owner.

"We have thus seen that even the most fortunate event for the working class, the speediest possible increase of capital, however much it may improve the material condition of the laborer, cannot abolish the opposition between his interests and those of the bourgeois or capitalist class. Profit and wages remain just as much as ever in inverse proportion.

"When capital is increasing fast, wages may rise, but the profit of capital will rise much faster. The actual position of the laborer has improved, but it is at the expense of his social position. The social gulf which separates him from the capitalist has widened.

"Finally, the meaning of fortunate conditions for wage-labor, and of the quickest possible increase of productive capital, is merely this; the faster the working classes enlarge and extend the hostile power that dominates over them, the better will be the conditions under which they will be allowed to labor for the further increase of bourgeois dominion and for the wider extension of the power of capital, and thus contentedly to forge for themselves the golden chains by which the bourgeois drags them in its train.

"But are the increase of productive capital and the rise of wages so indissolubly connected as the bourgeois economists assert? We can hardly believe that the fatter capital becomes, the more will its slave be pampered. The bourgeoisie is too much enlightened, and keeps its accounts much too carefully, to care for that privilege of the feudal nobility, the ostentation of splendor in its retinue. The very conditions of bourgeois existence compel it to keep careful accounts.

"We must therefore inquire more closely into the effect which the increase of productive capital has upon wages.

"With the general increase of the productive capital of a bourgeois society a manifold accumulation of labor-force takes place. The capitalists increase in number and in power. The increase in the number of capitalists increases the competition between capitalists. Their increased power gives them the means of leading into the industrial battle-field mightier armies of laborers furnished with gigantic implements of war.

"The one capitalist can only succeed in driving the other off the field and taking possession of his capital by selling his wares at a cheaper rate. In order to sell more cheaply without ruining himself, he must produce more cheaply, that is, he must heighten as much as possible the productiveness of labor. But the most effective way of making labor more productive is by means of a more complete subdivision of labor, or by the more extended use and continual improvement of machinery. The more numerous the departments into which labor is divided, and the more gigantic the scale in which machinery is introduced, in so much the greater proportion does the cost of production decline, and so much the more fruitful is the labor. Thus arises a manifold rivalry among capitalists with the object of increasing the subdivision of labor and machinery, and keeping up the utmost possible progressive rate of exploitation.

"Now if by means of a greater subdivision of labor, by the employment and improvement of new machines, or by the more skillful and profitable use of the forces of nature, a capitalist has discovered the means of producing a larger amount of commodities than his competitors with the same amount of labor; whether it be stored-up labor or direct—if he can, for instance, spin a complete yard of cotton in the time that his competitors take to spin half-a-yard—how will this capitalist proceed to act?

"He might go on selling half-a-yard at its former market price; but that would not have the effect of driving his opponents out of the field and increasing his own sale. But the need of increasing his sale has increased in the same proportion as his production. The more effective and more expensive means of production which he has called into existence enable him, of course, to sell his wares cheaper, but they also compel him to sell more wares and to secure a much larger market for them. Our capitalist will therefore proceed to sell his half-a-yard of cotton cheaper than his competitors.

"The capitalist will not, however, sell his complete yard so cheaply as his competitors sell the half, although its entire production does not cost him more than the production of half costs the others. For in that case he would gain nothing, but would only get back the cost of its production. The contingent increase in his receipts would result from his having set in motion a larger capital, but not from having made his capital more profitable than that of the others. Besides he gains the end he is aiming at, if he prices his goods a slight percentage lower than his competitors. He drives them off the field, and wrests from them at any rate a portion of their sale, if only he undersells them. And finally we must remember that the price current always stands either above or below the cost of production, according as the sale of a commodity is transacted at a favorable or unfavorable period of business. According as the market price of a yard of cloth is above or below its former cost of production, the percentage will alter in which the capitalist who has employed the new and profitable means of production exceeds in its sale the actual cost of its production to him.

"But our capitalist does not find his privilege very lasting. Other rival capitalists introduce with more or less rapidity the same machines and the same subdivision of labor; and this introduction becomes general, until the price of the yard of cloth is reduced not only below its old, but below its new cost of production.

"Thus the capitalists find themselves relatively in the same position in which they stood before the introduction of the new means of production; and if they are by these means enabled to offer twice the product for the same price, they now find themselves compelled to offer the doubled amount for less than the old price. From the standpoint of these new means of production the old game begins anew. There is greater subdivision of labor, more machinery, and a more rapid progress in the exploitation of both. Whereupon competition brings about the same reaction against this result.

"Thus we see how the manner and means of production are continually renewed and revolutionised; and how the division of labor necessarily brings in its train a greater division of labor; the introduction of machinery, a still larger introduction; and the rapidity of progress in the efficiency of labor, a still greater rapidity of progress.

"That is the law which continually drives bourgeois production out of its old track, and compels capital to intensify the productive powers of labor for the very reason that it has already intensified them—the law that allows it no rest, but for ever whispers in its ear the words, 'Quick March!'

"This is no other law than that which, cancelling the periodical fluctuations of business, necessarily identifies the price of a commodity with its cost of production.

"However powerful are the means of production which a particular capitalist may bring into the field, competition will make their adoption general; and the moment it becomes general, the sole result of the greater fruitfulness of his capital is that he must now for the same price offer ten, twenty, a hundred times as much as before. But as he must dispose of perhaps a thousand times as much, in order to outweigh the decrease in the selling price by the larger proportion of products sold; since a larger sale has now become necessary, not only to gain a larger profit, but also to replace the cost of production; and the implements of production, as we have seen, always get more expensive; and since this larger sale has become a vital question, not only for him, but also for his rivals, the old strife continues with all the greater violence, in proportion as the previously discovered means of production are more fruitful. Thus the subdivision of labor and the employment of new machinery take a fresh start, and proceed with still greater rapidity.

"And thus, whatever be the power of the means of production employed, competition does its best to rob capital of the golden fruit which it produces, by reducing the price of commodities to their cost of production; and, as fast as their production is cheapened, compelling by a despotic law the larger supply of cheaper products to be offered at the former price. Thus the capitalist will have won nothing by his exertions beyond the obligation to produce faster than before, and an enhancement of the difficulty of employing his capital to advantage. While competition continually persecutes him with its law of the cost of production, and turns against himself every weapon which he forges against his rivals; the capitalist continually tries to cheat competition by incessantly introducing further subdivision of labor, and replacing the old machines by new ones, which, though more expensive, produce more cheaply; instead of waiting till competition has rendered them obsolete.

"Let us now look at this feverish agitation as it affects the market of the whole world, and we shall understand how the increase, accumulation, and concentration of capital bring in their train an uninterrupted and extreme subdivision of labor, always advancing with gigantic strides of progress, and a continual employment of new machinery together with improvement of the old.

"But how do these circumstances, inseparable as they are from the increase of productive capital, affect the determination of the amount of wages?

"The greater division of labor enables one laborer to do the work of five, ten, twenty; it therefore multiplies the competition among laborers five, ten or twenty times. The laborers do not only compete when one sells himself cheaper than another; they also compete when one does the work of five, ten or twenty; and the division of labor which capital introduces and continually increases, compels the laborers to enter into this kind of competition with one another.

"Further; in the same proportion in which the division of labor is increased, the labor itself is simplified. The special skill of the laborer becomes worthless. It is changed into a monotonous and uniform power production, which can give play neither to bodily nor to intellectual elasticity. Its labor becomes accessible to everybody. Competitors therefore throng into it from all sides; and besides we must remember that the more simply and easily learnt the labor is, and the less it costs a man to make himself master of it, so much the lower must its wages sink; since they are determined, like the price of every other commodity, by its cost of production.

"Therefore exactly as the labor becomes more unsatisfactory and unpleasant, in that very proportion competition increases and wages decline. The laborer does his best to maintain the rate of his wages by performing more labor, whether by working for a greater number of hours, or by working harder in the same time. Thus, driven by necessity, he himself increases the evil of the subdivision of labor. So the result is this; the more he labors, the less reward he receives for it; and that for this simple reason—that he competes against his fellow-workmen, and thus compels them to compete against him, and to offer their labor on as wretched conditions as he does; and that he thus in the last result competes against himself as a member of the working class.

"Machinery has the same effect, but in a much greater degree. It supplants skilled laborers by unskilled, men by women, adults by children; where it is newly introduced, it throws the hand-laborers upon the streets in crowds; and where it is perfected or replaced by latter improvements and more inventions, discards them by slightly slower degrees. We have sketched above in hasty outlines the industral war of capitalists with one another; and the war has this peculiarty, that its battles are won less by means of enlisting than of discharging its industrial recruits. *The generals or capitalists vie with one another as to who can dispense with the greatest number of his soldiers.*

"The economists repeatedly assure us that the laborers who are rendered superfluous by the machines find new branches of employment.

"They have not the hardihood directly to assert that the laborers who are discharged enter upon the new branches of labor. The facts cry out too loud against such a lie as this. They only declare that for other divisions of the laboring class, as for instance, for the rising generation of laborers who were just ready to enter upon the defunct branch of industry, new means of employment will open out. Of course that is a great satisfaction for the dismissed laborers. The worshipful capitalists will not find their fresh supply of exploitable flesh and blood run short, and will let the dead bury their dead. This is indeed a consolation with which the bourgeois comfort *themselves* rather than the laborers. If the whole class of wage-laborers were annihilated by the machines, how shocking that would be for capital, which without wage-labor ceases to act as capital at all.

"But let us suppose that those who are directly driven out of their employment by machinery, and also all those of the rising generation who were expecting employment in the same line, find some new employment. Does any one imagine that this will be as highly paid as that which they have lost? Such an idea would be in direct contradiction to all the laws of economy. We have already seen that the modern form of industry always tends to the displacement of the more complex and the higher kinds of employment, by those which are more simple and subordinate.

"How then could a crowd of laborers, who are thrown out of one branch of industry by machinery, find refuge in another, without having to content themselves with a lower position and worse pay?

"The laborers who are employed in the manufacture of machinery itself have been instanced as an exception. As soon as a desire arises and a demand begins in an industry for more machinery, it is said that there must necessarily be an increase in the number of machines, and therefore in the manufacture of machines, and therefore in the employment of laborers in this manufacture; and the laborers who are employed in this branch of industry will be skilled, and indeed even educated laborers.

"Ever since the year 1840 this contention, which even before that time was only half true, has lost all its specious color. For the machine which are employed in the manufacture of machinery have been quite as numerous as those used in the manufacture of cotton; and the laborers who are employed in producing machines, instead of being highly educated, have only been able to play the part of utterly unskilled machines themselves.

"But in the place of the man who has been dismissed by the machine perhaps three children and one woman are employed to work it. And was it not necessary before that the man's wages should suffice for the support of his wife and his children? Was not the minimum of wages necessarily sufficient for the maintenance and propagation of the race of laborers? There is no difference, except that now the lives of four times as many laborers as before are used up in order to secure the support of one laborer's family.

"To repeat our deductions; the faster productive capital increases, the more does the division of labor and the employment of machinery extend. The more the division of labor and the employment of machinery extend, so much the more does competition increase among the laborers, and so much the more do their average wages dwindle.

"And besides, the laboring class is recruited from the higher strata of society; or else there falls headlong into it a crowd of small manufacturers and small proprietors, who thenceforth have nothing better to do than to stretch out their arms by the side of those of the laborers. And thus the forest of arms outstretched by those who are entreating for work becomes ever denser and the arms themselves grow ever leaner.

"That the small manufacturer cannot survive in a contest, whose first condition is production on a continually increasing scale, that is, that he cannot be at once both a large and a small manufacturer, is self-evident.

"That the interest on capital declines in the same proportion as the amount of capital increases and extends, and that therefore the small capitalist can no longer live on his interest, but must join the ranks of the workers and increase the number of the proletariat,—all this requires no further exemplification.

"Finally, in the proportion in which the capitalists are compelled by the causes here sketched out to exploit on an ever increasing scale yet more gigantic means of production, and with this object to set in motion all the mainsprings of credit, in this same proportion is there an increase of those earthquakes wherein the business world can only secure its own existence by the sacrifice of a portion of its wealth, its products, and even its powers of production to the gods of the world below—in a word, crises increase. They become at once more frequent and more violent; because in the same proportion in which the amount of production, and therefore the demand for an extension of the market, increases, the market of the world continually contracts, and ever fewer markets remain to be exploited; since every previous crisis has added to the commerce of the world a market which was not known before, or had been only superficially exploited by commerce. But capital not only *lives* upon labor. Like a lord, at once distinguished and barbarous, it drags with it to the grave the corpses of its slaves and whole hecatombs of laborers who perish in the crisis. Thus we see that if capital increases fast, competition among the laborers increases still faster, that is, the means of employment and subsistence decline in proportion at a still more rapid rate; and yet, none the less, the most fortunate conditions for wage-labor lie in the speedy increase of capital."

CHAPTER V.

CAPITALISM.—ORIGIN OF THE BOURGEOISIE AND PROLETARIAT.

In February, 1848, the now historical "Communist Manifesto" appeared in London, England. It was translated into all the European languages and spread broadcast by the workingmen's societies of those countries. An extract from it is here given as follows:

"From the serfs of the middle ages sprang the burgesses of the early Communes; and from this municipal class were developed the first elements of the bourgeoisie. The discovery of America, the circumnavigation of Africa, gave the bourgeoisie or middle class—then coming into being—new and wider fields of action. The colonization of America, the opening up of the East Indian and Chinese markets, the colonial trade, the increase of merchandise and of currency, gave an impetus—hitherto unknown—to commerce, shipping and manufactures, and aided the rapid development of the revolutionary element in the old decaying form of feudal society.

"The old feudal way of managing the industrial interests through guilds was found no longer sufficient for the increasing demands of new markets. It was replaced by the manufacturing system. Guilds gave way to the industrial middle class, and the division of labor between the different corporations was succeeded by the division of labor between the workmen of one and the same workshop.

"New markets multiplied; the demand still increased. The manufacturing system in its turn was found to be inadequate. Then industrial production was revolutionized by machinery and steam. The modern industrial system was then developed in all its gigantic proportions; instead of the industrial middle-class we find industrial millionaires, chiefs of whole industrial armies—the modern bourgeoisie, or middle-class capitalists. This system of modern industry founded a world-wide market, which the discovery of America had prepared, and thereby an immense development was given to commerce, and to the means of communication by sea and land. This again reacted upon the industrial system, and in the same degree that industry, trade, shipping and railroads have increased, so have the bourgeoisie developed and increased their capital, and at the same time have driven to the wall all classes then remaining from feudal times.

"We find, therefore, that the modern bourgeoisie are themselves the result of a long process of development, of a series of revolutions in the modes of production and exchange. Each of these stages in the evolution of the bourgeoisie was accompanied by corresponding progress. It was an oppressed class under the old feudal barons; in the mediæval communes it assumed the form of armed and self governing associations; in one county we find it existing as a commercial republic or free city; in another, as the third taxable estate of the monarchy; then during the prevalence of the manufacturing system (before the introduction of steam) the middle-class was a counterpoise to the nobility in absolute monarchies, and the groundwork of the powerful monarchial states generally. Finally, since the advent of the modern industrial system, with its world-wide markets, this class has gained exclusive possession of political power in modern representative states. Modern governments are merely committees for managing the affairs of industry in the interest of the bourgeoisie.

"The bourgeoisie have played an extremely revolutionary role in society!

"The bourgeoisie have destroyed all feudal, patriarchal and idylic relations wherever they have come into power. They relentlessly tore asunder the many-sided ties of that chain which bound men to their 'natural superiors,' and they left no bond of union between man and man, save that of bare self-interest—*of cash payments*. They resolved personal dignity into market value, and substituted the single unprincipled idea of freedom of trade for the numerous, well-earned, chartered liberties of the middle ages. Chivalrous enthusiasm, the emotions of piety, and all principles of personal honor have vanished before the icy breath of their selfish calculations. In a word, the bourgeoisie substituted shameless, direct open spoliation, for the previous system of spoliation concealed under religious and political illusions.

"The bourgeoisie divested of their sanctity all institutions heretofore regarded with pious veneration. They converted the physician, the jurist, the priest, the poet, the philosopher, into their paid tools and servants.

"The bourgeoisie have torn the tender veil of sentiment away from domestic ties and reduced the family relations to a mere question of dollars and cents.

"The bourgeoisie have demonstrated how the brutal force of the middle ages, which is so much admired by reactionists, has found its most befitting fulfilment to-day in the laziest ruffianism. They have also shown what human activity is capable of accomplishing. They have executed work more marvelous than Egyptian Pyramids, Roman Acqueducts, or Gothic Cathedrals; and their expeditions have surpassed by far all former crusades and migrations of nations.

"The bourgeoisie cannot exist, without continually revolutionizing machinery and the instruments of production, and consequently changing all our social institutions. Persistence in the established modes of production was, on the contrary, in former years, the first condition of existence for all other industrial classes. A continual change in the modes of production, a never ceasing state of agitation and social insecurity, distinguish the bourgeois epoch from all preceding ones. The ancient ties between men—their opinions and belief, hoary with antiquity—are fast disappearing, and new ones become worn out ere they become firmly rooted. Everything fixed and stable vanishes; everything holy and venerable is profaned; and men are forced to look at their mutual relations, at the problem of life, in the soberest, most matter-of-fact manner.

"The need of an ever increasing market for their produce drives the bourgeoisie all over the entire globe—they found settlements, form connections and set up means of communication everywhere. Through their control of the world's markets they have given a cosmopolitan tendency to the production and consumption of all countries. To the great regret of the reactionists the bourgeoisie have deprived modern industry of its national foundation. The old national manufactures have been in some cases annihilated and are still being destroyed. They are superseded by new modes of industry, the introduction of which is becoming a vital question for all civilized nations, where raw materials are not indigenous, but are brought from the remotest countries; and whose products are not merely consumed in the home market, but throughout the the whole world. Instead of the old primitive wants, supplied only by home production, we now find new wants supplied by the products of the most distant lands and climes. Instead of the old local, national feeling of independence and isolation, we find universal intercourse and inter-dependence among nations. The same fact obtains in the intellectual world! The intellectual productions of each nation become the common property of all nations. National partiality and prejudice are fast becoming impossible and a universal literature is being formed from the numerous local and national literatures.

"Through incessant improvements in machinery and the means of communication, the bourgeoisie draw the most barbarous nations into the magic circle of civilization. Cheap goods are their artillery for battering down Chinese walls and to overcome the obstinate hatred entertained towards strangers by semi-civilized nations. Under penalty of ruin, the bourgeoisie compel by competition the universal adoption of their system of production; they force all nations to accept what is called civilization—to become bourgeois—and thus the middle class shapes the world after its own image.

"The bourgeoisie have subjected the rural districts to the ascendancy of the town; they have created enormous cities, and by causing an immense increase of population in manufacturing districts, compared with agricultural, have removed a greater part of the population from the simplicity of country life. Not only have they made the country subordinate to the town, they have also made barbarous and half civilized tribes dependent on civilized nations, the agricultural on the manufacturing nations, the East on the West. The division of property, of the means of production disappear under the rule of the bourgeoisie. They agglomerate population, they centralize the means of production, and concentrate property in the hands of the few. Political centralization is the natural result. Independent provinces, with different interests, each affected by separate customs and under separate local government are brought together as one nation, under the same government, the same laws, customs, and tariff—under the same national class interest.

"The rule of the bourgeoisie has only prevailed for about a century, but during that time it has called into being greater gigantic powers of production than all preceding generations combined. The subjection of the elements of nature, the development of machinery, the application of chemistry to agriculture and manufactures, railways, telegraphs, steamships, the clearing and cultivation of whole continents, the canalizing of rivers,—large populations, whole industrial armies, springing up as if by magic. What preceding century ever even dreamed of these productive powers slumbering in the bosom of society?

"We have seen that these means of production and traffic which serve as the foundation of middle class development, originated in feudal times. At a certain stage in the evolution of these means, the conditions under which feudal society produced and exchanged—the feudal system of agriculture and industry—in a word the feudal conditions of property no longer sufficed for the increased productive powers of mankind. These conditions then became a hindrance to production; instead of an assistance, they were so many fetters which had to be broken and they were broken.

"They were superseded by unrestricted competition with its appropriate social and political constitutions, with the economic and political supremacy of the middle class. At the present moment a similar movement is going on. Modern middle class society which has revolutionized the conditions of property and called forth such collossal powers of production and exchange, resembles the wizard who loses control of the infernal powers he has conjured. The history of manufactures and commerce has been for many years the history of the revolts of the modern powers of production against the modern conditions of production—against the very conditions of property which are vital to the existence and supremacy of the middle class. It is sufficient to refer to the panics or commercial crises, which in their periodical recurrence, more and more endanger the existence of the middle class. In such a crisis is not only a larger quantity of social products destroyed, but also a large portion of the productive power itself.

"During such panics a social epidemic breaks forth, which in all former epochs whould have appeared a paradox—the epidemic of over-production. Society finds itself suddenly thrown back into momentary barbarism; famine or devastating war seem to have deprived it of the means of subsistence,—industry and trade appear destroyed. And is it because society possesses too much civilization, too much sustenance, too much industry, too much trade? The powers of production at the disposal of society, no longer serve to advance the middle class ownership of property; on the contrary they have become too powerful for these conditions; they are hampered by them and whenever these obstructions are overcome, they throw all middle class society into confusion and imperil the existence of middle class property. The social system of the middle class has become too narrow to hold the wealth it has called into being. How does the middle class try to withstand these panics? On the one hand by destroying masses of productive power, on the other hand by the conquest of new markets and by exhausting the old ones more thoroughly. That is they prepare the way for still more universal and dangerous panics and reduce the means of withstanding them.

"The weapons with which the middle class overthrew feudalism are now turned against itself. The middle class not only has forged the weapons for its own destruction, it has also produced the men who will wield these weapons—the modern workmen, the proletariat.

"In the same degree in which the bourgeoisie and capital have developed, so the proletariat has developed. And this is the class that live only when it can find work, and it finds work only as long as its toil will increase capital. These workers who must sell themselves piecemeal to the highest bidder, like all other articles of commerce, are equally exposed to all the variations of competition and to all the fluctuations of the market.

"Through the extension of machinery and the division of work, daily labor has lost all its independent character and all attraction for the workingman. He becomes merely an appendage to a machine, and only the simplest, most monotonous, and most easily learnt operation is demanded. The expenses of the workingman, are therefore almost entirely limited to the means of subsistence required for his support and for the propagation of his race.

"The price of a commodity, likewise of labor, is measured by its cost of production. In the same degree that the repulsiveness of labor increases, wages decrease. Still further in proportion as machinery and division of labor increase, the burdens of labor increase either through increase of the hours of labor, or in the quantity of work required in a given time, or through increased speed of machinery, etc.

"Modern industry has transformed the small workshop of the artisan into the larger factory of the capitalist. Masses of operatives crowded together in factories are organized on a military basis. They are placed as common soldiers, under the superintendence of a complete hierarchy of officers and subalterns. They are not alone slaves of the middle class, of the government; but they are also daily and hourly the slaves of the machine, the foreman, and above all the individual employer. This despotism is all the more hateful, contemptible and aggravating since it openly proclaims that *gain* is its only object and aim.

"The less skill and exertion of force manual labor requires, the more modern industry develops; the more the labor of men is displaced by that of women. Neither sex nor age have any social existence for the working class. They are merely so many instruments costing different sums according to age or sex.

"When the plundering of the workingman by the manufacturer has ceased in so far that he has been paid his cash wages, then step in the other portions of the middle class to prey upon the worker, *viz:* the landlord, storekeeper, pawnbroker, etc.

"The small middle class, the artisans, merchants, mechanics, shopkeepers, and farmers, are all doomed to fall into the ranks of the proletariat, because their small capital can not compete with that of the millionaire, and partly because their skill is depreciated by new modes of production. Thus the proletariat recruits from all classes of population.

"The proletariat has passed through many phases of development, but its struggle with the bourgeoisie dates from its birth. At first the struggle is waged by individual workingmen, then by the workingmen of one factory, next by the workingmen of an entire trade in the same locality against an individual employer who directly despoils them. They attack not only the capitalistic conditions of production, but even the instruments of production; they destroy competing merchandise from foreign countries, they break machines, burn factories and seek to regain the position of the workers in the middle ages. At this stage the workers form a disorganized mass scattered all over the country divided by competition. A more compact union then comes, not so much the effect of their own development, as it is the consequence of the organization of the bourgeoisie. This class requires and does set in motion the whole working class for the furtherance of its own political interests. And thus the working class do not fight their own enemies, but rather the enemies of their masters, such as absolute monarchy wherever it exists, the landowners, the non-employing capitalists, the shopkeepers; the benefits of every such movement are thus concentrated in the hands of the bourgeoisie, who are opposed to these classes; every victory thus gained is won for them.

"With the development of industry not only does the proletariat increase, it also concentrates into greater masses and learns its own strength and power. The interests and conditions of different trades are more and more equalized, because machinery destroys more and more the difference in labor and reduces wages to the same low level generally. The increasing competition of the bourgeoisie among themselves and the commercial panics resulting therefrom make the wages of workingmen more uncertain; the continual and rapid improvement in machinery makes their conditions in life more precarious. The collisions between individual workingmen and individual masters assume more and more the character of outbreaks between the two classes. The workingmen form coalitions against the masters, they unite in trade unions to maintain their wages. They form permanent associations for mutual aid and to prepare for these occasional outbreaks. And at times the struggle assumes the form of riots. From time to time the workingmen are victorious, but only momentarily. The actual result of their struggle is not immediate success, but leads to ever increasing combination among workingmen. Their unions are favored by the ever growing facility of communication, fostered by modern industry, whereby the workingmen of the remotest districts are placed in closer connection. All that is required is a closer union to centralize the many local struggles of the same character into one grand national struggle, into a class revolt. Every class struggle is a political one. The combination, which took the burghers of the middle ages with their common highways centuries to accomplish, can be now established in a few years by the modern working class, through the aid of railroads.

"This organization of the workingmen into a class and thereby into a political party is often destroyed by the competition of workingmen among themselves. Yet the organization of labor always reappears, and each time stronger, firmer and more extensive. It enforces the legal recognition of some particular interest of the workingmen, profiting by dissensions among the bourgeoisie—as in the case of the ten-hour law in England. The dissensions of the ruling class among themselves are favorable in many respects to the advancement of the proletariat. The bourgeoisie have always been in a state of perpetual warfare, first against the aristocracy, then against that part of its own class whose interests are opposed to the further development of industry, and thirdly against the bourgeoisie of other countries. In all these struggles it is obliged to appeal to the working class, to invoke their help, and so the working class is drawn into political movements. It therefore places in the hands of the proletariat its own means of advancement—and furnishes the weapons against itself.

"As we have already seen, the evolution of industry throws a large part of the ruling class into the ranks of the proletariat, or at least renders their condition in life more precarious. Thus a mass of enlightened elements are driven into the ranks of the working class.

"Finally, as the settlement of this class struggle nears an end, then the process of dissolution goes on so rapidly within the ruling class—within the worn out body politic—that a small fraction of this class separates from the bourgeoisie and unites with the revolutionary class—that class which holds the future in its own hands.

"As in former times, a part of the nobility joined the bourgeoisie, so now a part of the bourgeoisie joins the proletariat, and particularly that part of the bourgeoisie who have attained a theoretical and historical knowledge of the whole movement.

"The working class is the only true revolutionary class among all the enemies of the bourgeoisie to-day. The remaining classes are degenerating; destroyed by modern industry. The proletariat is its only product!

"The middle class, the artisans, the shopkeepers, mechanics and farmers, all oppose the bourgeoisie in order to defend their position as small capitalists. They are not revolutionary, but conservative. Yea more—they are reactionary, they seek to turn backward the wheels of history. When they are revolutionary, they are only so in view of their impending absorption by the proletariat, hence they do not defend their present but their future interests; they abandon their own position in order to take up that of the proletariat.

"The vagabond proletariat—the rowdies and bummers—that passive rot of the lowest strata of modern society, will be partially drawn into this movement but from its peculiar social status will be ever found a ready and venal tool for reactionary intrigues.

"The conditions of existence for modern society are already destroyed through the conditions imposed upon the working class. The workingman has no property; the relation in which he stands to his family has nothing in common with the bourgois family relation. Modern industrial labor, the modern slavery of labor to capital, the same in England as in France, in America as in Germany, has divested him of all national character. Law, morality, religion are for him only so much middle class prejudice, behind which are concealed so many middle class interests.

"All dominant classes in the past have sought to preserve the position they attained, by subjecting society to the conditions which gave those classes their possessions. The proletarians can gain control of the productive powers of society—of the instruments of labor—only by annihilating all acknowledged modes of spoliation by which they have been plundered, and with it the entire system of spoliation and robbery. The proletarians have nothing of their own to protect, they must destroy all existing capitalistic security and capitalistic guaranties.

"All previous movements were movements of minorities or in the interest of minorities. The labor movement is an independent movement of the immense majority in behalf of the immense majority. The proletariat, the lowest strata of existing society, cannot arise without disrupting the entire superstructure of classes above it, and that hold it down.

"Although the struggle of the proletariat against the bourgeoisie is *not* national in its nature, yet it is so in form. The proletariat of each country must naturally first settle accounts with the bourgeoisie of that country.

"We have thus sketched the general aspect presented by the development of the proletariat, and at the same time followed the more or less concealed civil war pervading modern society up to that point, where it must break forth into *open revolution*, and then the proletariat will arrive at supremacy through *the forcible downfall* of the bourgeoisie.

"All previous forms of society rested as we have seen, upon the antagonisms of oppressing and oppressed classes. But, in order to oppress a class, the conditions must be secured under which it can at least continue its slavish existence. The serf in the middle ages found it possible to become a member of the commune. The burghers could enter the middle class even under the yoke of feudal monarchy. The modern workingman on the contrary, instead of improving his condition with the progress of industry, is daily sinking lower and lower, even below the conditions of existence for his own class. The workingman is becoming a pauper, and pauperism develops even more rapidly than population and wealth. This clearly proves that the bourgeoisie is incapable of holding its position any longer as the ruling class. It can no longer force upon society its conditions as the rule of action. It is unable to rule because it is unable even to secure the existence of its slaves in their slavery, as it lets them sink into a lot where it must nourish them, instead of being nourished by them. Society can not longer exist under this class, as the existence of this class is no longer compatible with that of society.

"The most important condition for the existence and supremacy of the bourgeoisie, is accumulation of wealth in the hands of private individuals; the formation and increase of capital.

"The condition upon which capital depends is wages-labor. Wages-labor rests exclusively on the competition of the workingmen among themselves. The progress of industry, tends to supersede the isolated action of the workingmen by the revolutionary union of their class, and to replace competition by association. With the development of modern industry therefore the basis on which the bourgeoisie manages production and appropriates the products of labor is drawn from under its feet. Thus the bourgeoisie produces its own grave. Its downfall and the victory of the proletariat are alike unavoidable."

"But occult theft, theft which hides itself, even from itself, and is legal, respectable, and cowardly, corrupts the body and soul of man to the last fibre of them. And the guilty thieves of Europe, the real sources of all deadly war in it, are the capitalists—that is to say, people who live by percentages on the labor of others, instead of by fair wages for their own. The *real* war in Europe, of which this fighting in Paris is the inauguration, is between these and the workman, such as these have made him. They have kept him poor, ignorant and simple, that they might, without his knowledge, gather for themselves the produce of his toil. At last a dim insight into the fact of this dawns on him, and as they have made him, he meets them, and *will* meet.—*Extract from John Ruskin's letters to workmen and laborers* (FORS CLAVIGERA) *upon the Paris Commune of 1871.*

PART II.

CHAPTER I.

ANARCHY ON TRIAL.

"Black says they are humanitarians. Don't try, gentlemen, to shirk the issue. *Anarchy is on trial;* the defendants are on trial for treason and murder."
Mr. Black—The indictment does not charge treason; does it, Mr. Grinnell?
Mr. Grinnell—No, sir.—*Extract from closing speech of the State's Attorney.*

Not until this announcement, in the closing words of the last speech by the attorney representing the State, were the eight defendants apprised, officially, or otherwise, that the question at issue was anarchy; for professing which, a verdict of death was then demanded.

This announcement was all the more startling from the fact that frequent attacks had been made upon them as socialists and anarchists throughout the trial; and the defendants had demanded of their counsel the privilege of introducing witnesses, to explain to the judge, and the country, what was the meaning and purpose of the doctrine of which they were disciples, if not the apostles in America; and for entertaining which they were informed the death sentence was now invoked, not, however, until a few moments before the case was given to the jury.

Mr. Foster, who came into the case, with some local reputation in the State of his former residence as a criminal lawyer, persisted in trying the same, as one purely of homicide; to be determined upon the plain issue of law and facts pertaining to the alleged killing (as charged in the indictment) of one Matthias J. Degan.

He scouted the idea that either the court or jury would try the political opinions of the defendants; as a criminal issue to be adjudged worthy of death as social heretics. Mr. Foster's idea, however, prevailed, though not without opposition from Capt. Black, who was overruled by the majority.

In the words of a Wisconsin, Eau Claire, correspondent to a leading Chicago journal:

"Midway in the trial, while this question was still unsettled, there came a message from Chicago to Eau Claire summoning a well-known citizen of this city to appear at a conclave of the Chicago anarchists. The distinguished citizen was no other than Alderman Charles L. James, a person who, during a residence of over twenty years in this community, has been generally known as an advanced type of anarchistic socialism; that he had laid the literatures of several languages under contribution to furnish food for his theorizing, and, finally, that besides being a scholar himself, he was the youngest son of no less a scholar and *litterateur* than George P. R. James, the historiographer of William IV, the author of a whole library of romances—no other, indeed, than the 'Solitary Horseman.'

"Mr. James was one of the victims of that exclusive policy of Mr. Foster which choked the explanation of the propaganda. He came back from Chicago wearing a disappointment in his heart for that he was not allowed to speak. This disappointment, however, he shortly assuaged by addressing a communication embodying what he would have said, to the *North American Review*. The discriminating editor of that periodical published the letter in his July number, of which the following is an extract, and which is here given, because it is an embodyment of what would have been, and should have been, presented to the jury and the country, on the trial by Mr. James:

"'ANARCHY FROM AN ANARCHIST'S STANDPOINT.—Competition among capitalists is continually reducing the price of commodities to the cost of production. This necessitates increasingly minute subdivision of labor, destroying that technical skill which made the old-fashioned shoemaker or blacksmith independent; degrading the laborers into portions of the machine they operate; stimulating the competition for employment which prevails among them; increasing the frequency of those periods when they are thrown out of work and reduced from comfort to beggary, and of course contributing to increase the revolutionary discontent of educated men, nurtured in hope and enjoyment, who see themselves hopelessly distanced by those whom they can in no way regard as their superiors. The chasm which threatens to engulf our social system is still further widened by the destruction of small capitalists in the battle of competition and the growth of great monopolies, advancing *pari passu* with the pauperization of the laboring class. The miseries and dangers thus engendered by the very nature of modern trade and industry are greatly aggravated by the periodical gorging of the market with goods produced in excess of the demand during seasons of speculation, and the consequent forced migration of capital to other branches by the dreary road along which lie bankruptcy, stagnation, reduced consumption, reduced production, slow liquidation, and that gradual revival of business which closes a financial crisis. The critical character of these periodical revulsions is greatly aggravated by the fluctuations of that uncertain currency which speculative business has everywhere introduced. It has so far been palliated by the extension of the market into new countries—America, India, Egypt, China, etc. But when this process reaches an end and one commercial system extends over the world, then, if not sooner, prices will actually fall to the cost of production, and the catastrophe of production for profit will be reached. Anarchy, therefore, according to anarchists, is the inevitable end of the present drift and tendency of things. Trimmers may devise means to put it off; Napoleons and Bismarcks may, for a time, stifle it in blood, but the longer it is deferred the more violent will be the reaction which brings it in at last. That only is wise statesmanship which gives up moribund institutions to die. That only is reform which anticipates in a less painful manner the work of revolution.'

Dyer D. Lum, C. S. Griffin, Mrs. Lucy E. Parsons, Mrs. Holmes, Mrs. Ames, A. W. Simpson, John A. Henry, William Holmes, and many other well-known anarchists, including the eight prisoners at the bar, requested repeatedly throughout the trial permission to explain and define to the court and jury the speculative philosophy known as anarchism, but were always told by the lawyers for the defense that it was entirely unnessary, since their belief in the doctrines of "anarchy" was not upon trial. That anarchy really was on trial was made known when it was too late to explain or define it. At the close of the *trial* the prosecution sprung a new case upon the defendants, a charge which was not in the indictment, and against which *these defendants* were not permitted to defend themselves.

In their closing speeches the prosecution declared: "Law is upon trial. Anarchy is on trial. These men have been selected, picked out by the grand jury and indicted because they were leaders. They are no more guilty than the thousands who follow them. Gentlemen of the jury; convict these men, make examples of them, hang them and you save our institutions, our society."

It is mainly, if not wholly, on account of the declarations made by the prosecution in the paragraph quoted above that the author has written and compiled this work, towit: that not being permitted to defend or explain the belief we entertained; that having been condemned unheard for social heresy,—the world which is our final judge and to which we appeal, may know, as it has a right to know, in what our offense consisted.

CHAPTER II.

VIEWS OF THE PRISONERS.

Following are extracts from the speeches of the eight Chicago anarchists, relating to anarchy, made by them in reply to the question of the court why sentence should not be pronounced; including also other extracts from their writings:

AUGUST SPIES ON ANARCHY.

* * * "From their testimony one is forced to conclude that we had, in our speeches and publications, preached nothing else but destruction and dynamite. The court has this morning stated that there is no case in history like this. I have noticed, during this trial, that the gentlemen of the legal profession are not well versed in history. In all historical cases of this kind truth had to be perverted by the priests of the established power that was nearing its end.

"What have we said in our speeches and publications?

"We have interpreted to the people their conditions and relations in society. We have explained to them the different social phenomena and the social laws and circumstances under which they occur. We have, by way of scientific investigation, incontrovertibly proved and brought to their knowledge that the system of wages is the root of the present social iniquities—iniquities so monstrous that they cry to Heaven. We have further said that the wage system, as a specific form of social development, would, by the necessity of logic, have to make room for higher forms of civilization; that the wage system must prepare the way and furnish the foundation for a social system of co-operation—that is, *socialism.* That whether this or that theory, this or that scheme regarding future arrangements were accepted was not a matter of choice, but one of historical necessity, and that to us the tendency of progress seemed to be *anarchism*—that is, a free society without kings or classes—a society of sovereigns in which the liberty and economic equality of all would furnish an unshakable equilibrium as a foundation and condition of natural order.

"It is not likely that the honorable Bonfield and Grinnell can conceive of a social order not held intact by the policeman's club and pistol, nor of a free society without prisons, gallows, and State's attorneys. In such a society they probably fail to find a place for themselves. And is this the reason why anarchism is such a 'pernicious and damnable doctrine?'

"Grinnell has intimated to us that anarchism was on trial. The theory of anarchism belongs to the realm of speculative philosophy. There was not a syllable said about anarchism at the Haymarket meeting. At that meeting the very popular theme of reducing the hours of toil was discussed. But, 'anarchism is on trial' foams Mr. Grinnell. If that is the case, your honor, very well; you may sentence me, for I am an anarchist. I believe with Buckle, with Paine, Jefferson, Emerson, and Spencer, and many other great thinkers of this century, that the state of castes and classes—the state where one class dominates over and lives upon the labor of another class, and calls this *order*—yes; I believe that this barbaric form of social organization, with its legalized plunder and murder, is doomed to die, and make room for a free society, voluntary association, or universal brotherhood, if you like. You may pronounce the sentence upon me, honorable judge, but let the world know that in A. D. 1886, in the State of Illinois, eight men were sentenced to death because they believed in a better future; because they had not lost their faith in the ultimate victory of liberty and justice! 'You have taught the destruction of society and civilization,' says the tool and agent of the Bankers' and Citizens' Association, Grinnell. That man has yet to learn what civilization is. It is the old, old argument against human progress. Read the history of Greece, of Rome; read that of Venice; look over the dark pages of the church, and follow the thorny path of science. 'No change! No change! You would destroy society and civilization!' has ever been the cry of the ruling classes. They are so comfortably situated under the prevailing system that they naturally abhor and fear even the slightest change. Their privileges are as dear to them as life itself, and every change threatens these privileges. But civilization is a ladder whose steps are monuments of such changes! Without these social changes—all brought about against the will and the force of the ruling classes—there would be no civilization. As to the destruction of society which we have been accused of seeking, sounds this not like one of Æsop's fables—like the cunning of the fox? We, who have jeopardized our lives to save society from the fiend—the fiend who has grasped her by the throat; who sucks her life-blood, who devours her children—we, who would heal her bleeding wounds, who would free her from the fetters you have wrought around her; from the misery you have brought upon her—we her enemies!!

"Honorable judge, the demons of hell will join in the laughter this irony provokes!

"We have preached dynamite. Yes, we have predicted from the lessons history teaches, that the ruling classes of to-day would no more listen to the voice of reason than their predecessors; that they would attempt by brute force to stay the wheel of progress. Is it a lie, or was it the truth we told? Are not already the large industries of this once free country conducted under the surveillance of the police, the detective, the military and the sheriffs—and is this return to militancy not developing from day to day. American sovereigns—think of it—working like the galley convicts under military guards! We have predicted this, and predict that soon these conditions will grow unbearable. What then? The mandate of the feudal lords of our time is slavery, starvation and death! This has been their programme for the past years. We have said to the toilers, that science had penetrated the mystery of nature—that from Jove's head once more has sprung a Minerva—dynamite! If this declaration is synonymous with murder, why not charge those with the crime to whom we owe the invention? To charge us with an attempt to overthrow the present system on or about May 4th by force, and then establish anarchy, is too absurd a statement, I think, even for a political office-holder to make. If Grinnell belived that we attempted such a thing, why did he not have Dr. Bluthardt make an inquiry as to our sanity? Only mad men could have planned such a brilliant scheme, and mad people cannot be indicted or convicted of murder. If there had existed anything like a conspiracy or a pre-arrangement, does your honor believe that events would not have taken a different course than they did on that evening and later? This 'conspiracy' nonsense is based upon an oration I delivered on the anniversary of Washington's birthday at Grand Rapids, Mich., more than a year and a half ago. I had been invited by the Knights of Labor for that purpose. I dwelt upon the fact that our country was far from being what the great revolutionists of the last century had intended it to be. I said that those men if they lived to-day would clean the Augean stables with iron brooms, and that they, too, would undoubtedly be characterized as 'wild socialists.' It is not unlikely that I said Washington would have been hanged for treason if the revolution had failed. Grinnell made this 'sacreligious remark' his main arrow against me. Why? Because he intended to inveigh the know-nothing spirit against us. But who will deny the correctness of the statement? That I should have compared myself with Washington, is a base lie. But if I had, would that be murder? I may have told that individual who appeared here as a witness that the workingmen should procure arms, as force would in all probability be the *ultima ratio;* and that in Chicago there were so and so many armed, but I certainly did not say that we proposed to 'inaugurate the social revolution.' And let me say here: Revolutions are no more made than earthquakes and cyclones. Revolutions are the effect of certain causes and conditions. I have made social philosophy a specific study for more than ten years, and I could not have given vent to such nonsense! I do believe, however, that the revolution is near at hand—in fact, that it is upon us. But is the physician responsible for the death of the patient because he foretold that death? If any one is to be blamed for the coming revolution it is the ruling class who steadily refused to make concessions as reforms became necessary; who maintain that they can call a halt to progress, and dictate a stand-still to the enternal forces, of which they themselves are but the whimsical creation.

"The position generally taken in this case is that we are morally responsible for the police riot on May 4th. Four or five years ago I sat in this very court room as a witness. The workingmen had been trying to obtain redress in a lawful manner. They had voted, and among others, had elected their aldermanic candidate from the fourteenth ward. But the street car company did not like that man. And two of the three election judges of one precinct, knowing this, took the ballot box to their home and 'corrected' the election returns, so as to cheat the constituents of the elected candidate of their rightful representative, and give the representation to the benevolent street car monopoly. The workingmen spent $1,500 in the prosecution of the perpetrators of this crime. The proof against them was so overwhelming that they confessed to having falsified the returns and forged the official documents. Judge Gardner, who was presiding in this court, acquitted them, stating that 'that act had apparently not been prompted by criminal intent.' I will make no comment. But when we approach the field of moral responsibility, it has an immense scope! Every man who has in the past assisted in thwarting the efforts of those seeking reform is responsible for the existence of the revolutionists in this city to-day! Those, however, who have sought to bring about reforms must be exempted from the responsibility—and to these *I* belong.

"If the verdict is based upon the assumption of moral responsibility, your honor, I give this as a reason why sentence should not be passed.

"If the opinion of the court given this morning is good law, then there is no person in this country who could not lawfully be hanged. I vouch that, upon the very laws you have read, there is no person in this courtroom now who could not be 'fairly, impartially and lawfully' hanged! Fouche, Napoleon's right bower, once said to his master: 'Give me a line that any one man has ever written, and I will bring him to the scaffold.' And this court has done essentially the same. Upon that law every person in this country can be indicted for conspiracy, and, as the case may be, for murder. Every member of a trade union, Knights of Labor, or any other labor organization, can then be convicted of conspiracy, and in cases of violence, for which they may not be responsible at all, of murder, as we have been. This precedent once established, and you force the masses who are now agitating in a peaceable way into open rebellion! You thereby shut off the last safety valve—and the blood which will be shed, the blood of the innocent—it will come upon your heads!

"Seven policemen have died,' said Grinnell, suggestively winking at the jury. You want a life for a life, and have convicted an equal number of men, of whom it cannot be truthfully said that they had anything whatsoever to do with the killing of Bonfield's victims. The very same principle of jurisprudence we find among various savage tribes. Injuries among them are equalized, so to speak. The Chinooks and the Arabs, for instance, would demand the life of an enemy for every death that they had suffered at their enemy's hands. They were not particular in regard to the persons, just so long as they had a life for a life. This principle also prevails to-day among the natives of the Sandwich Islands. If we are to be hanged on this principle then let us know it, and let the world know what a civilized and christian country it is, in which the Goulds, the Vanderbilts, the Stanfords, the Fields, Armours, and other local money *hamsters* have come to the rescue of liberty and justice!

"Grinnell has repeatedly stated that our country is an enlightened country, (*sarcastically*.) The verdict fully corroborates the assertion! This verdict against us is the anathema of the wealthy classes over their despoiled victims—the vast army of wage workers and farmers. If your honor would not have these people believe this; if you would not have them believe that we have once more arrived at the Spartan Senate, the Athenian Areopagus, the Venetian Council of Ten, etc., then sentence should not be pronounced. But, if you think that by hanging us, you can stamp out the labor movement—the movement from which the downtrodden millions, the millions who toil and live in want and misery—the wage slaves—expect salvation—if this is your opinion, then hang us! Here you will tread upon a spark, but there, and there; and behind you, and in front of you, and everywhere, flames will blaze up. It is a subterranean fire. You cannot put it out.

"The ground is on fire upon which you stand. You can't understand it. You don't believe in magical arts, as your grandfathers did who burned witches at the stake, but you do believe in conspiracies; you believe that all these occurrences of late are the work of conspirators! You resemble the child that is looking for his picture behind the mirror. What you see, and what you try to grasp is nothing but the deceptive reflex of the stings of your bad conscience. You want to 'stamp out the conspirators'—the 'agitators?' Ah, stamp out every factory lord who has grown wealthy upon the unpaid labor for his employes. Stamp out every landlord who has amassed fortunes from the rent of over-burdened workingmen and farmers. Stamp out every machine that is revolutionizing industry and agriculture, that intensifies the production and ruins the producer, that increases the national wealth, while the creator of all these things stands amidst them, tantalized with hunger! Stamp out the railroads, the telegraph, the telephone, steam and yourselves—for everything breathes the revolutionary spirit.

"You, gentlemen, are the revolutionists! You rebel against the effects of social conditions which have tossed you, by the fair hand of fortune, into a magnificent paradise. Without inquiring, you imagine that no one else has a right in that place. You insist that you are the chosen ones, the sole proprietors. The forces that tossed you into the paradise, the industrial forces, are still at work. They are growing more active and intense from day to day. Their tendency is to elevate all mankind to the same level, to have all humanity share in the paradise you now monopolize. You, in your blindness, think you can stop the tidal wave of civilization, and human emancipation by placing a few policemen, a few gatling guns, and some regiments of militia on the shore—you think you can frighten the rising waves back into the unfathomable depths, whence they have risen, by erecting a few gallows in the perspective. You, who oppose the natural course of things, *you* are the real revolutionists. *You* and *you* alone are the conspirators and destructionists!

"Said the court yesterday, in referring to the board of trade demonstration: 'These men started out with the express purpose of sacking the board of trade building.' While I can't see what sense there would have been in such an undertaking, and while I know that the said demonstration was arranged simply as a means of propaganda against the system that legalizes the respectable business carried on there, I will assume that the three thousand workingmen who marched in that procession really intended to sack the building. In this case they would have differed from the respectable board of trade men only in this—that they sought to recover property in an unlawful way, while the others sack the entire country lawfully and unlawfully—this being their respectable profession. This court of "justice and equity" proclaims the principle that when two persons do the same thing, it is not the same thing. I thank the court for this confession. It contains all that we have taught, and for which we are to be hanged, in a nut shell! Theft is a felony when resorted to in self preservation by the other class. Rapine and pillage are the order of a certain class of gentlemen who find this mode of earning a livelihood easier and preferable to honest labor—this is the kind of order we have attempted, and are now trying, and will try as long as we live to do away with. Look on the economic battle fields. Behold the carnage and plunder of the christian patricians! Accompany me to the quarters of the wealth-creators in this city. Go with me to the half-starved miners of the Hocking Valley. Look at the pariahs in the Monongahela Valley, and many other mining districts in this country, or pass along the railroads of that great and most orderly and law-abiding citizen, Jay Gould. And tell me whether this order has in it any moral principle for which it should be preserved. I say that the preservation of such an order is criminal, is murderous. It means the preservation of the systematic destruction of children and women in factories. It means the preservation of enforced idleness of large armies of men and their degradation. It means the preservation of misery, want, and servility on one hand, and the dangerous accumulation of spoils, idleness, voluptuousness and tyranny on the other. It means the preservation of vice in every form.

"And last but not least, it means the preservation of the class struggle of strikes, riots and bloodshed. That is *your* 'order,' gentlemen; yes, and it is worthy of you to be the champions of such an order. You are eminently fitted for that role. You have my compliments!

"Grinnell spoke of Victor Hugo. I need not repeat what he said, but will answer him in the language of one of our German philosphers:

'Our bourgeoisie erect monuments in honor of the memory of the classics. If they had read them they would burn them!' Why, amongst the articles read here from the *Arbeiter-Zeitung*, put in evidence by the State, by which they intend to convince the jury of the dangerous character of the accused anarchists, is an extract from Goethe's Faust.

'Es erben sich Gesetz und Rechte,
We eine ew'ge Krankheit fort,' etc.

('Law and class privileges are transmitted like an hereditary disease.') And Mr. Ingham in his speech told the christian jurors that our comrades, the Paris communists, had in 1871, dethroned God, the Almighty, and had put up in his place a low prostitute. The effect was marvelous! The good christians were shocked.

"I wish your honor would inform the learned gentlemen that the episode related occurred in Paris nearly a century ago, and that the sacrilegious perpetrators were the cotemporaries of the founders of the Republic—and among them was Thomas Paine. Nor was the woman a prostitute, but a good *citoyenne de Paris*, who served on that occasion simply as an allegory of the goddess of reason.

"Referring to Most's letter, read here, Mr. Ingham said: 'They,' meaning Most and myself, 'They might have destroyed thousands of innocent lives in the Hocking Valley with that dynamite.' I have said all I know about the letter on the witness stand, but will add that two years ago I went through the Hocking Valley as a correspondent. While there I saw hundreds of lives in the process of slow destruction, gradual destruction. There was no dynamite, nor were they Anarchists who did that diabolical work. It was the work of a party of highly respectable monopolists, law-abiding citizens, if you please. It is needless to say the murderers were never indicted. The press had little to say, and the State of Ohio assisted them. What a terror it would have created if the victims of this diabolical plot had resented and blown some of those respectable cut-throats to atoms. When, in East St. Louis, Jay Gould's hirelings, 'the men of grit,' shot down in cold blood and killed six inoffensive workingmen and women, there was very little said, and the grand jury refused to indict the gentlemen. It was the same way in Chicago, Milwaukee and other places. A Chicago furniture manufacturer shot down and seriously wounded two striking workingmen last spring. He was held over to the grand jury. The grand jury refused to indict the gentleman.

"But when, on one occasion, a workingman in self defense resisted the murderous attempt of the police and threw a bomb, and for once blood flowed on the other side, then a terrific howl went up from the land: 'Conspiracy has attacked vested rights!' And eight victims are demanded for it. There has been much said about the public sentiment. There has been much said about the public clamor. Why, it is a fact, that no citizen dared express another opinion than that prescribed by the authorities of the State, for if one had done otherwise, he would have been locked up; he might have been sent to the gallows to swing, as they will have the pleasure of doing with us, if the decree of our 'honorable court' is consummated.

"'These men,' Grinnell said repeatedly, 'have no principles; they are common murderers, assassins, robbers,' etc. I admit that our aspirations and objects are incomprehensible to unprincipled ruffians, but surely for this we are not to be blamed. The assertion, if I mistake not, was based on the ground that we sought to destroy property. Whether this perversion of fact was intentional, I know not. But in justification of our doctrines I will say that the assertion is an infamous falsehood. Articles have been read here from the *Arbeiter-Zeitung* and *Alarm* to show the dangerous characters of the defendants. The files of the *Arbeiter-Zeitung* and *Alarm* have been searched for the past years. Those articles which generally commented upon some atrocity committed by the authorities upon striking workingmen were picked out and read to you. Other articles were not read to the court. Other articles were not what was wanted. The State's Attorney upon those articles (who well knows that he tells a falsehood when he says it), asserts that 'these men have no principle.'

"A few weeks before I was arrested and charged with the crime for which I have been convicted, I was invited by the clergymen of the Congregational Church to lecture upon the subject of socialism, and debate with them. This took place at the Grand Pacific Hotel. And so that it cannot be said that after I have been arrested, after I have been indicted, and after I have been convicted, I have put together some principles to justify my action, I will read what I said then—

"CAPT. BLACK: 'Give the date of the paper.'

"MR. SPIES: 'January 9, 1886.'

"CAPT. BLACK: 'What paper, the *Alarm?*'

"MR. SPIES: 'The *Alarm*. When I was asked upon that occasion what socialism was, I said this:

"Socialism is simply a resume of the phenomena of the social life of the past and present traced to their fundamental causes, and brought into logical connection with one another. It rests upon the established fact that the economic conditions and institutions of a people form the ground work of all their social conditions, of their ideas—aye, even of their religion, and further, that all changes of economic conditions, every step in advance, arises from the struggles between the dominating and dominated class in different ages. You, gentlemen, cannot place yourselves at this standpoint of speculative science; your profession demands that you occupy the opposite position, that which professes acquaintance with things as they actually exist, but which presumes a thorough understanding of matters which to ordinary mortals are entirely incomprehensible. It is for this reason that you cannot become Socialists (cries of 'Oh! oh!'). Lest you should be unable to exactly grasp my meaning, however, I will now state the matter a little more plainly. It cannot be unknown to you that in the course of this century there have appeared an infinite number of inventions and discoveries, which have brought about great, aye, astonishing changes in the production of the necessities and comforts of life. The work of machines has to a great extent replaced that of men.

"Machinery involves a great accumulation of power, and always a greater division of labor in consequence.

"The advantages resulting from this centralization of production were of such a nature as to cause its still further extension, and from this concentration of the means of labor and of the operations of laborers, while the old system of distribution was (and is) retained, arose those improper conditions which ails society to-day.

"The means of production thus came into the hands of an ever decreasing number, while the actual producers, through the introduction of machinery, deprived of the opportunity to toil, and being at the same time disinherited of the bounties of nature, were consigned to pauperism, vagabondage—the so-called crime and prostitution—all these evils which you gentlemen would like to exorcise with your little prayer-book.

"The socialists award your efforts a jocular rather than a serious attention—[symptoms of uneasiness]—otherwise, pray let us know how much you have accomplished so far by your moral lecturing toward ameliorating the condition of those wretched beings who through bitter want have been driven to crime and desperation? [Here several gentlemen sprang to their feet, exclaiming, 'We have done a great deal in some directions!'] Aye, in some cases you have perhaps given a few alms; but what influence has this, if I may ask, had upon societary conditions, or in affecting any change in the same? Nothing; absolutely nothing. You may as well admit it, gentlemen, for you cannot point me out a single instance.

"Very well. Those proletarians doomed to misery and hunger through the labor-saving of our centralized production, whose number in this country we estimate at about a million and a half, is it likely that they and the thousands who are daily joining their ranks, and the millions who are toiling for a miserable pittance, will suffer peacefully and with christian resignation their destruction at the hand of their theivish and murderous, albeit very christian wage-masters? They will defend themselves. It will come to a fight.

"The necessity of common ownership in the means of toil will be realized, and the era of socialism, of universal co-operation begins. The dispossesssing of the usurping classes—the socialization of these possessions—and the universal co-operation of toil, not for speculative purposes, but for the satisfaction of the demands which we make upon life; in short co-operative labor for the purpose of continuing life and of enjoying it—this in general outlines, is socialism. This is not, however, as you might suppose, a mere 'beautifully conceived plan,' the realization of which would be well worth striving for if it could only be brought about. No; this socialization of the means of production, of the machinery of commerce, of the land and earth, etc., is not only something desirable, but has become an imperative necessity, and where ever we find in history that something has once become a necessity there we always find that the next step was the doing away with that necessity by the supplying of the logical want.

"Our large factories and mines, and the machinery of exchange and transportation, apart from every other consideration, have become too vast for private control. Individuals can no longer monopolize them.

"Everywhere, wherever we cast our eyes, we find forced upon our attention the unnatural and injurious effects of unregulated private production. We see how one man, or a number of men, have not only brought into the embrace of their private ownership a few inventions in technical lines, but have also confiscated for their exclusive advantage all natural powers, such as water, steam, and electricity. Every fresh invention, every discovery belongs to them. The world exists for them only. That they destroy their fellow-beings right and left they little care. That, by their machinery, they even work the bodies of little children into gold pieces they hold to be an especially good work and a genuine christian act. They murder, as we have said, little children and women by hard labor, while they let strong men go hungry for lack of work.

"People ask themselves how such things are possible, and the answer is that the competitive system is the cause of it. The thought of a co-operative, social, rational, and well-regulated system of management irresistibly impresses the observer. The advantages of such a system are of such a convincing kind, so patent to observation—and where could there be any other way out of it? According to physical laws a body always moves itself, consciously or unconsciously, along the line of least resistance. So does society as a whole. The path to co-operative labor and distribution is leveled by the concentration of the means of labor under the private capitalistic system. We are already moving right in that track. We cannot retreat even if we would. The force of circumstances drives us on to socialism.

"'And now, Mr. S., won't you tell us how you are going to carry out the expropriation of the possessing classes?' asked Rev. Dr. Scudder.

"'The answer is in the thing itself. The key is furnished by the storms raging through the industrial life of the present. You see how penuriously the owners of the factories, of the mines, cling to their privileges, and will not yield the breadth of an inch. On the other hand, you see the half-starved proletarians driven to the verge of violence.'

"'So your remedy would be violence?'

"'Remedy? Well, I should like it better if it could be done without violence, but you, gentlemen, and the class you represent, take care that it cannot be accomplished otherwise. Let us suppose that the workingmen to-day go to their employers, and say to them: 'Listen! Your administration of affairs don't suit us any more; it leads to disastrous consequences. While one part of us are worked to death, the others out of employment, are starved to death; little children are ground to death in the factories, while strong, vigorous men remain idle; the masses live in misery while a small class of respectables enjoy luxury and wealth; all this is the result of your maladministration, which will bring misfortune even to yourselves; step down and out now; let us have your property, which is nothing but unpaid labor; we shall take this thing in our hands now; we shall administrate matters satisfactorily, and regulate the institutions of society; voluntarily we shall pay you a life-long pension.

Now, do you think the 'bosses' would accept this proposition? You certainly don't believe it. Therefore force will have to decide—or do you know of any any other way?

"'So you are organizing a revolution?'

"It was shortly before my arrest, and I answered: 'Such things are hard to organize. A revolution is a sudden upwelling—a convulsion of the fevered masses of society.

"We are preparing society for that, and insist upon it that workingmen should arm themselves and keep ready for the struggle. The better they are armed the easier will the battle be, and the less the bloodshed.

"'What would be the order of things in the new society?'

"'I must decline to answer this question, as it is, till now, a mere matter of speculation. The organization of labor on a co-operative basis offers no difficulties. The large establishments of to-day might be used as patterns. Those who will have to solve these questions will expediently do it, instead of working according to our prescriptions (if we should make anything of the kind); they will be directed by the circumstances and conditions of the time, and these are beyond our horizon. About this you needn't trouble yourselves.'

"'But, friend, don't you think that about a week after the division, the provident will have all, while the spendthrift will have nothing?'

"'The question is out of order,' interfered the chairman; 'there was not anything said about division.'

"Prof. Wilcox: 'Don't you think the introduction of socialism will destroy all invividuality?'

"'How can anything be destroyed which does not exist? In our times there is no individuality; that only can be developed under socialism, when mankind will be independent economically. Where do you meet to-day with real individuality? Look at yourselves, gentlemen! You don't dare to give utterance to any subjective opinion which might not suit the feeling of your bread-givers and customers. You are hypocrites [murmurs of indignation]; every business man is a hypocrite. Everywhere is mockery, servility, lies and fraud. And the laborers! There you feign anxiety about their individuality; about the individuality of a class that has been degraded to machines—used each day for ten or twelve hours as appendages of the lifeless machines! About their individuality you are anxious!'

"Does that sound as though I had at that time, as has been imputed to me, organized a revolution—a so-called social revolution, which was to occur on or about the 1st of May to establish anarchy in place of our present 'ideal order?' I guess not.

"So socialism does not mean the destruction of society. Socialism is a constructive and not a destructive science. While capitalism expropriates the masses for the benefit of the privileged class; while capitalism is that school of economics which teaches how one can live upon the labor (*i. e.*, property) of the other; socialism teaches how all may possess property, and further teaches that every man must work honestly for his own living, and not be playing the 'respectable board of trade man,' or any other highly (?) respectable business man or banker, such as appeared here as talesman in the jurors' box, with the fixed opinion that we ought to be hanged. Indeed, I believe they have that opinion! Socialism, in short, seeks to establish a universal system of co-operation, and to render accessible to each and every member of the human family the achievements and benefits of civilization, which, under capitalism, are being monopolized by a privileged class and employed, not as they should be, for the common good of all, but for the brutish gratification of an avaricious class. Under capitalism the great inventions of the past, far from being a blessing for mankind, have been turned into a curse! Under socialism the prophecy of the Greek poet, Antiporas, would be fulfilled, who, at the invention of the first water-mill, exclaimed: 'This is the emancipator of male and female slaves'; and likewise the prediction of Aristotle, who said: 'When, at some future age, every tool, upon command or by predestination, will perform its work as the art-works of Dædalus did, which moved by themselves; or like the three feet of Hephæstus, which went to their sacred work instinctively, when thus the weaver shuttles will weave by themselves, then we shall no longer require masters and slaves.' Socialism says this time has come, and can you deny it? You say: 'Oh, these heathens, what did they know?' True! They knew nething of political economy; they knew nothing of christendom. They failed to conceive how nicely these man-emancipating machines could be employed to lengthen the hours of toil and to intensify the burdens of the slaves. These heathens, yes, they excused the slavery of one on the ground that thereby another would be afforded the opportunity of human development. But to preach the slavery of the masses in order that a few rude and arrogant parvenues might become 'eminent manufacturers,' 'extensive packing-house owners,' or 'influential shoe-black dealers,' to do this they lacked that specific Christian organ.

"Socialism teaches that the machines, the means of transportation and communication are the result of the combined efforts of society, past and present, and that they are therefore rightfully the indivisible property of society, just the same as the soil and the mines and all natural gifts should be. This declaration implies that those who have appropriated this wealth wrongfully, though lawfully, shall be expropriated by society. The expropriation of the masses by the monopolists has reached such a degree that the expropriation of the expropriateurs has become an imperative nesessity, an act of social self-preservation. Society will reclaim its own, even though you erect a gibbet on every street corner. And anarchism, this terrible 'ism,' deduces that under a co-operative organization of society, under economic equality and individual independence, the 'State'—the political State—will pass into barbaric antiquity. And we will be where all are free, where there are no longer masters and servants, where intellect stands for brute force, there will no longer be any use for the policemen and militia to preserve the so-called 'peace and order'—the order that the Russian general spoke of when he telegraped to the Czar after he had massacred half of Warsaw, 'Peace reigns in Warsaw.'

"Anarchism does not mean bloodshed; does not mean robbery, arson, etc. These monstrosities are, on the contrary, the characteristic features of capitalism. Anarchism means peace and tranquility to all. Anarchism, or socialism, means the reorganization of society upon scientific principles and the abolition of causes which produce vice and crime. Capitalism first produces these social diseases and then seeks to cure them by punishment.

"Your honor has said this morning. 'we must learn their objects from what they have said and written,' and in pursuance thereof the court has read a number of articles.

"Now, if I had as much power as the court, and were a law-abiding citizen, I would certainly have the court indicted for some remarks made during this trial. I will say that if I had not been an anarchist at the beginning of this trial I would be one now. I quote the exact language of the court on one occasion. 'It does not necessarily follow that all laws are foolish and bad because a good many of them are so.' That is treason, sir! if we are to believe the court and the state's attorney. But, aside from that, I cannot see how we shall distinguish the good from the bad laws. Am I to judge of that? No; I am not. But if I disobey a bad law, and am brought before a bad judge, I undoubtedly would be convicted.

"In regard to a report in the *Arbeiter-Zeitung*, also read this morning, the report of the Board of Trade demonstration, I would say—and this is the only defense, the only word I have to say in my own defense, that I did not know of that article until I saw it in the paper, and the man who wrote it, wrote it rather as a reply to some slurs in the morning papers. He was discharged. The language used in that article would never have been tolerated if I had seen it.

"Now, if we cannot be directly implicated with this affair, connected with the throwing of the bomb, where is the law that says, 'that these men shall be picked out to suffer?' Show me that law if you have it. If the position of the court is correct, then half of this city—half of the population of this city—ought to be hanged, because they are responsible the same as we are for that act on May 4th. And if not half of the population of Chicago is hanged, then show me the law that says, 'eight men shall be picked out and hanged as scapegoats!' You have no such law. Your decision, your verdict, our conviction is nothing but an arbitrary will of this lawless court. It is true there is no precedent in jurisprudence in this case. It is true we have called upon the people to arm themselves. It is true that we have told them time and again that the great day of change was coming. It was not our desire to have bloodshed. We are not beasts. We would not be socialists if were beasts. It is because of our sensitiveness that we have gone into this movement for the emancipation of the oppressed and suffering. It is true we have called upon the people to arm and prepare for the stormy times before us.

"This seems to be the ground upon which the verdict is to be sustained.

"But when a long train of abuses and usurpations pursuing invariably the same object evinces a design to reduce the people under absolute despotism, it is their right, it is their duty, to throw off such government and provide new guards for their future safety."

"This is a quotation from the Declaration of Independence. Have we broken any laws by showing to the people how these abuses, that have occurred for the last twenty years, are invaribly pursuing one object, viz: to establish an *oligarchy* in this country as strong and powerful and monstrous as never before has existed in any country? I can well understand why that man Grinnell did not urge upon the grand jury to charge us with treason. I can well understand it. You cannot try and convict a man for treason who has upheld the constitution against those who try to trample it under their feet. It would not have been as easy a job to do that, Mr. Grinnell, as to charge 'these men' with murder.

"Now, these are my ideas. They constitute a part of myself. I cannot divest myself of them, nor would I, if I could. And if you think that you can crush out these ideas that are gaining ground more and more every day, if you think you can crush them out by sending us to the gallows—if you would once more have people to suffer the penalty of death because they have dared to tell the truth—and I defy you to show us where we have told a lie—I say, if death is the penalty for proclaiming the truth, then I will proudly and defiantly pay the costly price! Call your hangman. Truth crucified in Socrates, in Christ, in Giordano Bruno, in Huss, Gallileo, still lives—they and others whose number is legion have preceded us on this path. We are ready to follow!

Address of Michael Schwab.

* * * "To term the proceedings during the trial justice, would be a sneer. Justice has not been done, more than this, could not be done. If one class is arrayed against the other, it is idle and hypocritical to think about justice. Anarchy was on trial, as the state's attorney put it in his closing speech. A doctrine, an opinion hostile to brute force, hostile to our present murderous system of production and distribution. I am condemned to die for writing newspaper articles and making speeches. The state's attorney knows as well as I do that that alleged conversation between Mr. Spies and myself never took place. He knows a good deal more than that. He knows of all the beautiful work of his organizer, Furthman. When I was before the coroner's jury, two or three detectives swore very positively of having seen me at the Haymarket when Mr. Parsons finished his speech. I suppose they wanted at that time to fix the bomb-throwing on me. For the first dispatches to Europe said that M. Schwab had thrown several bombs at the police. Later on they sent detectives to Lake View, and found that would not do. And then Schnaubelt was the man.

"Anarchy was on trial. Little did it matter who the persons were to be honored by the prosecution. It was the movement the blow was aimed at; it was directed against the labor movement; against socialism, for to-day every labor movement must, of necessity, be socialistic.

"Talk about a gigantic conspiracy! A movement is not a conspiracy. All we did was done in open daylight.

"There were no secrets. We prophesied in word and writing the coming of a great revolution, a change in the system of production in all industrial countries of the globe. And the change will come, and must come. Is it not absurd, as the state's attorney and his associates have done, to suppose that this social revolution—a change of such immense proportions—was to be inaugurated on or about the first of May in the city of Chicago by making war on the police? The organizer, Furthman searched hundreds of numbers of the *Arbeiter-Zeitung*, and the *Alarm*, and so the prosecution must have known very well what we understood when we talked about the coming revolution. But the prosecuting attorney preferred to ignore these explanatory articles.

"The articles in evidence were carefully selected and paraded as samples of violent language, but the language used in them was just the same as newspapers used in general against us and their enemies. Even against the police and their practices they used words of the same kind as we did.

"The president of the Citizens' Association, Edwin Lee Brown, after the last election of Mayor Harrison, made a speech in north side Turner Hall in which he called on all good citizens to take possession of the court-house by force, even if they had to wade in blood. It seems to me that the most violent speakers are not to be found in the ranks of the Anarchists.

"It is not violence in word or action the attorneys of the State and their urgers-on are waging war against; it is our doctrine—anarchy.

"We contend for communism and anarchy—why? If we had kept silent, stones would have cried out. Murder was committed day by day. Children were slain, women worked to death, men killed inch by inch, and these crimes are never punished by law. The great principle underlying the present system is unpaid labor. Those who amass fortunes, build palaces, and live in luxury, are doing that by virtue of unpaid labor. Being directly or indirectly the possessors of land and machinery, they dictate their terms to the workingman. He is compelled to sell his labor cheap, or to starve. The price paid him is always far below the real value. He acts under compulsion, and they call it a free contract. This infernal state of affairs keeps him poor and ignorant; an easy prey for exploitation.

"I know what life has in store for the masses. I was one of them. I slept in their garrets, and lived in their cellars. I saw them work and die. I worked with girls in the same factory—prostitutes they were, because they could not earn enough wages for their living. I saw females sick from overwork, sick in body and mind on account of the lives they were forced to lead. I saw girls from ten to fourteen years of age working for a mere pittance. I heard how their morals were killed by the foul and vile language and the bad example of their ignorant fellow-workers, leading them on to the same road of misery, and as an individual I could do nothing. I saw families starving and able-bodied men worked to death. That was in Europe. When I came to the United States, I found that there were classes of workingmen who were better paid than the European workmen, but I perceived that the state of things in a great number of industries was even worse, and that the so-called better paid skilled laborers were degrading rapidly into mere automatic parts of machinery. I found that the proletariat of the great industrial cities was in a condition that could not be worse. Thousands of laborers in the city of Chicago live in rooms without sufficient protection from the weather, without proper ventilation, where never a stream of sunlight flows in. There are hovels where two, three and four families live in one room. How these conditions influence the health and the morals of these unfortunate sufferers, it is needless to say. And how do they live? From the ash-barrels they gather half-rotten vegetables, in the butcher shops they buy for some cents offal of meat, and these precious morsels they carry home to prepare from them their meals. The delapidated houses in which this class of laborers live need repairs very badly, but the greedy landlord waits in most cases till he is compelled by the city to have them done. Is it a wonder that diseases of all kinds kill men, women and children in such places by wholesale, especially children? Is this not horrible in a so-called civilized land where there is plenty of food and riches? Some years ago a committee of the Citizen's Association, or League, made an investigation of these matters, and I was one of the reporters that went with them. What these common laborers are to-day, the skilled laborers will be to-morrow. Improved machinery that ought to be a blessing for the workingman, under the existing condition turns for him to a curse. Machinery multiplies the army of unskilled laborers, makes the laborer more dependent upon the men who own the land and the machines. And that is the reason that socialism and communism got a foothold in this country. The outcry that socialism, communism and anarchism are the creed of foreigners, is a big mistake. There are more socialists of American birth in this country than foreigners, and that is much, if we consider that nearly half of all industrial workingmen are not native Americans. There are socialistic papers in a great many States edited by Americans for Americans. The capitalistic newspapers conceal that fact very carefully.

"Socialism, as we understand it, means that land and machinery shall be held in common by the people. The production of goods shall be carried on by producing groups which shall supply the demands of the people. Under such a system every human being would have an opportunity to do useful work, and no doubt would work. Four hours' work every day would suffice to produce all that, according to statistics, is necessary for a comfortable living. Time would be left to cultivate the mind, and to further science and art.

"That is what the socialists propose. Some say it is un-American! Well, then, is it American to let people starve and die in ignorance? Is exploitation and robbery of the poor, American? What have the great political parties done for the poor? Promised much; done nothing, except corrupting them by buying their votes on election day. A poverty-stricken man has no interest in the welfare of the community. It is only natural that in a society where women are driven to sell their honor, men should sell their votes.

"But we 'were not only socialists and communists; we were anarchists.'

"What is anarchy?

"Is it not strange that when anarchy was tried nobody ever told what anarchy was. Even when I was on the witness stand, and asked the state's sttorney for a definition of anarchy, he declined to give it. But in their speeches he and his associates spoke very frequently about anarchy, and it appeared that they understood it to be something horrible —arson, rapine, murder. In so speaking, Mr. Grinnell and his associates did not speak the truth. They searched the *Alarm* and the *Arbeiter-Zeitung*, and hunted up articles written years before the month of May, 1886. In the columns of these papers it is very often stated what we, the 'anarchists,' understood by the term anarchy. And we are the only competent judges in this matter. As soon as the word is applied to us and our doctrine, it carries with it the meaning which we, the anarchists, saw fit to give to it. 'Anarchy' is Greek, and means, verbatim, without rulership; not being ruled. According to our vocabulary, anarchy is a state of society, in which the only government is reason.

"A state of society in which all human beings do right for the simple reason that it is right, and hate wrong because it is wrong. In such a society, no laws, no compulsion will be necessary. The attorney of the State was wrong when he said: 'Anarchy is dead.' Anarchy, up to the present day, has existed only as a doctrine, and Mr. Grinnell has not the power to kill any doctrine whatever. You many call anarchy, as defined by us, an idle dream, but that dream was dreamed by Gotthold Ephraim Lessing, one of the great German poets and the most celebrated German critic of the last century. If anarchy were the thing the state's attorney makes it out to be, how could it be that such eminent scholars as Prince Kropotkin, and the greatest living geographer, Elisee Reclus, were avowed anarchists, even editors of anarchistic papers? Anarchy is a dream, but only in the present. It will be realized. Reason will grow in spite of all obstacles. Who is the man that has the cheek to tell us that human development has already reached its culminating point? I know that our ideal will not be accomplished this or next year, but I know that it will be accomplished as near as possible, some day, in the future. It is entirely wrong to use the word anarchy as synonymous with violence. Violence is one thing and anarchy is another. In the present state of society violence is used on all sides, and, therefore, we advocated the use of violence against violence. but against violence only, as a necessary means of defense.

* * * * *

"If I had never seen life as it is, I never would have taken to foretelling the coming downfall of this murderous system, and might now cry out like the learned and the ignorant mobsters: 'Hang the anarchists!' instead of living in the shadow of the gallows. Seeing the terrible abuses with my own eyes, seeing how girls became prostitutes, before they knew it, observing the slaughter of the little ones, the killing of workingmen by slow degrees, corruption, misery, crime, hypocrisy, poverty, dirt, ignorance, brutality and hunger everywhere, and conceiving that all these things are the legitimate children of the capitalistic system, which, by establishing the right for single persons to possess the means of production and the land, makes the mass of the people wretched, I became a 'kicker.' For an honest and honorable man only one course was left, and I became an opponent to the existing order of things, and was soon called an anarchist. What are my views? If we socialists, communists and anarchists held the views malicious or ignorant hirelings impute to us in their writings, we would simply be madmen who should be confined in an insane asylum forever. But if it were true that modern socialism, communism and anarchism were methodical madness, how could it be that these doctrines spread all over the world in so short a time? No doctrine whatever made so quick its march around the world; no doctrine ever gained so many converts in so few years! Our martyrs alone count hundreds of thousands in a score of years—men, women, yea even children. They perished by bullets, gallows, the sword, the guillotine; they perished in dungeons, in the wilderness, in the snow, and the mines of Siberia, under the tropical sun, they were driven from town to town, from country to country, outcast by their families, and some ended in madness brought about by persecutions such as only modern civilization could invent. Girls brought up in palatial mansions, with a life of ease and luxury before them; youths of rich and aristocratic parents worked as common factory hands, leading a life of misery, with no hope of ever gaining a reward, often enough despised and betrayed even by the class for whom they endured all this—only to preach the gospel of the saving of mankind—socialism, communism, anarchism. Of some of these heroes not even the names are known. Even one of your famous American poets—Joaquin Miller—could not help to say, in a poem written to the praise of that noble anarchist girl, Sophia Perovskaya, who was hung, that he would rather die with her on the gallows, than live as the Russian Czar. There is certainly truth in an idea, which has such martyrs. If our doctrine was wrong, our enemies would state the facts and it would then be comparatively easy to show the absurdity of the same. I have been a socialist for thirteen years, but never, never did I see our views correctly stated by a capitalistic newspaper. They fabricate wind mills, call them socialism, communism and anarchism and begin fighting them.

"The modern communist holds that labor is the fountain of all wealth and all culture and that, because useful labor only is possible by association of all mankind, the fruits of labor belong to all mankind. Even land has no value except where it can be put into use by labor. No empty lot in a city would have the least value, if labor had not built around it houses and streets, if business was not going on near that lot. We know further, that labor is not paid its full value; if this were the case, it would be unprofitable to employ labor and would not be done. Let one man work alone for himself, he never could grow rich, although even in such a case his knowledge would be the fruit of the work of others, the labor of generations. And because the latter is the case, the communist wants education, culture and knowledge for all. The land was common property thousands and thousands of years, and the private property system is—to speak historically—but of yesterday. And how was it introduced! Queen Elizabeth, that highly praised monster of murderous lust and brutality, for instance, had during her reign two millions of Irishmen killed in the usual way—battles, gallows, etc., took their land and gave it to favorites.

It is not for me now to give a history how the common lands in England were stolen and robbed, but it is a historical fact that it was acquired by the forefathers of the present owners by murder, arson, theft and lesser crimes. Let the hired men of the press fill their columns with history of the crimes or land-robbing, if they dare. The sentence: 'Property is robbery,' is literally true—if you call robbery what the law calls so of the property of the British landholders. The socialists and communists know further that the capitalistic system requires always expansion. The so-called profits—that is, the fruit of the labor withheld by the employer—are transformed into capital, to gain for him new profits. New factories are built, more machines set to work, new markets are sought for, if necessary by war. More and more nations are drawn into competition. It begins to become difficult to find buyers for the goods; each nation, each corporation, each capitalist wages war against the other for supremacy. He who sells cheapest holds the market. But not only this is required; he who is first in the market, he who can supply the demand in any emergency quick and cheap, will win the battle.

"This brings in speculation. The demand of the market is but limited, but the capitalists of all industrial countries are busy to glut it, to overflood it with the products of their factories. To come out all right from this insane race for money, it is necessary to supply cheap and quick, so as to leave other competitors behind. The greater the plant, the better the machines, the cheaper the workmen, the more probable is victory. The smaller manufacturer is soon driven from the contest and forced to close his establishment; new inventions of labor saving machines throw workmen out of employment and compel these forces to look out for new work, as machines tend to transform skilled labor into common labor. The competition for work among workingmen grows to fearful dimensions and brings wages down to a minimum. But this in turn has its effect on production, and the battle wages more fearful than ever. But now reaction sets in. Millions of workmen are starving and leading the lives of vagabonds. Even the most ignorant wage-slave commences to think. The common misery makes it clear to them that they must combine, and they do it. The great levellers, the machines, destroyed the guild-pride of olden times. The carpenter feels that he has a common interest with the farm hand, and the printer with the hod-carrier, the German learns that his interest is that of Negro, of the Frenchman, of the American, and passing I would like to state, that in my opinion it is the greatest merit of the order of the Knights of Labor to have carried out that principle in America in such an immense way. The workingmen learn that the capitalistic system, although necessary for some time, must make room for universal co-operation; that the land and means of production must pass from the hands of speculators, private individuals into the hands of the producing masses; this is communism.

"Any thinking man must concede that strikes, boycotts, co-operation on a small scale and other means will not and cannot better the condition of the working-classes, even not so-called factory laws can bring the sought for result about. It is true the workingmen cannot help to use these insufficient means, often enough they are forced upon him. They must be looked on as means of education. Man learns by failures. A little baby who commences to stand on his feet, tumbles down many and many a time, before his limbs gain sufficient strength to walk. Many and many a time it tries to raise itself, till at last the great feat is accomplished. In all these fights, in striking, boycotting, going into politics, yes, even in street riots the young Hercules collects strength to throttle the serpent— the capitalistic system. The workingmen may be sometimes wrong, why not, the baby sometimes tries to raise itself by means of the table-cloth, thus bringing down the dishes, but his impulse to raise is all right, and therefore the workingman should continue to try raising his condition, even if he sometimes brings down the dishes.

"Now as to anarchism. Anarchism is order without government. We anarchists say that anarchism will be the natural outgrowth of universal co-operation (communism). We say that, when poverty has vanished and education is common property of the people, that then reason will reign supreme. We say that crime will belong to the past and that the misdeeds of erring brethren can be righted by other means than those of to-day. Most of the crimes of our days are engendered directly by the system of to-day, the system which creates ignorance and misery.

"We anarchists do believe that the time is near at hand when the working people will demand their rights of their exploiters, and we further believe, that the slave-holders of to-day will rebel against the majority of the people, aided by the slums of the cities and duped people of the country. This struggle, in our opinion, is inevitable.

Oscar Neebe's Remarks.

* * * "I saved for the men from four to five hours a day less work. I have saved the bakers from six to eight hours work a day, and that gives them time for education. We socialists are great believers that the laboring men should educate themselves; not to be ignoramuses, as some people express themselves, 'as the ignorant anarchists are.' We are great friends of education and a reduction of the hours of labor was my principal aim, and I have done some good work to bring it about. I have been in the labor movement since 1875. I have seen how the police have trodden on the constitution of this conntry, and crushed the labor organizations. I have seen from year to year how they were trodden down, where they were shot down, where they were 'driven into their holes like rats,' as Mr. Grinnell said to the jury. But they will come out! Remember that within three years before the beginning of the French Revolution, when laws had been stretched like rubber, that the rubber stretched too long, and broke a result which cost a good many state's attorneys at that time their necks, and a good many honorable men their necks.

"We socialists hope such times may never come again; we do everything in our power to prevent it by reducing the hours of labor and increasing wages. But you capitalists won't allow this to be done. You use your power to perpetuate a system by which you may make your money for yourselves and keep the wage-workers poor. You make them ignorant and miserable, and you are responsible for it. You won't let the toilers live a decent life.

"We want to educate the masses and keep them back from destroying life and property, but we are not able to hold the masses when starvation brings them out of their holes like rats. I have walked along the streets of this city and I have seen the rats come from their holes by the hundreds in the basements, where they pay five and ten cents for lodgings. I have seen the miserable wretches lying there in the day begging for a piece of bread, and in the night they lie there in an air that nobody hardly could live in. I have been in there at ten, twelve, and two o'clock at night, and when those rats are let out of their holes once and get desperate I would not like to be near them. The time will come that you will see them. You rich men don't want the workingmen educated. You don't want anybody to be educated. You want to keep them down in the mud so you can squeeze the last drop of blood out of their bones. We asked the capitalists once at one meeting to discuss the question of labor, and Mr. Gary was invited and each one of them was invited, and nobody appeared. They didn't want to discuss the question; they didn't care for it. What is the next question? No discussion, more Gatling guns, more militia, and three hundred more police. For what? To catch the thieves? I read the daily papers and see burglaries all over the city, but I don't see that they catch any. There are some 1.200 and odd policemen in the city of Chicago, and every day so many burglaries. May be they need them to make a case sometimes, and they don't arrest them; but when it comes to arresting a poor workingman they are all there. On May 9, when, I came home, my wife, who is delicate, told me that the patrol wagon, with twenty-five police came to search my house. I must be a very dangerous man to take so many police. They searched the whole house and found a revolver. That is a deadly weapon and a dangerous weapon. I don't think anybody else has revolvers but anarchists and socialists and labor agitators.

"They found a red flag. too—a flag of that size (about a foot square) that my little boy played with, and my wife used at a masquerade ball. My wife told me that the police—these honorable men to protect law and order—when they got on that wagon they waved that flag and hollered and hurrahed just like a lot of wild Indians— and they were wild Indians in those days. They searched hundreds of houses, and money was stolen by searching houses, and watches were stolen, and nobody knew whether they were stolen by the police or not. Captain Schaack knows it. His gang was one of the worst in this city. You need not laugh about it, Captain Schaack. You are one of them. You are an anarchist, as you understand it. You are all anarchists, in this sense of the word, I must say. Well, these are all the crimes I have committed. They found a revolver in my house. and a red flag there. I organized trades unions. I was for reduction of the hours of labor, and the education of laboring men, and the re-establishment of the *Arbeiter-Zeitung*—the workingmen's newspaper. There is no evidence to show that I was connected with the bomb-throwing, or that I was near it, or anything of that kind. So I am only sorry, your honor—that is, if you can stop it or help it—I will ask you to do it—that is, to hang me, too; for I think it is more honorable to die suddenly than to be killed by inches. I have a family and children; and if they know their father is dead, they will bury him. They can go to the grave, and kneel down by the side of it; but they can't go to the penitentiary and see their father, who was convicted for a crime that he hasn't had anything to do with. That is all I have got to say. Your honor, I am sorry I am not to be hung with the rest of the men.

ADOLPH FISCHER.

"Being familiar with the doctrines of socialism from my earliest youth I have held it my duty to spread these principles so dear to me whenever and wherever I could. What induced me to become a socialist, you may ask? This I will relate in a few words:

"It happened during the last year of my school days that our tutor of historical science one day chanced to refer to socialism, which movement was at that time beginning to flourish in Germany, and which he told us meant 'division of property.' I am inclined to believe now that it was a general instruction given by the government to the patriotic pedagogues to periodically describe to their elder pupils socialism as a most horrible thing. It is, as is well known, a customary policy on the part of the respective monarchial governments of the old world to prejudice the undeveloped minds of the youth against everything which is disagreeable to the despots through the medium of the school teachers. For instance, I remember quite distinctly that before the outbreak and during the Franco-German war we were made to believe by our teachers that every Frenchman was at least a scoundrel, if not a criminal. On the other hand, the kings were praised as the representatives of God, and obedience and loyalty to them was described as the highest virtues. Thus the minds of the children are systematically poisoned, and the fruits of this practice are made use of when the little ones become men and women. [Enough at the mentioned occasion our teachers told us that the socialists were a lot of drunkards, swindlers and idlers, who were opposed to work.] 'The time draws nigh,' that worthy said, placing his forefinger significantly alongside of his roman nose, 'when you young men will have to earn your daily bread in the sweat of your brow. Some of you may acquire wealth, while others will be less fortunate. Now, these socialists—mark you, who are a lazy set of people—intend to forcibly make you divide with them everything you possess at the termination of every year. For instance, if you should call two pairs of boots your own, one of these socialistic scoundrels will kindly relieve you of one pair. How would you like this?' Certainly, we thought we did not like this at all. Neither would I consent to anything of that sort to-day. Most decidedly not. Such an arrangement, I fancied, would be absurd. Now I knew it to be a fact that my father took part in socialistic meetings very frequently, and I wondered that day why he—whom I thought to be so good—should have intercourse with such a bad class of men, whose object it was to lead a lazy life and to make the sober, industrious working people, at the termination of each year, divide their earnings with them. When I reached home that day I intimated to my father what (according to what the teacher had told us) bad people the socialists must be. Much to my surprise my dear father laughed aloud and embraced me very affectionately. 'Dear Adolph,' he said, 'if socialism is what your teacher explained it to be, why then the very same institutions which prevail now, would be socialistic.' And my father went on to show me how, in fact, there were many idlers and indolent people under the now existing form of society, whose were living in palatial houses and living luxuriously at the expense of the sober and industrious working people, and that socialism had the mission to abolish such unjust division. After this day I accompanied my father to socialistic gatherings, and soon became convinced of the truth of what he had said.

"I began to study. Wandering about the streets I often saw groups of hard-fisted men who were working in quarries and other places of toil, and handling heavy picks and clumsy shovels from early morning until late at night. Standing a little aside I would notice an elegantly dressed individual, smoking a Havana, and seemingly interested in the work of the toilers. The hands of the idler were covered with kid gloves, in the bosom of his snow-white shirt glittered a diamond pin, and from his vest dangled a valuable gold watch and chain. You can guess, dear reader, who this gentleman was—the 'employer.' The busy toilers, notwithstanding the many hours of strained work, could scarcely earn enough to keep themselves and families from want. I saw they inhabited miserable hovels, and the pleasures and comforts of life were unkown to them. Their children were hollow-eyed and resembled fence posts covered with human skin more than human beings. Following, on one occasion, the fine gentleman whom I had seen standing idly by, and who had commanded the workingmen, I saw him enter a wonderfully beautiful house—a palace. Costly pictures decorated the massive walls of its parlors, precious carpets covered the floors and golden chandeliers were suspended from the ceilings. The safes and pantries were bursting with its tempting contents, and the tables covered with choice wines and delicacies. In short, everything good and agreeable could be enjoyed here in abundance. This contrast between the busy toiler and the idle bystander did not fail to impress itself upon my mind, especially as I observed that these conditions existed everywhere and in all branches of industry. I perceived that the diligent, never resting human working bees, who create all wealth and fill the magazines with provisions, fuel and clothing, enjoy only a minor part of their products and lead a comparatively miserable life, whilst the drones, the idlers, keep the ware-houses locked up and revel in luxury and voluptuousness. Was I wrong, or was the world wrong? I saw men who manufactured shoes and boots and had helped fill the storehouse with these products ever since their boyhood, and yet they lingered to leave their shanties after rainy weather for fear of getting wet feet, and in many cases the toes of their children's feet peeped speakingly out of the top of the shabby shoes. Bricklayers were busy building houses from sunrise until sunset for several decades, yet as I looked about me, I discovered but very few who called a house their own; they were bound to pay rent for the very same houses which they had built. The clothing stores I knew to be crammed with goods, but it was not a rare spectacle in my native city to see tailors walk about in the streets with pants patched to such an extent, that they resembled chess boards. Whilst the journeymen bakers were half-roasting in the hot bake-house, sixteen out of twenty-four hours a day, their wives in many instances did not know where to get a loaf of bread. My father's neighbor worked in a butcher shop, but his wages were so low that his family could afford the luxury of one pound of meat only once a week—on Sunday. All these circumstances convinced me that 'there must be something rotten in the state of Denmark,' and it did not even require a profound thinker or a sorcerer to discover that the prevailing social institutions were based upon the extortion of one class by another.

"The capitalistic papers of this country sneered at a certain Indian chief; I think Red Cloud, who, they reported had said: 'What we (the Indians) want is white men to plant our corn, hoe it, harvest it, and put it into barns which they will build for us.' Now, I cannot comprehend why the capitalistic press considers this utterance of Red Cloud as a peculiar one. Have not the capitalists put this very same idea into practice? Let us investigate. Instead of the words 'white men,' use the expression 'workingmen,' and it will read thus: 'What we (the capitalists, the privileged class) want is workingmen to plant our corn, hoe it, harvest it, and put it into barns which they will build for us.' Well, nevertheless, these conditions exist to-day. The wage-slaves really produce everything, and store their products away into warehouses which they build for their masters; and besides they build for them also palaces such as Red Cloud never had on his programme. Yes; and the toilers do more than that; they decorate their masters with diamonds, and over-burden them with luxuries and riches of which Red Cloud never dreamed. Who can deny this fact?

"In order to illustrate the existing social 'order,' I will draw the following parable:

"A long time ago the forests of a tropical land were populated by a happy lot of monkeys. They lived together like a large family and quarrelling and discontentedness were qualities totally unknown to them. For a livelihood they searched the surroundings for food for themselves and their young ones in a harmonious way and without grudge. They were happy, indeed. One day some cunning monkeys were overcome by a very smart idea. They erected fences around the best parts of the forests and forbade their fellow-monkeys to hunt for food inside of the hedged regions. They named these pieces of land 'property.' Now, the propertyless monkeys were in utter despair, for they did not know where to get food for themselves and families. They called upon the property-owners and complained of their impossibility of making a livelihood. The propertied monkeys said unto them: 'We may allow you to seek food on our property under the condition that you will give us half of the result of your labor.' This offer the poor propertyless monkeys were compelled to accept, as there was no other way of making a living. No other choice was left open to them as either to accept or starve. The propertyless monkeys had to build large ware-houses for their 'employers,' into which to store away their products. As a compensation they received so much for their services as was sufficient to keep themselves and families alive. This was called 'means.' The property-owning monkeys became very wealthy, and were living in luxury and idleness. And why should they not? Did not the poor monkeys work for them, and thus enable them to be idle and yet debauch in abundance?

"For a long time the working monkeys did not grumble, but were very obedient. Generations thus passed, and the monkeys thought that the 'social institutions' could not be otherwise and that there had to be rich and poor monkeys, because these were the conditions which existed already when they were born. But the employers grew continually richer whilst the portion of the products of the workers, which they received as a compensation, were reduced to the lowest standard. Consequently the poor working monkeys were living in destitution and misery, notwithstanding the fact that the warehouses were filled with food. Discontentedness among the workers was the natural result of the growing wealth on one side and increasing poverty on the other. In order to keep the grumbling monkeys in subjection and maintain the respect for the existing institutions (which were called 'law and order') the propertied classes hired numbers of able-bodied monkeys from the ranks of the propertyless classes. Those men were called police, sheriffs, malitia, a. s. f.

"Now, the dissatisfied monkeys assembled frequently for the purpose of seeking remedy for the existing evils. As the opinions as to ways and means to secure better conditions were very different they formed various organizations. Some of the workers aimed at 'higher wages' and others wanted to work less time. Still another class of workers held that the 'wage-system' should be abolished entirely. They said that the propertied monkeys had accumulated their riches by robbing the workers out of the major part of the results of their labor. Furthermore, they claimed that the wealthy classes had no right to monopolize the natural resources of existence and thereby force their fellow-monkeys into their services, but that the mother-earth and her products belonged to the monkey race in common. The monkeys who confessed the latter ideas were considered very dangerous by the privileged class. 'Law and order is endangered,' the wealthy cried. 'Those anarchists want to overthrow our glorious institutions and turn everything topsy-turvy. We must do away with those bloodthirsty rascals, who want to take our property and who are undermining our free and glorious institutions.' The propertied monkeys were also opposed to that part of the working monkeys who only demanded a larger compensation for their work; but their hate against those who wanted to abolish their privileges altogether was immeasurable.

"The capitalistic press, and even numerous labor journals, define anarchism as murder, plunder, arson and outrage upon society in general. These 'learned' journalists, or at least a majority of them thus defining anarchism, misrepresent the object and aims of this teaching maliciously. Anarchism does not mean plunder and outrage upon society; contrarily, its mission is to outroot the systematical plunder of a vast majority of the people by a comparatively few—the working classes by the capitalists. It aims at the extermination of the outrages committed by the reigning classes upon the wage-slaves, under the name of 'law and order.' Murder, plunder, robbery, outrages. 'Is an anarchist really the impersonation of all crimes, of everything dastardly and damnable?' The 'International Working Peoples' Association,' the organization of the anarchists, has the following platform, which was agreed upon at the congress at Pittsburg in October, 1883. Let this platform be the answer to the question I have raised before:

"1. Destruction of the existing class rule, by all means, i. e., by energetic, relentless, revolutionary and international action.

"2. Establishment of a free society based upon co-operative organition of production.

"3. Free exchange of equivalent products by and between the productive organizations without commerce and profit-mongery.

"4. Organization of education on a secular, scientific and equal basis for both sexes.

"5. Equal rights for all without distinction to sex or race.

"6. Regulation of all public affairs by free contracts between the autonomous (independent) communes and associations, resting on a federalistic basis.

"Does this sound like outrages and crime?

"In the course of my observations I will dwell more thoroughly on the aims and objects of anarchy.

"Many people undoubtedly long to know what the relationship between anarchism and socialism is, and whether these two doctrines have anything in common with each other. A number of persons claim that an anarchist cannot be a socialist, and a socialist not an anarchist. This is wrong. The philosophy of socialism is a general one, and covers several subordinate teachings. To illustrate, I will cite the word 'Christianity.' There are Catholics, Lutherans, Methodists, Baptists, Congregationalists, and various other religious sects, all of whom call themselves Christians. Although every Catholic is a Christian, it would not be correct to say that every Christian believes in Catholicism. Webster defined socialism thus: 'A more orderly, equitable and harmonious arrangement of social affairs than has hitherto prevailed.' Anarchism is aiming at this: anarchism is seeking a more just form of society. Therefore every anarchist is a socialist but every socialist is not necessarily an anarchist. The anarchists again are divided into two factions: the communistic anarchists and the Proudhon or middle-class anarchists. The 'International Working Peoples' Association' is the representative organization of the communistic anarchists. Politically we are anarchists, and economically, communists or socialists. With regard to political organization the communistic anarchists demand the abolition of political authority, the state; we deny the right of a single class or single individual to govern or rule another class or individual. We hold that, as long as one man is under the dictation of another, as long as one man can in any form subjugate his fellow man, and as long as the means of existence can be monopolized by a certain class or certain individuals, there can be no liberty. Concerning the economical form of society, we advocate the communistic or co-operative method of production.

"As to the distribution of products, a free exchange between the organizations of productions without profit-mongery would take place. Machinery and the means of production in general would be the common servant, and the products certainly the common property of the whole of the people. In what respect do the social-democrats differ from the anarchists? The state-socialists do not seek the abolition of the state, but they advocate the centralization of the means of production in the hands of the government; in other words, they want the government to be the controller of industry. Now, a socialist who is not a state-socialist must necessarily be an anarchist. It is utterly ridiculous for men like Dr. Aveling to state that they are neither state-socialists nor anarchists. Dr. Aveling has to be either one or the other.

"The term 'anarchism' is of Greek origin and means 'without government,' or, in other words, 'without oppression.' I only wish that every workingman would understand the proper meaning of this word. It is an absurd falsehood if the capitalists and their hired editors say that anarchism is identical with disorder and crime. On the contrary, anarchism wants to do away with the now existing social disorder; it aims at the establishment of the real—the natural—order. I think every sensible man ought to conceive, that where ruling is existing on one hand, there must be submission on the other. He who rules is a tyrant, and he who submits is a slave. Logically there can be no other outlet, because submission is the antithesis of rule. Anarchists hold that it is the natural right of every member of the human family to control themselves. If a centralized power—government—is ruling the mass of people (no matter whether this government 'represents the will of the majority of the people' or not) it is enslaving them, and a direct violation of the laws of nature. When laws are made there must be certain interests which cause their issue. Now every statute law, and consequently every violation thereof—crime—can be traced back to the institution of private property. The state protects the interests of the owners of private property (wealthy class), and therefore does not and cannot possibly protect the interests of the non-possessing people (the wage-workers), because the interests of both are of an opposite nature. The capitalists who have taken possession of the means of production—factories, machinery, land; etc., are the masters, and the workingmen who have to apply to the capitalists for the use of the means of production (for which they receive a small compensation in order to live), are the slaves. The interests of the capitalistic class are backed by the state (militia, sheriffs, and police) while the interests of the non-possessing people are not protected. Anarchists say that there should be no class interests, but that every human being should have free access to the means of existence and that the pantries of mother-earth should be accessible to all of her children. One part of the great human family has no right to deprive their brothers and sisters of their legitimate place at the common table, which is set so richly by generous mother-nature for all. Anarchists, as well as all other thinking people, claim, that in the present society, a great number of people are deprived of a decent existence. We demand the re-installation of the disinherited! Is this a crime? Is this an outrage upon society? Are we therefore dangerous criminals, whose lives should be taken in the interests of the common good of society?

* * * * *

"Yes, the anarchists demand the re-installation of the disinherited members of the human family. It is, therefore, quite natural that the privileged classes should hate them. Why, do not wrong doing parties always hate those who disclose the nature of their transactions and open the eyes of their ignorant victims? Certainly they do. The anarchists are very much hated by the extortioners; indeed, they are proud of it. To them, this is a proof that they are on the right road. But the ruling classes very cunningly play the role of the thief, who, when pursued by his discoverers, cries out, 'stop the thief,' and by this manipulation succeeds in making good his escape. The anarchists have proven that the existing form of society is based upon the exploitation of one class by another; in plain words, upon legalized robbery. They say that few persons have no right whatever, to monopolize the resources of nature; and they urge the victims, the toilers, to take possession of the means of production, which belong to the people in common, and thus secure the full benefit of their toil. Anarchists do not want to deprive the capitalists of their existence, but they protest against the capitalists depriving the toilers of their right to a decent existence. Should the communistic form of production prevail, the capitalists of to-day would not have to starve; they would be situated just as comfortably and would be just as happy (yea, happier than they are now) as the rest of the people. But, certainly they would have to take an active part in the production and be satisfied with their respective share of the results of labor, performed in common with their fellowmen. The strongest bulwark of the capitalistic system is the ignorance of its victims. The average toiler shakes his head like the incredulous Thomas, when one tries to make plausible to him that he is held in economic bondage. And yet this is so easily to be seen if one only takes the pains to think a little. Working at my trade alongside my colleagues, whom I tried to convince of my ideas, I used to tell them a story about some foxes: 'Several foxes, in speculating about some scheme which would enable them to live without hunting for food themselves, succeeded at last in discovering one. They took possession of all the springs and other water-places. Now, as the other animals came to quench their thirst, the foxes said unto them: The water-places belong to us; if you want to drink, you must bring us something in return, you must bring us food for compensation. The other animals were foolish enough to obey, and, in order to drink, they had to hunt the whole day for food for the foxes, so that they themselves had to live very meagerly. I asked one of my colleagues, who was prominent as a denunciator of socialism, what his opinion was concerning the just mentioned story. He said that the animals who were thus swindled by the foxes were very foolish in obeying them, and ought to drive the latter away from the water-places. When I directed his attention to the fact that a similar practice was being cultivated in modern society, with the only difference that the role of the foxes was occupied by the capitalists, and the water-places were represented by the means of production, and that he (my colleague) was very inconsistent in condemning the one and defending the other, he owed me the answer. This, for instance, illustrates the ignorance and indifference of the average workingmen. In the case of the foxes, they see no more and no less than robbery in their schemes, whilst in the case of the capitalists they approve of their methods.

"Many inconsistent objections to anarchism are being made by its opponents. Some people have the impression that in an anarchistic society, where there is nobody to govern and nobody to be governed, every person would be isolated. This is false. Men have implanted by nature an impulse to associate with their fellow men. In a free society men would form economic as well as social associations; but all organizations would be voluntary, not compulsory. As I have asserted before, laws and the violations thereof, crimes, are attributed to the institution of private property, especially to the unequal distribution of the means of existence, to degradation and want. When the institution of private property will be abolished; when economic and social equalities will be established; when misery and want will belong to the past, then crime will be unknown and laws will become superfluous. It is a wrong assertion when people claim that a man is a criminal because of a natural disposition to crime. A man, as a rule, is but the reflex of the conditions which surround him. In a society, which places no obstacles in the road of free development of men, and which gives everybody an equal share to the pursuit of happiness, there will be no course which will induce men to become bad.

"The legalized private-property system gives birth to crime and at the same time punishes it because it exists. The mother punishes her own child because it is born. Do away with the systems that produce evils and the latter will vanish. The removal of the cause is synonymous with the removal of the effects; but the social diseases will never be cured if you declare war against the victims and on the other hand defend the cause which produced them. If one has the small-pox it would not cure the disease if one would scratch the scabs off. The disease in this case is the system of private-property, and the scabs its evil effects.

"How will the anarchists realize their ideas? What means do they intend to employ to accomplish the realization of a free society. Much has been written and talked on this subject, and, as an avowed anarchist, I will in plain terms give my individual opinion to the readers of this journal. The 'anarchism' itself does not indicate force; on the contrary it means peace. But I believe that everybody who has studied the true character of the capitalistic form of society, and who will not deceive himself, will agree with me that now and never will the ruling classes abandon their privileges peaceably. Anarchism demands a thorough transformation of society, the total abolition of the private-property system. Now, history shows us that even reforms within the frame of the existing society have never been accomplished without the force of arms. Feudalism received its death blow through the great French revolution a century ago, which at the same time gave form to modern capitalism. Capitalism now is speedily attaining its most extreme character, that is, it is developing into monopolism. Wealth concentrates itself more and more in a few hands and the misery and poverty of the great mass of people is consequently enlarging in the same degree. The rich get richer and the poor poorer. Like the ruling classes in the eighteenth century, so the same classes at the eve of the nineteenth century are deaf to the complaints and warnings of the disinherited, and blind to the misery and degradation which surround their luxuriously outfitted palaces. The natural result will be that perhaps before the nineteenth century will wing its last hours the people will arise *en masse*, expropriate the privileged and proclaim the freedom of the human race. It is wrong if people assert that the anarchists will be responsible for the coming revolution. No, the drones of society are the parties who will have to answer to the charge of being the cause of the prospective uprising of the people; for the rich and mighty have ears and hear not, and eyes and yet see not.

"To abolish chattel slavery in this country a long and awful war took place. Notwithstanding the fact that indemnification was offered for their losses, the slaveholders would not bestow freedom upon their slaves. Now, in my judgment, he who believes that the modern slave holders—the capitalists—would voluntarily, without being forced to do so, give up their privileges and set free their wage-slaves, are poor students. Capitalists possess too much egotism to give way to reason. Their egotism is so enormous that they even refuse to grant subordinate and insignificant concessions. Capitalists and syndicates, for instance, rather lose millions of dollars than to accept the eight-hour labor system. Would a peaceable solution of the social question be possible, the anarchists would be the first ones to rejoice over it.

"But is it not a fact that on the occasion of almost every strike the minions of the institution of private property—militia, police, deputy sheriffs, yea, even federal troops—are being called to the scenes of the conflict between capital and labor, in order to protect the interests of capital. Did it ever happen that the interests of labor were guarded by these forces? What peaceable means should the toilers employ? There is, for example, the strike. If the ruling classes want to enforce the 'law' they can have every striker arrested and punished for 'intimidation' and conspiracy. A strike can only be successful if the striking workingmen prevent their places being occupied by others. But this prevention is a crime in the eyes of the law. Boycott! In several states the 'courts of justice' have decided that the boycott is a violation of the law, and in consequence thereof a number of boycotters have had the pleasure of examining the inner construction of penitentiaries 'for conspiracy' against the interests of capital. 'But,' says some apostle of harmony, 'there is something left which will help us; there is the ballot.' No doubt many people who say this are honest in their belief.

"But scarcely did the workingmen participate in the elections as a class, many representatives of 'law and order' advocate a limitation (in many instances even the total abolition) of the right of the proletarian to vote. People who read the Chicago *Tribune* and *Times* and other representative capitalistic organs, will confirm my statement. The propaganda among capitalists in favor of limiting the right to vote to tax payers—

property owners—only, is increasing constantly, and will be realized whenever the political movement of the workingmen becomes really dangerous to the interests of capital. The 'Law and Order League' of capitalists, recently organized all over the country to defeat the demands of organized labor, has declared that the workingmen must not be allowed to obtain power over the ballot box. They have so resolved everywhere.

"The anarchists are not blind. They see the development of things and predict that a collision between the plebeians and patricians is inevitable. Therefore in time for the coming struggle—to arms! If threatening clouds are visible on the horizon, I advise my fellow-man to carry an umbrella with him, so he will not get wet. Am I then the cause of the rain? No. So let me say plainly that, in my opinion, only by the force of arms can the wage slaves make their way out of capitalistic bondage.

"As the court as well as the states-attorney have plainly said, the verdict of death was rendered for the purpose of crushing the anarchistic and the socialistic movement. But I am satisfied that just the contrary has been accomplished by this barbarous measure. Thousands of workingmen have been led by our 'conviction' to study anarchism, and if we are executed, we can ascend the scaffold with the satisfaction that by our death, we have advanced our noble cause more than we could possibly have done had we grown as old as Methusalah."

Address of Louis Lingg.

"Court of Justice! With the same irony with which you have regarded my efforts to win, in this 'free land of America,' a livelihood such as human kind is worthy to enjoy, do you now, after condemning me to death, concede me the liberty of making a final speech.

"I accept your concession; but it is only for the purpose of exposing the injustice, the calumnies, and the outrages which have been heaped upon me.

"You have accused me of murder, and convicted me: what proof have you brought that I am guilty?

"In the first place, you have brought this fellow Seliger to testify against me. Him I have helped to make bombs, and you have further proven that with the assistance of another, I took those bombs to No. 58 Clybourne avenue, but what you have not proven—even with the assistance of your bought 'squealer,' Seliger, who would appear to have acted such a prominent part in the affair—is that any of those bombs were taken to the haymarket.

"A couple of chemists also, have been brought here as specialists, yet they could only state that the metal of which the haymarket bomb was made bore a certain resemblance to those bombs of mine, and your Mr. Ingham has vainly endeavored to deny that the bombs were quite different. He had to admit that there was a difference of a full half inch in their diameters, although he suppressed the fact that there was also a difference of a quarter of an inch in the thickness of the shell. This is the kind of evidence upon which you have convicted me.

"It is not murder, however, of which you have convicted me. The judge has stated that much only this morning in his resume of the case, and Grinnell has repeatedly asserted that we were being tried, not for murder, but for anarchy, so that the condemnation is—that I am an anarchist!

"What is anarchy? This is a subject which my comrades have explained with sufficient clearness, and it is unneccessary for me to go over it again. They have told you plainly enough what our aims are. The state's attorney, however, has not given you that information. He has merely criticized and condemned not the doctrines of anarchy, but our methods of giving them practical effect, and even here he has maintained a discreet silence as to the fact that those methods were forced upon us by the brutality of the police. Grinnell's own proffered remedy for our grievances is the ballot and combination of trades unions, and Ingham has even avowed the desirability of a six-hour movement! But the fact is, that at every attempt to wield the ballot, at every endeavor to combine the efforts of workingmen, you have displayed the brutal violence of the police club, and this is why I have recommended rude force, to combat the ruder force of the police.

"You have charged me with despising 'law and order.' What does your 'law and order' amount to? Its representatives are the police, and they have thieves in their ranks. Here sits Captain Schaack. He has himself admitted to me that my hat and books have been stolen from him in his office—stolen by policemen. These are your defenders of property rights!

"The detectives again, who arrested me, forced their way into my room like house breakers, under false pretences, giving the name of a carpenter, Lorenz, of Burlington street. They have sworn that I was alone in my room, therein perjuring themselves. You have not subpœnaed this lady, Mrs. Klein, who was present, and could have sworn that the aforesaid detectives broke into my room under false pretenses, and that their testimonies are perjured.

"But let us go further. In Schaack we have a captain of the police, and he also has perjured himself. He has sworn that I admitted to him being present at the Monday night meeting, whereas, I distinctly informed him that I was at a carpenter's meeting at Zepf's Hall. He has sworn again that I told him that I had learned how to make bombs from Herr Most's book. That, also, is a perjury.

"Let us go still a step higher among these representatives of law and order. Grinnell and his associates have permitted perjury, and I say that they have done it knowingly. The proof has been adduced by my counsel, and with my own eyes I have seen Grinnell point out to Gilmer, eight days before he came upon the stand, the persons of the men whom he was to swear against.

"While I, as I have stated above, believe in force for the sake of winning for myself and fellow-workmen a livelihood such as men ought to have, Grinnell, on the other hand, through his police and other rogues, has suborned prejury in order to murder seven men, of whom I am one.

"Grinnell had the pitiful courage here in the courtroom, where I could not defend myself, to call me a coward! The scoundrel! A fellow who has leagued himself with a parcel of base, hireling knaves, to bring me to the gallows. Why? For no earthly reason save a contemptible selfishness—a desire to 'rise in the world'—to 'make money,' forsooth.

"This wretch—who, by means of the perjuries of other wretches is going to murder seven men—is the fellow who calls me 'coward!' And yet you blame me for despising such 'defenders of the law'—such unspeakable hypocrites!

"Anarchy means no domination or authority of one man over another, yet you call that 'disorder.' A system which advocates no such 'order' as shall require the services of rogues and thieves to defend it you call 'disorder.'

"The Judge himself was forced to admit that the state's attorney had not been able to connect me with the bomb throwing. The latter knows how to get around it, however. He charges me with being a 'conspirator.' How does he prove it? Simply by declaring the International Workingmens' Association to be a 'conspiracy.' I was a member of that body, so he has the charge securely fastened on me. Excellent! Nothing is too difficult for the genius of a state's attorney!

"It is hardly incumbent upon me to review the relations which I occupy to my companions in misfortune. I can say truly and openly that I am not as intimate with my fellow prisoners as I am with Captain Schaack.

"The universal misery, the ravages of the capitalistic hyena have brought us together in our agitation, not as persons, but as workers in the same cause. Such is the 'conspiracy' of which you have convicted me.

"I protest against the conviction, against the decision of the court. I do not recognize your law, jumbled together as it is by the nobodies of bygone centuries, and I do not recognize the decision of the court. My own counsel have conclusively proven from the decisions of equally high courts that a new trial must be granted us. The state's attorney quotes three times as many decisions from perhaps still higher courts to prove the opposite, and I am convinced that if, in another trial, these decisions should be supported by twenty-five volumes, they will adduce one hundred in support of the contrary, if it is anarchists who are to be tried. And not even under such a law, a law that a schoolboy must despise, not even by such methods have they been able to 'legally' convict us.

"They have suborned perjury to boot.

"I tell you frankly and openly, I am for force. I have already told Captain Schaack, 'if they use cannons against us, we shall use dynamite against them.'

"I repeat that I am the enemy of the 'order' of to-day, and I repeat that, with all my powers, so long as breath remains in me, I shall combat it. I declare again, frankly and openly, that I am in favor of using force. I have told Captain Schaack, and I stand by it, 'if you cannonade us we shall dynamite you.' You laugh! Perhaps you think, 'you'll throw no more bombs;' but let me assure you that I die happy on the gallows so confident am I that the hundreds and thousands to whom I have spoken will remember my words; and when you shall have hanged us, then, mark my words, they will do the bomb-throwing! In this hope do I say to you: 'I despise you. I despise your order; your laws, your force-propped authority.' HANG ME FOR IT!

George Engell, on Anarchism.

"This is the first occasion of my standing before an American court, and on this occasion it is murder of which I am accused. And for what reasons do I stand here? For what reasons am I accused of murder? The same that caused me to leave Germany—the poverty—the misery of the working classes.

"And here, too, in this 'free republic,' in the richest country of the world, there are numerous proletarians for whom no table is set; who, as outcasts of society, stray joylessly through life. I have seen human beings gather their daily food from the garbage heaps of the streets, to quiet therewith their knawing hunger.

"I have read of occurrences in the daily papers which proves to me that here, too, in this great 'free land,' people are doomed to die of starvation. This brought me to reflection, and to the question: What are the peculiar causes that could bring about such a condition of society? I then began to give our political institutions more attention than formerly. My discoveries brought to me the knowledge that the same society evils exist here that exist in Germany. This is the explanation of what induced me to study the social question, to become a socialist. And I proceeded with all the means at my command, to make myself familiar with the new doctrine.

"When in 1878, I came here from Philadelphia, I strove to better my condition, believing it would be less difficult to establish a means of livelihood here than in Philadelphia, where I had tried in vain to make a living. But here, too, I found myself disappointed. I began to understand that it made no difference to the proletarian, whether he lived in New York, Philadelphia, or Chicago. In the factory in which I worked I became acquainted with a man who pointed out to me the causes that brought about the difficult and fruitless battles of the workingmen for the means of existence. He explained to me, by the logic of scientific socialism, how mistaken I was in believing that I could make an independent living by the toil of my hands, so long as machinery, raw material, etc., were guaranteed to the capitalists as private property by the State. That I might further enlighten my mind in regard to these facts, I purchased with money earned by myself and family, sociological works, among them those of LaSalle, Marx, and Henry George. After the study of these books, it became clear to me why a workingman could not decently exist in this rich country. I now began to think of ways and means to remedy this. I hit upon the ballot box; for it had been told me so often that this was the means by which workingmen could better their condition.

"I took part in politics with the earnestness of a good citizen; but I was soon to find that the teachings of a 'free ballot box' are a myth, and that I had again been duped. I came to the opinion that as long as workingmen are economically enslaved they cannot be politically free. It became clear to me that the working classes would never bring about a form of society guaranteeing work, bread, and a happy life by means of the ballot.

"Before I had lost my faith in the ballot-box the following occurrences transpired which proved to me that the politicians of this country were through and through corrupt. When, in the fourteenth ward, in which I lived and had the right to vote, the social-democratic party had grown to such dimensions as to make it dangerous for the republican and democratic parties, the latter forthwith united and took stand against the social democrats. This, of course, was natural; for are not their interests identical? And as the social-democrats nevertheless elected their candidates, they were beaten out of the fruits of their victory by the corrupt schemes of the old political parties. The ballot-box was stolen and the votes so 'corrected' that it became possible for the opposition to proclaim their candidates elected. The workingmen sought to obtain justice through the courts, but it was all in vain. The trial cost them fifteen hundred dollars, but their rights they never obtained.

"Soon enough I found that political corruption had burrowed through the ranks of the social-democrats. I left this party and joined the International Working People's Association, that was just being organized. The members of that body have the firm conviction that the workingman can free himself from the tyranny of capitalism only through force; just as all advances of which history speaks, have been brought about through force alone. We see from the history of this country that the first colonists won their liberty only through force; that through force slavery was abolished, and just as the man who agitated against slavery in this country, had to ascend the gallows, so also must we. He who speaks for the workingman to-day must hang. And why? Because this republic is not governed by people who have obtained their office honestly.

"Who are the leaders at Washington that are to guard the interests of this nation? Have they been elected by the people, or by the aid of their money? They have no right to make laws for us, because they were not elected by the people. These are the reasons why I have lost all respect for American laws.

"The fact that through the improvement of machinery so many men are thrown out of employment, or at best, working but half the time, brings them to reflection. They have leisure, and they consider how their conditions can be changed. Reading matter that has been written in their interest gets into their hands, and faulty though their education may be, they can nevertheless cull the truths contained in those writings. This, of course, is not pleasant for the capitalistic class, but they cannot prevent it. And it is my firm conviction that in a comparatively short time the great mass of proletarians will understand that they can be freed from their bonds only through socialism. One must consider what Carl Schurz said scarcely eight years ago: That, 'in this country there is no space for socialism;' and yet to-day socialism stands before the bars of the court.

For this reason it is my firm conviction that if these few years suffice to make socialism one of the burning questions of the day, it will require but a short time more to put it in practical operation.

"All that I have to say in regard to my conviction is, that I was not at all surprised; for it has ever been that the men who have endeavored to enlighten their fellow man have been thrown into prison or put to death, as was the case with John Brown. I have found, long ago, that the workingman has no more rights here than anywhere else in the world. The state's attorney has stated that we were not citizens. I have been a citizen this long time; but it does not occur to me to appeal for my rights as a citizen, knowing as well as I do that this does not make a particle of difference. Citizen or not—as a working man I am without rights, and therefore I respect neither your rights nor your laws, which are made and directed by one class against the other; the working class.

"Of what does my crime consist?

"That I have labored to bring about a system of society by which it is impossible for one to hoard millions, through the improvements in machinery, while the great masses sink to degradation and misery. As water and air are free to all, so should the inventions of scientific men be applied for the benefit of all. The statute laws we have are in opposition to the laws of nature, in that they rob the great masses of their rights to 'life, liberty, and the pursuit of happiness.'

"I am too much a man of feeling not to battle against the societary conditions of to-day. Every considerate person must combat a system which makes it possible for the individual to rake and hoard millions in a few years, while, on the other side, thousands become tramps and beggars.

"Is it to be wondered at that under such circumstances men arise who strive and struggle to create other conditions, where the humane humanity shall take precedence of all other considerations. This is the aim of socialism, and to this I joyfully subscribe.

"The state's attorney said here that 'anarchy' was 'on trial.'"

"Anarchism and socialism are as much alike, in my opinion, as one egg is to another. They differ only in their tactics. The anarchists have abandoned the way of liberating humanity which socialists would take to accomplish this. I say: Believe no more in the ballot, and use all other means at your command. Because we have done so we stand arraigned here to-day—because we have pointed out to the people the proper way. The anarchists are being hunted and persecuted for this in every clime, but in the face of it all anarchism is gaining more and more adherents, and if you cut off our opportunities of open agitation, then will all the work be done secretly. If the state's attorney thinks he can root out socialism by hanging seven of our men and condemning the other to fifteen years servitude, he is laboring under a very wrong impression. The tactics simply will be changed—that is all. No power on earth can rob the workingman of his knowledge of how to make bombs— and that knowledge he possessess. I do not wish for state's attorney Grinnell and his assistant, Furthman, the fate of the Chief of Police Rumpff.

"If anarchism could be rooted out, it would have been accomplished long ago in other countries. On the night on which the first bomb in this country was thrown, I was in my apartments at home. I knew nothing of the conspiracy which the state's attorney pretends to have discovered.

"It is true I am acquainted with several of my fellow defendants; with most of them, however, but slightly, through seeing them at meetings, and hearing them speak. Nor do I deny that I too have spoken at meetings, saying that, if every working man had a bomb in his pocket, capitalistic rule would soon come to an end.

"That is my opinion, and my wish; it became my conviction, when I mentioned the wickedness of the capitalistic conditions of the day.

"When hundreds of workingmen have been destroyed in mines in consequence of faulty preparations, for the repairing of which the owners were too stingy, the capitalistic papers have scarcely noticed it. See with what satisfaction and cruelty they make their report, when here and there workingmen have been fired upon, while striking for a few cents increase in their wages, that they might earn only a scanty subsistence.

"Can any one feel any respect for a government that accords rights only to the privileged classes, and none to the workers? We have seen but recently how the coal barons combined to form a conspiracy to raise the price of coal, while at the same time reducing the already low wages of their men. Are they accused of conspiracy on that account? But when workingmen dare ask an increase in their wages, the militia and the police are sent out to shoot them down.

"For such a government as this I can feel no respect, and will combat them despite their power, despite their police, despite their spies.

"I hate and combat, not the individual capitalist, but the system that gives him those privileges. My greatest wish is that workingmen may recognize who are their friends and who are their enemies.

"As to my conviction, brought about as it was, through capitalistic influence, I have not one word to say.

Samuel Fielden on Socialism and Anarchism.

"I came to the United States in 1868. I have preached in Ohio, and I came to Chicago in 1869. There are monuments of beauty, of stability, and evidences of progress in the city of Chicago, and you can hardly go through a street in this city that I have not dropped my sweat upon, that had been produced by the labor of my hand. And just here let me tell you that when the indictment had been procured against me and my comrades here, it was accompanied by the statement that these men had been deluding their dupes in order to make money out of them. When the trial was in progress the only man who could have answered the question as to whether we had made money out of our organization was Zeller, the Secretary of the Central Labor Union, and when he was asked the question whether we ever received any money for speaking and organizing unions in that organization, the gentlemen who had been instrumental in attaching that to the indictment in order to prejudice the people against us before the trial should come on against us— for there is nothing in the world that can prejudice a man so much as to be charged with having imposed on some one for mercenary motives, and this is creditable to society—when the trial came on and this man who could have testified to that—who could have substantiated it if it had been true—was asked the question, each one of the gentlemen who were interested in its being proven true for their side of the case at once sprang to their feet and objected to the question being asked. We have been tried by a jury that have found us guilty. You will be tried by a jury now that will find you guilty.

"Being of an inquiring disposition or turn of mind, and having observed that there was something wrong in our social system, I attended some meetings of workingmen and compared what they said with my own observation. I knew there was something wrong. My ideas did not become settled as to what was the remedy, but when they did I carried the same energy and the same determination to bring about that remedy that I had applied to ideas which I had possessed years before. There is always a period in every individual's life when some sympathetic chord is touched by some other person. That is the open sesame that carries conviction. The ground may have all been prepared. The evidence may all have been accumulated, but it has not formed any shape. In fact, the child has not been born. The new idea has not impressed itself thoroughly when that sympathetic chord is touched, and the person is thoroughly convinced of the truth of the idea. It was so in my investigation of political economy. I knew there was something wrong, but I did not know what the remedy was; but discussing the condition of things and the different remedies one day, a person said to me that socialism meant equal opportunities—and that was the touch. From that time I became a socialist; I learned more and more what it was. I knew that I had found the right thing; that I had found the medicine that was calculated to cure the ills of society. Having found it I had a right to advocate it, and I did. The constitution of the United States, when it says: 'The right of free speech shall not be abridged,' gives every man the right to speak his thoughts. I have advocated the principles of socialism and social economy, and for that and no other reason am I here, and is sentence of death to be pronounced upon me? What is socialism? Taking somebody else's property? That is what socialism is in the common acceptation of the term. No. But if I were to answer it as shortly and as curtly as it is answered by its enemies, I would say it is preventing somebody else from taking your property. But socialism is equality. Socialism recognizes the fact that no man in society is responsible for what he is; that all the ills that are in society are the production of poverty; and scientific socialism says you must go to the root of the evil. There is no criminal statistician in the world but will acknowledge that all crime, when traced to its origin, is the product of poverty. It has been said that it was inflammatory for me to say that the present social system degraded men until they became mere animals. Go through this city into the low lodging houses where men are huddled together into the smallest possible space, living in an infernal atmosphere of death and disease, and I will ask you to draw your silks and your broadcloths close to you when these men pass you. Do you think that these men deliberately, with a full knowledge of what they are doing, choose to become that class of animals? Not one of them. They are the products of conditions, of certain environments in which they were born, and which have impelled them resistlessly into what they are. And we have this loadstone. You who wish it could be taken from the shoulders of society. What is it? When those men were children, put them into an environment where they have the best results of civilization around them, and they will never willfully choose a condition like that. Some cynic might say that this would be a very nice thing for these men. Society, with its rapidity of production of the means of existence, is capable of doing that without doing injury to a single individual; and the great masses of wealth owned by individuals in this and the old world have been produced in exactly the same proportion as these men have been degraded—and they never could have been accumulated in any other way. I do not charge that every capitalist willfully and maliciously conspires to bring about these results; but I do charge that it has been done, and I do charge that it is a very undesirable condition of things, and I claim that socialism would cure the world of that ulcer. These are my ideas in short, on socialism. The ultra patriotic sentiment of the American people—and I suppose the same comparative sentiment is felt in England and France and Germany—is that no man in this country need be poor. The class who are not poor think so. The class who are poor are beginning to think differently; that under existing conditions it is impossible that some people should not be poor.

"Why is it that we have 'over-production?' And why is it that our warehouses are full of goods, and our workshops have to shut up, and our workmen are turned out on the highway because there is nothing to do? What is this tending to? Let me show the change of conditions as shown in Boston in forty years. Charles Dickens, a man of acute perceptions, visited this country forty years ago, and he said that the sight of a beggar in the streets of Boston at that time would have created as much consternation as the sight of an angel with a drawn sword.

"A Boston paper in the winter of 1884–5 stated that there were some quarters in Boston where to own a stove was to be a comparative aristocrat. The poor people who lived in the neighborhood paid a certain sum of money to rent the holes on the top of the stove that belonged to the aristocrats. You see the change, and there is this comparative change in the working classes of that city, and in every large city in the Union. It is a noted fact that within the last twenty or thirty years the farms of this country have been gradually going out of the possession of the actual cultivators until to-day there is a little more than a quarter of the actual cultivators of farms in this country who are renters; and within twenty years in the states of Iowa and Illinois the mortgages on farms have increased thirty-three per cent of the actual value of the farms. Is it not enough to make any thinking man ask if there is not something wrong somewhere? Possibly it would be answered 'yes, a man has a right to inquire whether there is something wrong or not, but for God's sake, don't think that socialism will do it any good, or if you do we will hang you! It is all right to think, but we will punish you for your conclusions.' Parsons, in his testimony, repeated what he had said at the haymarket on the night of May 4, when he stated that this was an American question, because the patriotic tricksters who have been telling the people to worship the American flag, while they quietly put their hands in their pockets and robbed them—they have said that this is merely a European question. It is an American question, and the close contact of nations cemented by the facilities of civilization, is bringing all the questions that affect one people to affect all people equally all over the world. What affects the European laborer and his employer affects the American laborer and his American employer, and the relationship is the same between the two classes. In the winter of 1884–5 one hundred and twenty American girls of fourteen and sixteen years of age were driven from their homes by the shutting down of the Merrimac mills in Connecticut, and they were compelled to walk through the bleak New England hills and find refuge in out-houses and hay-stacks, and numbers of them undoubtedly found their way to lives of shame. And I say here and now that the man who can look upon suffering like this and not feel stirred to do something to change such conditions, has not got anything in his heart but the feelings of the tiger, hungry for prey. In this city of Chicago children are working at very tender ages. Going home one very cold night in the winter of 1884, two little girls ran up to me and begged of me to go home with them. I asked them why. They said: 'A man down there has been offering us money.' It was 7 o'clock at night and snowing; I asked them where they had been so late. They said: 'We have been working in such a store.' Children, babies turned out from their mother's heart to make a living, their fathers perhaps dead—in this case they were. The civilization that will not and cannot support a widow so that she will not have to turn her children out to such temptations as that is not worth respecting, and the man who will not try to change it is no man.

"It is a known fact that there is no possibility of a young, unmarried woman, who has not a brother or father to assist her, getting a living in the city of Chicago, with a few exceptions. A friend of mine, a labor agitator, was asked by a young lady to procure her a position. He went to one of your large establishments, and they said: 'Yes, we can give her a position, but she has got to dress tastily and nicely and neatly, and look well, and we will give her from three to five dollars a week;' and you propose to get rid of these things by fining those who are compelled to resort to such extremes to live. I tell you these things to show you that the question is an American question. It is a question of the nineteenth century.

Albert R. Parsons on Anarchy.

"In the effort of the prosecution to hold up our opinions to public execration they lost sight of the charge of murder. Disloyalty to their class, and their boasted civilization is in their eyes a far greater crime than murder.

"Anarchy, in the language of Grinnell, is simply a compound of robbery, incendiarism and murder. This is the official statement of Mr. Grinnell, and against his definition of anarchy I would put that of Mr. Webster. I think that is pretty near as good authority as that gentleman's.

"What is anarchy? What is the nature of the dreadful thing—this anarchy, for the holding of which this man says we ought to suffer death?

"The closing hours of this trial, yes, for five days the representatives of a privileged, usurped power and of despotism sought to belie, misrepresent, and vilify the doctrine in which I believe. Now, sir, let me speak of that for a moment.

"What is anarchism? What is it—what are its doctrines?

"General Parsons—for which you are called upon to die.

"Mr. Parsons—For which I am called upon to die. First and foremost it is my opinion, or the opinion of an anarchist, that government is despotism; government is an organization of oppression, and law, statute law is its agent. Anarchy is anti-government, anti-rulers, anti-dictators, anti-bosses and drivers. Anarchy is the negation of force; the elimination of all authority in social affairs; it is the denial of the right of domination of one man over another. It is the diffusion of rights, of power, of duties, equally and freely among all the people.

"But anarchy, like many other words, is defined in Webster's dictionary as having two meanings. In one place it is defined to mean, 'without rulers or governors.' In another place it is defined to mean, 'disorder and confusion.' This latter meaning is what we call 'capitalistic anarchy,' such as is now witnessed in all portions of the world and especially in this court-room; the former, which means without rulers, is what we denominate communistic anarchy, which will be ushered in with the social revolution.

"Socialism is a term which covers the whole range of human progress and advancement. Socialism is defined by Webster—I think I have a right to speak of this matter, because I am tried here as a socialist. I am condemend as a socialist, and it has been of socialism that Grinnell and these men had so much to say, and I think it right to speak before the country, and be heard in my own behalf, at least. If you are going to put me to death, then let the people know what it is for. Socialism is defined by Webster as 'A theory of society which advocates a more precise, more orderly, and more harmonious arrangement of the social relations of mankind that has hitherto prevailed.' Therefore everything in the line of progress, in civilization in fact, is socialistic. There are two distinct phases of socialism in the labor movement throughout the world to-day. One is known as anarchism, without political government or authority, the other is known as state socialism or paternalism, or governmental control of everything. The state socialist seeks to ameliorate and emancipate the wage laborers by means of law, by legislative enactments. The state socialistis demand the right to choose their own rulers. Anarchists would have neither rulers nor law-makers of any kind. The anarchists seek the same ends by the abrogation of law, by the abolition of all government, leaving the people free to unite or disunite as fancy or interest may dictate; coercing no one, driving no party.

"Now, sir, we are supported in this position by a very distinguished man indeed, no less a man than Buckle, the author of 'The History of Civilization.' He states that there have been two opposing elements to the progress of civilization of man. The first of these two is the church, which commands what a man shall believe. And the other is the state, which commands him what to do. Buckle says that the only good laws passed in the last three or four hundred years have been laws that repealed other laws. That is the view exactly of anarchists. Our belief is that all these laws should be repealed, and that is the only good legislation that could possibly take place.

"Now, law is license, and consequently despotic. A legal enactment is simply something which authorizes somebody to do something for somebody else that he could not do were it not for the statute. Now then the statute is the divestment and the denial of the right of another, and we hold that to be wrong; we consider that the invasion of a man's natural right. Mark you, we do not object to all laws: The law which is in accordance with nature is good. The Constitution of the United States, when it guarantees me the right of free speech, a free press, of unmolested assemblage, and the right of self-defense, why—your Constitution of the United States is good, because it sanctions it. Why? Because it is in conformity with natural law. It don't require any statute law to provide such a safeguard as that. That is inalienable, and it is a natural right, inherited by the very fact of my existence, and the mere fact that it is embraced in the Constitution does not make it any more sacred at all. On the contrary it shows how foolish it is to do by constitution that which kind mother nature has already freely and graciously done for us. The more we are governed the less we are free. I do not believe your honor will deny that.

"The law-abiding citizen—especially if he is called upon to do something, you understand, under a law that enslaves him, is an uncomplaining slave to the power that governs him. Imagine a chattel slave down south who was law-abiding, who was obedient; what does that mean? That means he did not have any objections; he did not have anything to say against the law that makes him another man's slave. Now, the workingman to-day in this country who says nothing, who makes no objection to any of these enactments, with no protest at all against these infamous things that are practiced by legislation, that workingman is a law-abiding, obedient workingman. He is a nice, quiet, peaceful, genteel citizen.

"Anarchists are not that kind. We object to those laws. Whether the government consists of one over the million, or a million over one, an anarchist is opposed to the rule of majorities as well as minorities. If a man has a right, he has that right, whether that right is denied by a million or by one. Right is right, and the majority that sets itself up to dictate to minorities, they simply transform themselves into tyrants, they become usurpers; they deny the natural right of their fellow men. Now, sir, this will put an end to the law factory business. What would become of your law-makers? Why a human law-maker, in my humble judgment, is a human humbug. Yes, sir, and I believe that these law-factories that we have throughout the country, the legislatures of our states and the Union, where they manufacture laws just as we go to a factory to manufacture a pair of boots—why, your honor, the same pair of boots won't fit every man; how can you make a law that will apply to the individual cases of each one?

"Now, your honor, I suppose that you would hold, like they did in the days of old—I don't know whether you will or not, but there are some men who would hold that a man who would adhere to these kind of opinions ought to die. That this world has got no use for him. Well, that remains to be seen.

"The natural and the imprescriptible right of all is the right of each to control oneself. Anarchy is a free society where there is no concentrated or centralized power, no state, no king, no emperor, no ruler, no president, no magistrate, no potentate of any character whatever. Law is the enslaving power of man. Blackstone defines the law to be a rule of action. I believe that is it. Colonel Foster, I would like to ask your opinion if that quotation is correct? Blackstone describes the law to be a rule of action, prescribing what is right and prohibiting what is wrong. Now, very true. Anarchists hold that it is wrong for one person to prescribe what is the right action for another person, and then compel that person to obey that rule. Therefore, right action consists in each person attending to his business and allowing everybody else to do likewise.

"Whoever prescribes a rule of action for another to obey is a tyrant, usurper, and an enemy of liberty. This is precisely what every statute does. Anarchy is the natural law, instead of the man-made statute, and gives men leaders in the place of drivers and bosses. All political law, statute and common, gets its right to operate from the statute; therefore all political law is statute law. A statute law is a written scheme by which cunning takes advantage of the unsuspecting, and provides the inducement to do so, and protects the one who does it. In other words, a statute is the science of rascality, or the law of usurpation. If a few sharks rob mankind of all the earth, turn them all out of house and home, make them ragged slaves and beggars, and freeze and starve them to death, still they are expected to obey the statute because it is sacred. This ridiculous nonsense that human laws are sacred, and that if they are not respected and continued we cannot prosper, is the stupidest and most criminal nightmare of the age. Statutes are the last and greatest curse of man, and when destroyed the world will be free. The statute book is a book of laws by which one class of people can safely trespass upon the rights of another. Every statute law is always used to oppose some natural law, or to sustain some other equally vicious statute. The statute is the great science of rascality by which alone the few trample upon and enslave the many. There are natural laws provided for every want of man. Natural laws are self-operating. They punish all who violate them, and reward all who obey them. They cannot be repealed, amended, dodged or bribed, and it costs neither time, money nor attention to apply them. It is time to stop legislating against them. We want to obey laws, not men, nor the tricks of men. Statutes are human tricks. The law—the statute law—is the coward's weapon, the tool of the thief, and more—the shield and buckler of every gigantic villany, and frightful parent of all crimes. Every great robbery that was ever perpetrated upon a people has been by virtue of and in the name of law. By this tool of thieves the great mass of the people who inhabit our planet have been robbed of their equal right to the use of the soil and of all other natural opportunities. In the name of this monster (statute law) large sections of our race have been bought and sold as chattels; by it the vast majority of the human race are to-day held in the industrial bondage of wage-slavery, and in its name our fair earth has been times without number deluged in human blood. By the instrumentality of this tool, cowards and thieves, tyrants and usurpers, are robbing their fellows of their substance, despoiling them of their natural rights, and depriving them of liberty. Man's legal rights are everywhere in collision with man's natural rights; hence the deep-rooted and wide-spread unrest of modern civilization. The only sacred right of property is the natural right of the workingman to the product, which is the creation of his labor. The legal right of the capitalist to rent and interest and profit is the absolute denial of the natural right of labor. Free access to the means of production is the natural right to labor. Free access to the means of production is the natural right of every man able and willing to work. It is the legal right of the capitalist to refuse such access to labor, and to take from the laborer all the wealth he creates over and above a bare subsistence for allowing him the privilege of working.

"A laborer has the natural right to life, and as life is impossible without the means of production the equal right to life involves an equal right to the means of production. The legal right of the capitalist is virtually the assertion that one man has a greater right to life than another man, since it denies the equality of natural conditions. Our present social system, therefore, is based upon the legalization of robbery, slavery and murder. The laborer who does not get more than a bare subsistence as the fruit of his toil is robbed. The laborer who is forced to beg for work, and has to accept it on any terms or starve, is a slave. The laborer who, being unable to get work, but who in turn has too much manhood to beg, steal or become a pauper, is by the refined process of slow starvation murdered.

"Laws—just laws—natural laws—are not made, they are discovered. Law enancting is an insult to divine intelligence, and law enforcing is the impeachment of God's integrity and His power. I make, as an anarchist, this declaration for the benefit of our christian ministry, who, while professing loyalty for God's laws, never forget to pray and work for the supremacy of man's laws and man's government. Those pious frauds who profess their faith in the 'power' of God, while they employ the police, the militia and other armed hirelings to enforce their man-made laws and maintain their 'power' over their fellow men. Oh, consistency, indeed thou art a jewel! These hypocrites, who always did, and do to-day, employ brute force to compel their fellow men to obey and serve them, while they whine and snivel behind their sanctimonious masks about their 'love for man and the power of God.' I hope some of them will preach in their pulpits next Sunday morning on this topic.

"In the opinion of an anarchist, the sum total of human ills is expressed in one word—authority. The economic regulates and controls the social status of man; the mode and manner of procuring our livelihood affects our whole life; the all-pervading cause is economic, not political, moral or religious; and social institutions of every kind and degree result from, grow out of, and are created by the economic or industrial regulations of society. Every human being, consciously or unconsciously, is affected and controlled by it in what they think, or say, or do. There is no escape, no evasion from its consequences. It is logic. It is cause and effect. Evil exists on every hand; the well-disposed, philanthropic, and generous, and the good, seek relief from these evil influences by moral suasion, by self-denial, by religion, by politics, etc., etc., but in vain, in vain! The evils remain, and not only remain, but grow worse and worse. Why, if the fountain is corrupt, can the stream be pure? If the cause remains, must not the effects follow? Jails, judges and executioners, police, armies and navies, pestilence, misery and ignorance and debauchery, and evils of all kinds of high and low degree, all flow from one fountain. That flowing fountain of human woe is the economic or industrial subjection and enslavement of man to man. Every human ill is produced by the denial or violation of man's natural rights, or by the neglect or refusal of man to conform his life to the requirements of nature. Wickedness, wretchedness, ignorance, vice, crime, poverty, are the penalties which nature inflicts upon her disobedient children. The natural man is a happy man. He is virtuous and rich; truly so. Whoever violates the right of another, sooner or later punishes himself. Nature is inexorable. From her penalty there is no escape. But in a court of law—of so-called 'justice'—if you are a member of the Citizen's Association, or if you have a big bank account, in other words, if you are a member of the propertied class, you crawl out of anything you want to, for law is for sale; that is to say, whoever can purchase the lawyers, stock the jury and bribe the court can win. There is only one law for the poor, to wit: Obey the rich.

"The existing economic system has placed on the markets for sale man's natural rights. What are these rights? Well, among the many I will enumerate one or two. The right to live, for instance, is an inalienable right. So too, is the right to liberty and the pursuit of happiness. Now, how can I possess these rights and enjoy them, when the very conveniences of life and the means for their procurement are owned by and belong to another?

"Shakespeare makes Shylock say at the bar of the Venetian court, 'You do take my life when you take the means whereby I live.' Now, the means of life are monopolized; the necessary means for the existence of all has been appropriated and monopolized by a few. The land, the implements of production and communication, the resources of life, are now held as private property, and its owners exact tribute from the propertyless. In this way the privileged class become millionaires. They deny the equal right of every one to freely use our natural inheritance, the earth. The denial of that right is death to whom it is denied. The right to live is made a privilege by law, granted by law, which is granted or denied by the possessor to the disposessed. Human rights are for sale, 'If thou wilt not work, neither shaft thou eat,' says the scripture. This finds immunity, however, among those who can pay for it. Those who work eat not; and those who eat work not. They do not have to; they hire some hungry, poor devil to do the work for them. The hired man—the hired man whom the capitalist press gloats on the idea of, and whom the pious frauds declare is the dispensation of divine providence, whom we will always have among us is a social fungus, the outgrowth of a rotten, corrupt industrial regime.

"In conclusion I will say, compulsion is slavery, and those disinherited of their natural rights must hire out and serve and obey the oppressing class or starve. There is no other alternative. Some things are priceless, chief among which are life and liberty. A freeman is not for sale or for hire.

"You accuse the anarchists of using or advising the use of force; it is false. 'Out of your own mouth you stand condemned.' The present existing state of society is based upon and maintained by and perpetuated by force, This capitalistic system that we have to-day would not exist twenty-four hours if it were not held together by the bayonets and the clubs of the militia and police. No, sir, it would not! Now, sir, we object to this. We protest against it. But you accuse us, or the prosecution here accuses us, of that very thing which they themselves are guilty of. It is the old, old story of Æsop's fable, the lamb standing in the water and the wolf above him; he looks up; the water has run down, the wolf stands above him; he looks down toward the lamb, and says he, 'Ho, there! you are making the water muddy.' The lamb observes, 'My friend, I am below you in the stream.' 'That don't matter; you are my meat, anyhow.' And he goes for him and eats him up. That is just the way of the capitalist toward the anarchist. You are doing the very thing you accuse us of, and against which we protest. Now any institution that is based upon force is self-condemned; it does not need any argument, in my opinion, to show it.

"The political economy that prevails was written to justify the taking of something for nothing; it was written to hide the blushes of the rich when they look into the faces of the poor. These are they who brand anarchy as a compound of 'incendiarism, robbery and murder:' these are they who despoil the people; they love power and hate equality; they who dominate, degrade and exploit their fellow men, they who employ brute force, violence and wholesale murder, to perpetuate and maintain their privileges.

"This labor question is not a question of emotion: the labor question is not a question of sentiment; it is not a religious matter; it is not a political problem: no, sir, it is a stern economic fact, a stubborn and immovable fact. It has, it is true, its emotional phase; it has its sentimental, religious, political aspects, but the sum total of this question is the bread and butter question, the how and wherefore we will live and earn our daily bread. And until the right of existence is settled upon the basis of equal and perfect liberty to all, there will never be peace among men. This is the labor movement. It has a scientific basis. It is founded upon fact.

"Labor is a commodity and wages is the price paid for it. The owner of this commodity—of labor—sells it, that is himself, to the owner of capital in order to live. Labor is the expression of energy, the power of the laborer's life. This energy of power he must sell to another person in order to live. It is his only means of existence. He works to live, but his work is not simply a part of his life; it is the sacrifice of it. His labor is a commodity which under the guise of free labor, he is forced by necessity to hand over to another party. The reward of the wage laborer's activity is not the product of his labor—far from it. The silk he weaves, the palace he builds, the ores he digs from out the mines—are not for him—oh, no. The only thing he produces for himself is his wage, and the silk, the ores and the palace which he has built are simply transformed for him into a certain kind of means of existence, namely, a cotton shirt, a few pennies, and the mere tenantcy of a lodging-house. In other words, his wages represent the bare necessities of his existence, and the unpaid-for or 'surplus' portion of his labor product constitutes the vast superabundant wealth of the non-producing or capitalist class. That is the capitalist system. It is the capitalist system that creates these classes, and it is these classes that produces this conflict. This conflict intensifies as the power of the privileged classes over the non-possessing or propertyless classess increases and intensifies, and this power increases as the idle few become richer and the producing many become poorer, and this produces what is called the labor movement. Wealth is power, poverty is weakness. If I had time I might answer some suggestions that probably arise in the minds of some persons not familiar with this question. I imagine I hear your honor say, 'Why, labor is free. This is a free country.' Now, we had in the southern states for nearly a century a form of labor known as chattel slave labor. That has been abolished, and I hear you say that labor is free; that the war has resulted in establishing free labor all over America. Is this true? Look at it. The chattel slave of the past—the wage slave of to-day; what is the difference? The master selected under chattel slavery his own slaves. Under the wage slavery system the wage slave selects his master.

"Formerly the master selected the slave; to-day the slave selects his master and he has got to find one or else he is carried down here to my friend, the goaler, and occupy a cell along side of myself. He is compelled to find one. So the change of the industrial system, in the language of Jefferson Davis, ex-president of the southern confederacy, in an interview with the New York *Herald* upon the question of the chattel slave system of the south and that of the so-called 'free laborer,' and their wages. Jefferson Davis has stated positively that the change was a decided benefit to the former chattel slave owners who would not exchange the new system of wage labor at all for chattel labor, because now the dead had to bury themselves and the sick take care of themselves, and now they don't have to employ overseers to look after them. They give them a task to do—a certain amount to do. They say: 'Now, here, perform this piece of work in a certain length of time,' and if you don't (under the wage system, says Mr. Davis), why, when you come around for your pay next Saturday, you simply find in the envelope containing your money, a note which informs you of the fact that you have been discharged. Now, Jefferson Davis admitted in his statement that the leather thong dipped in salt brine, for the chattel slave, had been exchanged under the wage slave system for the lash of hunger, an empty stomach and the ragged back of the wage-slave, who, according to the census of the United States for 1880, constitute more than nine-tenths of our entire population. But you say the wage slave has advantage over the chattel slave. The chattel slave couldn't get away from it. Well, if we had the statistics, I believe it could be shown that as many chattel slaves escaped from bondage with the bloodhounds of their masters after them as they tracked their way over the snow-beaten rocks of Canada, and via the underground grapevine road. I believe the statistics would show to-day that as many chattel slaves escaped from their bondage under that system as could, and as many as do escape to-day from wage bondage into capitalistic liberty. I am a socialist, I am one of those, although myself a wage slave, who holds that it is wrong, wrong to myself, wrong to my neighbor and unjust to my fellowmen, for me, wage slave that I am, to undertake to make my escape from wage slavery by becoming a master. I refuse to do it, I refuse equally to be a slave or the owner of slaves. Had I chosen another path in life, I might be upon the avenue of the city of Chicago to-day, surrounded in my beautiful home with luxury and ease and slaves to do my bidding. But I chose the other road, and instead I stand here to-day upon the scaffold. This is my crime. Before high heaven this and this alone is my crime. I have been false, I have been untrue, and I am a traitor to the infamies that exist to-day in capitalistic society. If this is a crime in your opinion I plead guilty to it. Now, be patient with me; I have been with you, or rather, I have been patient with this trial. Follow me, if you please, and look at the impressions of this capitalistic system of industry. Every new machine that comes into existence comes there as a competitor with the man of labor. Every machine under the capitalistic system that is introduced into industrial affairs comes as a competitor, as a drag and menace and a prey to the very existence of those who have to sell their labor in order to earn their bread. The man is turned out to starve and whole occupations and pursuits are revolutionized and completely destroyed by the introduction of machinery, in a day, in an hour as it were. I have known it to be the case in the history of my own life—and I am yet a young man—that whole pursuits and occupations have been wiped out or revolutionized by the invention of machinery.

"What becomes of these people? Where are they? Tens of thousands are thrown out of employment, and they become competitors of other laborers and are made to reduce wages and increase the work hours. Many of them are candidates for the gibbet, they are candidates for your prison cells. Build more penitentiaries; erect new scaffolds, for these men are upon the highway of crime, of misery, of death. Your honor, there never was an effect without a cause. The tree is known by its fruit.

Socialists are not those who blindly close their eyes and refuse to look, and who refuse to hear, but having eyes to see, they see, and having ears to hear, they hear. Look at this capitalistic system; look at its operation upon the small dealers, the middle class. *Bradstreet's Commercial Statistics* tells us in last year's report that there were 11,000 small business men financially destroyed the past twelve months. What became of those people? Where are they, and why have they been wiped out? Has there been any less wealth? No; that which they had possessed has simply transferred itself into the hands of some other person. Who is that other? It is he who has greater capitalistic facilities. It is the monopolist, the man who can run corners, who can create rings and squeeze these men to death and wipe them out like dead flies from the table into his monopolistic basket. The middle classes, destroyed in this manner, join the ranks of the proletariat. They become what? They seek out the factory gate, they seek in the various occupations of wage labor for employment. What is the result? Then there are more men upon the market. This increases the number of those who are applying for employment. What then? This intensifies the competition, which in turn creates greater monopolists, and with it wages go down until the starvation point is reached, and then what?

"Socialism comes to the people and asks them to look into this thing, to discuss it, to reason, to examine it, to investigate it, to know the facts, because it is by this, and this alone, violence will be prevented and bloodshed will be avoided, because, as my friend here has said, men in their blind rage, in their ignorance, not knowing what ails them, knowing that they are hungry, that they are miserable and destitute, strike blindly, and do as they did with Maxwell here, and fight the labor-saving machinery. Imagine such an absurd thing, and yet the capitalistic press has taken great pains to say that socialists do these things; that we fight machinery; that we fight poverty. Why, sir, it is an absurdity; it is ridiculous; it is preposterous. No man ever heard an utterance from the mouth of a socialist to advise anything of the kind. They know to the contrary. We don't fight machinery; we don't oppose these things. It is only the manner and methods of employing it that we object to. That is all. It is the manipulation of these things in the interests of a few; it is the monopolization of them that we object to. We desire that all the forces of nature, all the forces of society, of the gigantic strength which has resulted from the combined intellect and labor of the ages of the past shall be turned over to man, and made his servant, his obedient slave forever. This is the object of socialism. It asks no one to give up anything. It seeks no harm to anybody. But, when we witness this condition of things, when we see little children huddling around the factory gates, the poor little things whose bones are not yet hard; when we see them clutched from the hearthstone, taken from the family altar, and carried to the bastiles of labor and their little bones ground up into gold dust to bedeck the form of some aristocratic Jezebel, then it stirs me and I speak out. We plead for the little ones; we plead for the helpless; we plead for the oppressed, we seek redress for those who are wronged; we seek knowledge and intelligence for the ignorant; we seek liberty for the slave; socialism secures the welfare of every human being.

"The evil effects of our existing social system naturally flow from the established social relations, which are founded upon the economic subjection and dependence of the man of labor to the monopolizer of the means of labor— the resources of life. All the ills that afflict society— social miseries, mental degradations, political dependence—all result from the economic subjection and dependence of the man of labor upon the monopolizer of the means of existence; and as long as the cause remains the effect must certainly follow. Seventy-five per cent. of the farms of America are to-day under mortgage. The man who a few years ago owned the soil that he worked, is to-day a tenant at will. A mortgage is placed upon his soil, and when he, the farmer whose hand tickles the earth and causes it to blossom as the rose and bring forth its rich fruits for human sustenance —even while this man is asleep the interest upon the mortgage continues. It grows and it increases, rendering it more and more difficult for him to get along or make his living. In the meantime the railway corporations place upon the traffic all that the market will bear. The board of trade sharks run their corners until— what? Until it occurs, as stated in the Chicago *Tribune* about three months ago, that a freight train of corn from Iowa consigned to a commission merchant in Chicago, had to be sold for less than the cost of freight. The freightage upon that corn was three dollars more than the corn brought in the market. So it is with the tenant farmers of America. Your honor, we do not have to go to Ireland to find the evils of landlordism. We do not have to cross the Atlantic ocean to find Lord Leitrim's rackrenters— landlords who evict their tenants. We have them all around us. There is Ireland right here in Chicago and everywhere else in this country. Look at Bridgeport where the Irish live! Look! Tenants at will, huddled together as State's Attorney Grinnell calls them, like rats; living as they do in Dublin, living precisely as they do in Limerick—taxed to death, unable to meet the extortions of the landlord.

"We were told by the prosecution that law was on trial; that government was on trial; that anarchy was on trial. That is what the gentlemen on the other side stated to the jury. The law is on trial, and government is on trial. Well, up to near the conclusion of this trial we, the defendants, supposed that we were indicted and being tried for murder. Now, if the law is on trial, and the government is on trial, and anarchy is on trial, who has placed it upon trial? And I leave it to the people of America whether the prosecution in this case have made out a case; and I charge it here now frankly that in order to bring about this conviction the prosecution, the representatives of the state, the sworn officers of the law, those whose obligation it is to the people to obey the law and preserve order—I charge upon them a willful, a malicious, a purposed violation of every law which guarantees every right to every American citizen. They have violated free speech. In the prosecution of this case they have violated a free press. They have violated the right of public assembly. Yea, they have even violated and denounced the right of self-defense. I charge the crime home to them. These great blood-bought rights, for which our forefathers spent centuries of struggle, they have violated and betrayed and we, who defend these rights, it is attempted to run like rats into a hole by the prosecution in this case. Why, gentlemen, law is upon trial; government is upon trial, indeed. Yea, they are themselves guilty of the precise thing of which they accuse me. They say that I am an anarchist, and refuse to respect the law. 'By their works ye shall know them,' and out of their own mouths they stand condemned. They are the real anarchists in this case, while we stand upon the constitution of the United States. I have violated no law of this country. Neither I nor my colleagues here have violated any legal right of American citizens. We stand upon the right of free speech, free press, of public assemblage, unmolested and undisturbed. We stand upon the constitutional right of self-defense, and we defy the prosecution to rob the people of America of these dearly bought rights. But the prosecution imagines that they have triumphed because they propose to put to death seven men. Seven men to be exterminated in violation of law, because they insist upon the rights guaranteed them by the constitution. Seven men are to be exterminated because they demand the right of free speech and exercise it. Seven men by this court of law are to be put to death because they claim their right of self-defense. Do you think, gentlemen of the prosecution, that you will have settled the case when you are carrying my lifeless bones to the potter's field? Do you think that this trial will be settled by my strangulation and that of my colleagues? I tell you that there is a greater verdict yet to be heard from. The American people will have something to say about this attempt to destroy their rights, which they hold sacred. The American people will have something to say as to whether or not the Constitution of the United States can be trampled under foot at the dictation of monopoly.

*　　　*　　　*　　　*

"We are charged with being the enemies of 'law and order,' as breeders of strife and confusion. Every conceivable bad name and evil design was imputed to us by the lovers of power and haters of freedom and equality. Even the workingmen in some instances, caught the infection and many of them joined in the capitalistic hue and cry against the anarchists. Being satisfied of ourselves that our purpose was a just one, we worked on undismayed, willing to labor and to wait, for time and events to justify our cause. We began to allude to ourselves as anarchists and that name which was at first imputed to us as a dishonor, we came to cherish and defend with pride. What's in a name? But names sometimes express ideas; and ideas are everything. What, then, is our offense, being anarchists? The word anarchy is derived from the two Greek words *an*, signifying no, or without, and *arche*, government; hence anarchy means no government. Consequently anarchy means a condition of society which has no king, emperor, president or ruler of any kind. In other words ararchy is the social administration of all affairs by the people themselves; that is to say, self-government, individual liberty. Such a condition of society denies the right of majorities to rule over or dictate to minorities. Though every person in the world agree upon a certain plan and only one objection thereto, the objector would, under anarchy, be respected in his natural right to go his own way? And when such person is thus held responsible by all the rest for the violation of the inherent right of any one how then can injustice flourish or right triumph? For the greatest good to the greatest number anarchy substitutes the equal right of each and every one. The natural law is all sufficient for every purpose, every desire and every human being. The scientist then becomes the natural leader, and is accepted as the only authority among men. Whatever can be demonstrated will by self interest be accepted, otherwise rejected. The great natural law of power derived alone from association and co-operation will of necessity and from selfishness be applied by the people in the production and distribution of wealth, and what the trades unions and labor organizations seek now to do, but are prevented from doing because of obstructions and coercions, will under perfect liberty—anarchy—come easiest to hand. Anarchy is the extension of the boundaries of liberty until it covers the whole range of the wants and aspirations of man—not men, but man.

"Power is might, and might always makes its own right. Thus in the very nature of things, might makes itself right whether or no. Government, therefore, is the agency or power by which some person or persons govern or rule other persons, and the inherent right to govern is found wherever the power or might to do so is manifest. In a natural state, intelligence of necessity control ignorance, the strong the weak, the good the bad, etc. Only when the natural law operates is this true, however. On the other hand when the statute is substituted for the natural law, and government holds sway, then, and only then, power centers itself into the hands of a few, who dominate, dictate, rule, degrade and enslave the many. The broad distinction and irreconcilable conflict between wage laborers and capitalists, between those who buy labor or sell its products, and the wage-worker who sells his labor (himself) in order to live, arises from the social institution called government; and the conflicting interests, the total abolition of warring classes, and the end of domination and exploitation of man by man is to be found only in a free society, where all and each are equally free to unite or disunite, as interest or inclination may incline. The anarchists are the advance guard in the impending social revolution. They have discovered the cause of the world-wide discontent which is felt but not yet understood by the toiling millions as a whole. The effort now being made by organized and unorganized labor in all countries to participate in the making of laws which they are forced to obey will lay bare to them the secret source of their enslavement to capital. Capital is a thing—it is property. Capital is the stored up, accumulated savings of past labor, such as machinery, houses, food, clothing, all the means of production (both natural and artificial) of transportation and communication—in short the resources of life, the means of subsistence. These things are, in a natural state, the common heritage of all for the free use of all, and they were so held until their forcible seizure and appropriation by a few. Thus the common heritage of all seized by violence and fraud, was afterwards made the property—capital—of the usurpers, who erected a government and enacted laws to perpetuate and maintain their special privileges. The function, the only function of capital is to appropriate or confiscate the labor product of the propertyless, non-possessing class, the wage-workers. The origin of government was in violence and murder. Government disinherits and enslaves the governed. Government is for slaves; free men govern themselves. Law—statute—man-made law, is license. Anarchy—natural law—is liberty. Anarchy is the cessation of force. Government is the rulership or control of man by men, in the name of law—by means of statute law—whether that control be by one man (*mon*-arche) or by a majority (*mob*-arche). The effort of the wage-slaves (now being made) to participate in the making of laws will enable them to discover for the first time that a human law-maker is a human humbug. That laws, true, just and perfect laws, are discovered, not made. The law-making class—the capitalists—will object to this; they (the capitalists) will remonstrate, they will fight, they will kill, before they permit laws to be made, or repealed, which deprives them of their power to rule and rob. This fact is demonstrated in every strike which threatens their power; by every lock-out, by every discharge, by every black-list. Their exercise of these powers is based upon force, and every law, every government in the last analysis is resolved into force. Therefore, when the workers, as they are now everywhere preparing to do, insist upon and demand a participation in, or application of democratic principles in industrial affairs, think you the request will be conceded? Nay, nay. The right to live, to equality of opportunity, to liberty and the pursuit of happiness, is yet to be acquired by the producers of all wealth. The Knights of Labor unconsciously stand upon a state socialist programme. They will never be able to seize the state by ballot, but when they do seize it (and seize it they must) they will abolish it. Legalized capital and the state stand or fall together. They are twins. The liberty of labor makes the state not only unnecessary, but impossible. When the people—the whole people—become the state, that is, participate equally in governing themselves, the state of necessity ceases to exist. Then what? Leaders, natural leaders, take the place of the overthrown rulers; liberty takes the place of statute laws, of license; the people voluntarily associate or freely withdraw from association, instead of being bossed or driven, as now. They unite and disunite, when, where, and as they please. Social administration is substituted for governmentalism, and self-preservation becomes the actuating motive, as now, minus the dictation, coercion, driving and domination of man by man. Do you say this is a dream? That it is the millenium? Well, the crisis is near at hand. Necessity, which is its own law, will force the issue. Then whatever is most natural to do will be the easiest and best to do. The workshops will drop into the hands of the workers, the mines will fall to the miners, and the land and all other things will be controlled by those who possess and use them. There will be, there can then be no title to anything aside from its possession and use. Only the statute law and government stand to-day as a barrier to this result, and all efforts to change them failing, will inevitably result in their total abolition.

"Anarchy, therefore, is liberty; is the negation of force, or compulsion, or violence. It is the precise reverse of that which those who hold and love power would have their oppressed victims believe it is.

"Anarchists do not advocate or advise the use of force. Anarchists disclaim and protest against its use, and the use of force is justifiable only when employed to repel force. Who, then, are the aiders, abettors and users of force? Who are the real revolutionists? Are they not those who hold and exercise power over their fellows? They who use clubs and bayonets, prisons and scaffolds? The great class conflict now gathering throughout the world is created by our social system of industrial slavery. Capitalists could not if they would, and would not if they could, change it. This alone is to be the work of the proletariat, the disinherited, the wage-slave, the sufferer. Nor can the wage-class avoid this conflict. Neither religion or politics can solve it or prevent it. It comes as a human, an imperative necessity. Anarchists do not make the social revolution; they prophesy its coming. Shall we then stone the prophets? Anarchists do not use or advise the use of force, but point out that force is ever employed to uphold despotism to despoil man's natural rights. Shall we therefore kill and destroy the anarchists? And capital shouts, 'Yes, yes! exterminate them!'

"In the line of evolution and historical development, anarchy—liberty—is next in order. With the destruction of the feudal system, and the birth of commercialism and manufactories in the sixteenth century, a contest long and bitter and bloody, lasting over a hundred years, was waged for mental and religious liberty. The seventeenth and eighteenth centuries, with their sanguinary conflicts, gave to man political equality and civil liberty, based on the monopolization of the resources of life, capital—with its 'free laborers'—freely competing with one another for a chance to serve king capital, and 'free competition' among capitalists in their endeavors to exploit the laborers and monopolize the labor products. All over the world the fact stands undisputed that the political is based upon, and is but the reflex of the economic system, and hence we find that whatever the political form of the government, whether monarchial or republican, the average social status of the wage-workers is in every country identical. The class struggle of the past century is history repeating itself; it is the evolutionary growth preceding the revolutionary denoument. Though liberty is a growth, it is also a birth, and while it is yet to be, it is also about to be born. Its birth will come through travail and pain, through bloodshed and violence. It cannot be prevented. This, because of the obstructions, impediments and obstacles which serve as a barrier to its coming. An anarchist is a believer in liberty, and as I would control no man against his will, neither shall any one rule over me with my consent. Government is compulsion; no one freely consents to be governed by another, therefore there can be no just power of government. Anarchy is perfect liberty, is absolute freedom of the individual. Anarchy has no schemes, no programmes, no systems to offer or to substitute for the existing order of things. Anarchy would strike from humanity every chain that binds it, and say to mankind: 'Go forth! you are free! Have all; enjoy all!'

"Anarchism or anarchists neither advise, abet nor encourage the working people to the use of force or a resort to violence. We do not say to the wage-slaves: 'You ought, you should use force.' No. Why say this when we know they must—they will be driven to use it in self-defense, in self-preservation, against those who are degrading, enslaving and destroying them.

"Already the millions of workers are unconsciously anarchists. Impelled by a cause, the effects of which they feel but do not wholly understand, they move unconsciously, irresistibly forward to the social revolution. Mental freedom, political equality, industrial liberty!

"This is the natural order of things, the logic of events. Who so foolish as to quarrel with it, obstruct it, or attempt to stay its progress? It is the march of the inevitable; the triumph of progress."

Parsons' Plea for Anarchy.

[From the N. Y. Herad, August 30, 1886.]

"So much is written and said nowadays about socialism or anarchism, that a few words on this subject from one who holds to these doctrines may be of interest to the readers of your great newspaper.

"Anarchy is the perfection of personal liberty or self-government It is the free play of nature's law, the abrogation of the statute. It is the negation of force or the domination of man by man. In the place of the law maker it puts the law discoverer and for the driver, or dictator, or ruler, it gives free play to the natural leader. It leaves man free to be happy or miserable, to be rich or poor, to be mean or good. The natural law is self-operating, self-enacting, and cannot be repealed, amended or evaded without incurring a self-imposed penalty. The statute law is license. Anarchy is liberty. The socialistic or anarchistic programme leaves the people perfectly free to unite or disunite for the purpose of production and consumption. It gives absolute freedom of contract by and between individuals or associations, and places the means of life—capital—at the disposal of the people. To those persons who may regard these aspirations as merely sentimental or utopian, I invite their attention to the operation of our capitalistic system, as outlined by Marx and others.

"The capitalist system originated in the forcible seizure of natural opportunities and rights by a few, and converting these things into special privileges, which have since become vested rights formally entrenched behind the bulwarks of statute law and government. Capital could not exist unless there also existed a class, a majority class, who are propertyless—that is, without capital. A class whose only mode of existence is by selling their labor to capitalists. Capitalists maintained, fostered and perpetuated by law. In fact, capital is law, statute law, and law is capital.

"Labor is a commodity, and wages is the price paid for it. The owner of the commodity, labor, sells it (himself) to the owner of capital in order to live. Labor is the expression of the energy or power of the laborer's life. This energy or power he must sell to another person in order to live. It is his only means of existence. He works to live. But his work is not simply a part of his life. On the contrary, it is the sacrifice of it. It is a commodity which under the guise of 'free labor' he is forced by necessity to hand over to another party. The aim of the wage laborer's activity is not the product of his labor. Far from it. The silk he weaves, the palace he builds, the ores he digs from out the mine are not for him. The only thing he produces for himself is his wage, and silk, ores and palace are merely transformed for him into a certain quantity of means of existence —viz: a cotton shirt, a few pennies and the mere tenancy of a lodging house.

"And what of the laborer who for twelve or more hours weaves, spins bores, turns, builds, shovels, breaks stones, carries loads, and so on? Does his twelve hours weaving, spinning, boring, turning, building, shoveling, etc., represent the active expression or energy of his life? On the contrary, life begins for him exactly where this activity, this labor of his ceases—viz: at his meals, in his tenement house, in his bed. His twelve hours work represents for him as a weaver, builder, spinner, etc., only so much earnings as will furnish him his meals, clothes and rent. Capital ever grows with what it feeds on—viz: the life, the very existence, the flesh and blood of the men, women and children of toil. The wage slaves are 'free' to compete with each other for the opportunity to serve capital and capitalists to compete with each other in monopolizing the laborer's products. This law of 'free' competition establishes the iron law of subsistence wages. Thus in every country the average wage of the working people is regulated by what it takes to maintain a bare subsistence and perpetuate their class.

"The increase of capital grows with every stroke of the laborers. So does his dependence. To-day there are but two classes in the world—to wit: the capitalist class and the wage class; the latter a hereditary serving class, dependent upon the former for work and bread; the former a dictating class, dominating and exploiting the latter.

"The struggle of classes, the conflict between capital and labor is for possession of the labor product of the laborers. As profits rise wages fall, and as wages rise profits fall. As the share of the capitalist (his profit) increases, the share of the laborer (his wages) diminishes, and the interest of the capitalist class is in direct antagonism to the interests of the wage class. Profit and wages for every class are in inverse proportion. Wage laborers are doomed by the capitalist system to forge for themselves the golden chains which bind them more securely in industrial slavery. Thus the industrial war wages—to wit: the captains and generals of industry contest with each other as to who can dispense with the greatest number of industrial soldiers. This brings on a rapid sub-division and simplification of the productive process, the employment of women and children, and the introduction of labor-saving machinery. Result, surplus laborers.

"The United States Commissioner of Labor Statistics tells us in last year's report that over one million able-bodied men were in compulsory idleness, and that the general average of wages for the whole wage class was estimated at fifty-five cents per day. As the struggle for existence intensifies among the laborers the struggle among capitalists for profits intensifies also. The crisis? What is it? When the dead level of cost of production is reached, which is near if not already at hand—the capitalist system—being no longer able to preserve the lives of its slaves—the wage workers—will collapse, will fall of its own weight, and fail because of its own weakness. Modern enterprise and commercialism is the old-time piracy of our fathers legalized, made respectable and safe. The homeless, the destitute, hungry and ragged, and ignorant and miserable, are the victims, the creatures, the offspring, the product of our modern system of legalized piracy. The capitalist system has its morality—a plastic, convenient morality—which it puts on or off like a coat.

"The golden rule of the carpenter's son is made subservient to the laws of trade, whose morality and religion are expounded in the churches (temples of Mammon) where the clergy propagate that good philosophy which teaches man (poor man) that he is here to suffer, denouncing as atheistic and anarchistic that other philosophy which says to man: 'Go! the earth is the gift of God to the whole human race. Discover nature's laws, apply them and be happy.'

"To quarrel with socialism is silly and vain. To do so is to quarrel with history; to denounce the logic of events; to smother the aspirations of liberty. Mental freedom, political freedom, industrial freedom—do not these follow in the line of progress? Are they not the association of the inevitable? A. R. PARSONS."

Lucy E. Parsons on Anarchy.

[We are frequently asked, 'what is anarchy and what do the anarchists want?' We are free to confess that in all we have read and heard from anarchists about how they expected to attain their ends, we never read or heard just what those ends were. In an interview with the *New York World*, Mrs. Lucy E. Parsons, the well-known lecturess in this new school of social economy, gave the most succinct account we have ever seen; and in answer to the question, 'what is anarchy,' reprint the interview.—*Editor Knights of Labor, Chicago.*]

"In reply to the reporter's inquiry as to the prospects of anarchy in this country and the world in general, the woman anarchist dropped her eyes for a moment in deep thought and said:

"'This is the evolutionary stage of anarchism. The revolutionary period will be reached when the great middle classes are practically extinct. The great monopolies and corporations and syndicates met with on every hand are now rapidly extinguishing the middle classes, which we regard as the one great bulwark between the monopoly or wealthy class and the great producing or working class. There will come a time when there will be in this world only two classes—the possessing class and the non-possessing but producing class, the middle classes have been forced into the wage.class, owing to the enormous capital now needed to remain in the field of production. These two classes will therefore find themselves arrayed against each other; a struggle, the revolutionary stage will come and the order of things in the world will be changed by the people themselves'.

"'Will the change come peaceably?'

"'I think not, for all history shows that every attempt to wrest from the wealthy and powerful that which they have, has been made by force. The vanguard of this struggling army will be found in America, because Americans will never submit to being forced to the conditions of the European masses. All the signs of the times show that the fight will begin here. Witness the strikes without number that have swept up and down this broad land like a grand cyclone. Millionaires are made here in one generation, whereas it takes centuries in Europe, and that is a fact that proves that Americans will respond to the call the quicker. The wage system in this country has now reached its full development. It no longer satisfies the needs and wants and aspirations of the people, facts which are illustrated by the poverty and starvation to be met with in the midst of plenty.'

"'When this struggle comes and culminates in the sovereignty of the people, what then? What sort of a state will follow under anarchism?'

"'Well, first let us look at the derivation of anarchy. It means without rule. We pre-suppose that the wage system has been abolished. There wage-slavery ends and anarchy begins, but you musn't confuse this state with the revolutionary period, as people are in the habit of doing. We hold that the granges, trade-unions, Knights of Labor assemblies, etc., are the embryonic groups of the ideal anarchistic society. Under anarchy the different groups, including all the industrial trades, such as the farmer, the shoemaker, the printer, the painter, the hatter, the cigar-maker, etc., will maintain themselves apart and distinct from the whole. We ask for the decentralization of power from the central government into the groups or classes. The farmers will supply so much of the land products, the shoemaker so many shoes, the hatters so many hats. and so on, all of them measuring the consumption by statistics which will be accurately compiled and published. Land will be in common, and there will be no rent, no interest and no profit. Therefore there will be no Jay Goulds, no Vanderbilts, no corporations and no moneyed power.

"'Drudgery, such as exists to-day will be reduced to a minimum. The children will be taken from the factories and sent to museums and schools. The number of hours of labor will be reduced, and people will have more time for pleasure and cultivation of the mind. We base all these results on natural reasons, believing that nature has implanted in every man, in common with all his fellows, certain instincts and certain capacities. If a man won't work nature makes him starve, so in our state, you must work or starve. But we claim that the sum of human happiness will be increased, while the drudgery and poverty and misery of the world of to-day, all due to the powerful concentration of capital, will be done away with. It will be impossible for a man to accumulate Gould's wealth, because there would be no such thing as profit, and no man could get more for his work than he produces. There would be no over-production, because only enough of any one article would be proluced to meet the demand. There will be no political parties, no capitalists, no rings, no kings, no statesmen and no rulers.'

"'How is this change to be brought about?'

"'That comes in the revolutionary stage and will happen, as I said, when the final great struggle of the masses against the moneyed powers takes place. The money and wages now found in the possession of the wage class represent the bare coarse necessaries of life, nothing over when the bills from one week to another are paid. The rest goes to the profit-taking class, and that is why we call the system wage-slavery.'

"'What criticism of the present form of government do you make?'

"'All political government must necessarily become despotic, because all government tends to become centralized in the hands of the few, who breed corruption among themselves, and in a very short time disconnect themselves from the body of the people. The American republic is a good illustration. Here we have the semblance of a republic, of a democracy, but it has fallen into the hands of a powerful few, who rule with a despotism absolutely impossible in Europe. I have but to refer you to Carter Harrison's interview not long ago in the *World*, in which he remarked that the atrocities committed on the anarchists in Chicago would not have been suffered in any monarchy.'"

CHAPTER III.

The Scientific Basis of Anarchy.

By Peter (Prince) Kropotkin.

Anarchy, the no-government system of socialism, has a double origin. It is an outgrowth of the two great movements of thought in the economical and the political fields which characterise our century, and especially its second part. In common with all socialists, the anarchists hold that the private ownership of land, capital, and machinery has had its time; that it is condemned to disappear; and that all requisites for production must, and will, become the common property of society, and be managed in common by the producers of wealth. And, in common with the most advanced representatives of political radicalism, they maintain that the ideal of the political organization of society is a condition of things where the functions of government are reduced to a minimum, and the individual recovers his full liberty of initiative and action for satisfying, by means of free groups and federations—freely constituted—all the infinitely varied needs of the human being. As regards socialism, most of the anarchists arrive at its ultimate conclusion, that is, at a complete negation of the wage system and at communism. And with reference to political organization, by giving a further development to the above mentioned part of the radical programme, they arrive at the conclusion that the ultimate aim of society is the reduction of the functions of government to *nil*

—that is, to a society without government, to an-archy. The anarchists maintain, moreover, that such being the ideal of social and political organization, they must not remit it to future centuries, but that only those changes in our social organization which are in accordance with the above double ideal, and constitute an approach to it, will have a chance of life and be beneficial for the commonwealth.

As to the method followed by the anarchist thinker, it differs to a great extent from that followed by the utopists. The anarchist thinker does not resort to metaphysical conceptions (like the "natural rights," the "duties of the State," and so on) for establishing what are, in his opinion, the best conditions for realizing the greatest happiness of humanity. He follows, on the contrary, the course traced by the modern philosophy of evolution—without entering, however, the slippery route of mere analogies so often resorted to by Herbert Spencer. He studies human society as it is now and was in the past; and, without either endowing men altogether, or separate individuals, with superior qualities which they do not possess, he merely considers society as an aggregation of organisms trying to find out the best ways of combining the wants of the individual with those of co-operation for the welfare of the species. He studies society and tries to discover its tendencies, past and present, its growing needs, intellectual and economical; and in his ideal he merely points out in which direction evolution goes. He distinguishes between the real wants and tendencies of human aggregations and the accidents (want of knowledge, migrations, wars, conquests) which prevented these tendencies from being satisfied, or temporarily paralyzed them. And he concludes that the two most prominent, although often unconscious, tendencies throughout our history were: a tendency towards integrating our labor for the production of all riches in common, so as finally to render it impossible to discriminate the part of the common production due to the separate individual; and a tendency towards the fullest freedom of the individual for the prosecution of all aims, beneficial both for himself and for society at large. The ideal of the anarchist is thus a mere summing-up of what he considers to be the next phase of evolution. It is no longer a matter of faith; it is a matter for scientific discussion.

In fact, one of the leading features of our century is the growth of socialism and the rapid spreading of socialist views among the working classes. How could it be otherwise? We have witnessed during the last seventy years an unparalleled sudden increase of our powers of production, resulting in an accumulation of wealth which has outstripped the most sanguine expectations. But, owing to our wage system, this increase of wealth—due to the combined efforts of men of science, of managers, and workmen as well—has resulted only in an unprevented accumulation of wealth in the hands of the owners of capital; while an increase of misery for the great numbers, and an insecurity of life for all, have been the lot of the workmen. The unskilled laborers, in continuous search for labor, are falling into an unheard-of destitution; and even the best paid artisans and skilled workmen, who undoubtedly are living now a more comfortable life than before, labor under the permanent menace of being thrown, in their turn, into the same conditions as the unskilled paupers, in consequence of some of the continuous and unavoidable fluctuations of industry, and caprices of capital. The chasm between the modern millionaire who squanders the produce of human labor in a gorgeous and vain luxury, and the pauper reduced to a miserable and insecure existence, is thus growing more and more, so as to break the very unity of society—the harmony of its life—and to endanger the progress of its further development. At the same time, the working classes are the less inclined patiently to endure this division of society into two classes, as they themselves become more and more conscious of the wealth-producing power of modern industry, of the part played by labor in the production of wealth, and of their own capacities of organization. In proportion as all classes of the community take a more lively part in public affairs, and knowledge spreads among the masses, their longing for equality becomes stronger, and their demands of social reorganization become louder and louder. They can be ignored no more. The worker claims his share in the riches he produces; he claims his share in the management of production; and he claims not only some additional well-being, but also his full rights in the higher enjoyments of science and art. These claims, which formerly were uttered only by the social reformer, begin now to be made by a daily growing minority of those who work in the factory or till the acre; and they so conform with our feelings of justice, that they find support in a daily growing minority amidst the priviledged classes themselves. Socialism becomes thus the idea of *the* nineteenth century; and neither coercion nor pseudo-reforms can stop its further growth.

Much hope of improvement was laid, of course, in the extension of political rights to the working classes. But these concessions, unsupported as they were by corresponding changes in the economical relations proved delusory. They did not materially improve the conditions of the great bulk of the workmen. Therefore, the watchword of socialism is: "Economical freedom, as the only secure basis for political freedom." And as long as the present wage system, with all its bad consequences, remains unaltered, the socialist watchword will continue to inspire the workmen. Socialism will continue tc grow until it has realized its programme.

Side by side with this great movement of thought in economical matters, a like movement was going on with regard to political rights, political organization, and the functions of government. Government was submitted to the same criticism as capital. While most of the radicals saw in universal suffrage and republican institutions the last word of political wisdom a further step was made by the few. The very functions of government and the State, as also their relations to the individual, were submitted to a sharper and deeper criticism. Representative government having been experimented on a wider field than before, its defects became more and more prominent. It became obvious that these defects are not merely accidental, but inherent to the system itself. Parliament and its executive proved to be unable to attend to all the numberless affairs of the community and to conciliate the varied and often opposite interests of the separate parts of a State. Election proved unable to find out the men who might represent a nation, and manage, otherwise than in a party spirit, the affairs they are compelled to legislate upon. These defects became so striking that the very principles of the representative system were criticised and their justness doubted. Again, the dangers of a centralized government became still more conspicuous when the socialists came to the front and asked for a further increase of the powers of government by entrusting it with the management of the immense field covered now by the economical relations between individuals. The question was asked, whether a government, entrusted with the management of industry and trade, would not become a permanent danger for liberty and peace, and whether it even would be able to be a good manager?

The socialists of the earlier part of this century did not fully realize the immense difficulties of the problem. Convinced as they were of the necessity of economical reforms, most of them took no notice of the need of freedom for the individual; and we have had social reformers ready to submit society to any kind of theocracy, dictatorship, or even Cæsarism, in order to obtain reform in a socialist sense. Therefore we saw, in this country and also on the continent, the division of men of advanced opinions into political radicals and socialists—the former looking with distrust on the latter, as they saw in them a danger for the political liberties which have been won by the civilized nations after a long series of struggles. And even now, when the socialists all over Europe are becoming political parties, and profess the democratic faith, there remains among most impartial men a well-founded fear of the *Volksstaat* or "popular State" being as great a danger for liberty as any form of autocracy, if its government be entrusted with the management of all the social organization, including the production and distribution of wealth.

The evolution of the last forty years prepared, however, the way for showing the necessity and possibility of a higher form of social organization which might guarantee economical freedom without reducing the individual to the role of a slave to the State. The origins of government were carefully studied, and all metaphysical conceptions as to divine or "social contract" derivation having been laid aside, it appeared that it is among us of a relatively modern origin, and that its powers grew precisely in proportion as the division of society into the privileged and unprivileged classes was growing in the course of ages. Representative government was also reduced to its real value—that of an instrument which has rendered services in the struggle against autocracy, but not an ideal of free political organization. As to the system of philosophy which saw in the State (the *Kultur-Staat*) a leader to progress, it was more and more shaken as it became evident that progress is the more effective when it is not checked by State interference. It thus became obvious that a further advance in social life does not lie in the direction of a further concentration of power and regulative functions in the hands of a governing body, but in the direction of decentralization, both territorial and functional— in a subdivision of public functions with respect both to their sphere of action and to the character of the functions; it is in the abandonment to the initiative of freely constituted groups of all those functions which are now considered as the functions of government.

This current of thought found its expression not merely in literature, but also, to a limited extent, in life. The uprise of the Paris commune, followed by that of the commune of Cartagena—a movement of which the historical bearing seems to have been quite overlooked in this country—opened a new page of history. If we analyze not only this movement in itself, but also the impression it left in the minds and the tendencies which were manifested during the communal revolution, we must recognize in it an indication showing that in the future human agglomerations which are more advanced in their social development will try to start an independent life; and that they will endeavor to convert the more backward parts of a nation by example, instead of imposing their opinions by law and force, or submitting themselves to the majority rule, which always is a mediocrity rule. At the same time the failure of representative government within the commune itself proved that self-government and self-administration must be carried on further than in a mere territorial sense; to be effective they must be carried on also with regard to the various functions of life within the free community; a merely territorial limitation of the sphere of action of government will not do—representative government being as deficient in a city as it is a nation. Life gave thus a further point in favor of the no-government theory, and a new impulse to anarchist thought.

Anarchists recognize the justice of both the just-mentioned tendencies towards economical and political freedom, and see in them two different manifestations of the very same need of equality which constitutes the very essence of all struggles mentioned by history. Therefore, in common with all socialists, the anarchist says to the political reformer: "No substantial reform in the sense of political equality, and no limitation of the powers of government, can be made as long as society is divided into two hostile camps, and the laborer remains, economically speaking, a serf, to his employer." But to the popular state socialist we say also: "You cannot modify the existing conditions of property without deeply modifying at the same time the political organization. You must limit the powers of government and renounce parliamentary rule. To each new economical phasis of life corresponds a new political phasis. Absolute monarchy—that is, court-rule—corresponded to the system of serfdom. Representative government corresponds to capital-rule. Both, however, are class rule. But in a society where the distinction between capitalist and laborer has disappeared, there is no need of such a government: it would be an anachronism, a nuisance. Free workers would require a free organization, and this cannot have another basis than free agreement and free cooperation, without sacrificing the autonomy of the individual to the all-pervading interference of the State. The no-capitalist system implies the no-government system."

Meaning thus the emancipatian of man from the oppressive powers of capitalist and government as well, the system of anarchy becomes a synthesis of the two powerful currents of thought which characterize our century.

In arriving at these conclusions anarchy proves to be in accordance with the conclusions arrived at by the philosophy of evolution. By bringing to the light the plasticity of organizaton, the philosophy of evolution has shown the admirable adaptivity of organisms to their conditions of life, and the ensuing development of such faculties as render more complete both the adaptations of the aggregates to their surroundings and those of each of the constituent parts of the aggregate to the needs of free co-operation. It familiarized us with the circumstance that throughout organic nature the capacities for life in common are growing in proportion as the integration of organisms into compound aggregates becomes more and more complete; and it enforced thus the opinion already expressed by social moralists as to the perfectibility of human nature. It has shown us that, in the long run of the struggle for existence, "the fittest" will prove to be those who combine intellectual knowledge with the knowledge necessary for the production of wealth, and not those who are now the richest because they, or their ancestors, have been momentarily the strongest. By showing that the "struggle for existence" must be conceived, not merely in its restricted sense of a struggle between individuals for the means of subsistence, but in its wider sense of adaptation of all individuals of the species to the best conditions for the survival of the species, as well as for the greatest possible sum of life and happiness for each and all, it permitted us to deduce the laws of moral science from the social needs and habits of mankind. It showed us the infinitesimal part played by positive law in moral evolution, and the immense part played by the natural growth of altruistic feelings, which develop as soon as the conditions of life favor their growth. It thus enforced the opinion of social reformers as to the necessity of modifying the conditions of life for improving man, instead of trying to improve human nature by moral teachings while life works in an opposite direction. Finally, by studying human society from the biological point of view, it came to the conclusions arrived at by anarchists from the study of history and present tendencies, as to further progress being in the line of socialization of wealth and integrated labor, combined with the fullest possible freedom of the individual.

It is not a mere coincidence that Herbert Spencer, whom we may consider as a pretty fair expounder of the philosophy of evolution, has been brought to conclude, with regard to political organization, that "that form of society towards which we are progressing" is "one in which government will be reduced to the smallest amount possible, and freedom increased to the greatest amount possible." When he opposes in these words the conclusion of his synthetic philosophy to those of Auguste Comte, he arrives at very nearly the same conclusion as Proudhon and Bakunin. More than that, the very methods of argumentation and the illustrations resorted to by Herbert Spencer (daily supply of food, postoffice, and so on) are the same which we find in the writings of the anarchists. The channels of thought were the same, although both were unaware of each other's endeavors.

Again, when Mr. Spencer so powerfully and even not without a touch of passion, argues (in his appendix to the third edition of the *Data of Ethics*) that human societies are marching towards a state when a further indentification of altruism with egoism will be made "in the sense that personal gratification will come from the gratification of others;" when he says that "we are shown, undeniably, that it is a perfectly possible thing for organisms to become so adjusted to the requirements of their lives, that energy expended for the general welfare may not only be adequate to check energy expended for the individual welfare, but may come to subordinate it so far as to leave individual welfare no greater part than is necessary for the maintenance of individual life"—provided the conditions for such relations between the individual and the community be maintained—he derives from the study of nature the very same conclusions which the forerunners of anarchy, Fourier, and Robert Owen, derived from a study of human character.

When we see further Mr. Bain so forcibly elaborating the theory of moral habits, and the French philosopher, M. Guyau, publishing his remarkable work on morality without obligation or sanction; when J. S. Mill so sharply criticises representative government, and when he discusses the problem of liberty, although failing to establish its necessary conditions; when Sir John Lubbock prosecutes his admirable studies on animal societies, and Mr. Morgan applies scientific methods of investigation to the philosophy of history—when, in short, every year, by bringing some new arguments to the theory of anarchy—we must recognize that this last although differing as to its starting points, follows the same sound methods of scientific investigation. Our confidence in its conclusions is still more increased. The difference between anarchists and the just-named philosophers may be immense as to the presumed speed of evolution, and as to the conduct which one ought to assume as soon as he has had an insight into the aims toward which society is marching. No attempt, however, has been made scientifically to determine the ratio of evolution, nor have the chief elements of the problem (the state of mind of the masses) been taken into account by the evolutionist philosophers. As to bringing one's action into accordance with his philosophical conceptions, we know that, unhappily, intellect and will are too often separated by a chasm not to be filled by mere philosophical speculations, however deep and elaborate.

There is, however, between the just-named philosophers and the anarchists a wide difference on one point of primordial importance. This difference is the stronger as it arises on a point which might be discussed figures in hand, and which constitutes the very basis of all further deduction, as it belongs to what biological sociology would describe as the physiology of nutrition.

There is, in fact, a widely spread fallacy, maintained by Mr. Spencer and many others, as to the causes of the misery which we see round about us. It was affirmed forty years ago, and it is affirmed now by Mr. Spencer and his followers, that misery in civilized society is due to our insufficient production, or rather to the circumstance that "population presses upon the means of subsistence." It would be of no use to inquire into the origin of such a misrepresentation of facts, which might be easily verified. It may have its origin in inherited misconceptions which have nothing to do with the philosophy of evolution. But to be maintained and advocated by philosophers, there must be, in the conceptions of these philosophers, some confusion as to the different aspects of the struggle for existence. Sufficient importance is not given to the difference between the struggle which goes on among organisms which do *not* co-operate for providing the means of subsistence, and those which *do* so. In this last case again there must be some confusion between those aggregates whose members find their means of subsistence in the ready produce of the vegetable and animal kingdom, and those whose members artificially grow their means of subsistence and are enabled to increase (to a yet unknown amount) the productivity of each spot of the surface of the globe. Hunters who hunt, each of them for his own sake, and hunters who unite into societies for hunting, stand quite differently with regard to the means of subsistence. But the difference is still greater between the hunters who take their means of subsistence as they are in nature, and civilized men who grow their food and produce all requisites for a comfortable life by machinery. In this last case—the stock of potential energy in nature being little short of infinite in comparison with the present population of the globe—the means of availing ourselves of the stock of energy are increased and perfected precisely in proportion to the density of population and to previously accumulated stock of technical knowledge: so that for human beings who are in possession of scientific knowledge, and co-operate for the artificial production of the means of subsistence and comfort, the law is quite the reverse to that of Malthus. The accumulation of means of subsistence and comfort is going on at a much speedier rate than the increase of population. The only conclusion which we can deduce from the laws of evolution and multiplication of effects is that the available amount of means of subsistence increases at a rate which increases itself in proportion as population becomes denser—unless it be artificially (and temporarily) checked by some defects of social organization. As to our *powers* of production (our potential production), they increase at a still speedier rate; in production as scientific knowledge grows, the means for spreading it are rendered easier, and inventive genius is stimulated by all previous inventions.

If the fallacy as to the pressure of population on the means of subsistence could be maintained a hundred years ago, it can be maintained no more, since we have witnessed the effects of science on industry, and the enormous increase of our productive power during the last hundred years. We know, in fact, that while the growth of population of England has been from $16\frac{1}{2}$ millions in 1844 to $26\frac{3}{4}$ millions in 1883, showing thus an increase of 62 per cent., the growth of national wealth (as testified by schedule A of the Income Tax Act) has increased at a twice speedier rate; it has grown from 221 to $507\frac{1}{2}$ millions—that is, by 130 per cent. And we know that the same increase of wealth has taken place in France, where population remains almost stationary, and that it has gone on at a still speedier rate in the United States, where population is increasing every year by immigration.

But the figures just mentioned, while showing the increase of production, give only a faint idea of what our production might be under a more reasonable economical organization. We know well that the owners of capital, while trying to produce more wares with fewer "hands," are also continually endeavouring to limit the production, in order to sell at higher prices. When the benefits of a concern are going down, the owner of the capital limits the production, or totally suspends it, and prefers to engage his capital in foreign loans or shares of Patagonian gold-mines. Just now there are plenty of pitmen in England who ask for nothing better than to be permitted to extract coal and supply with cheap fuel the households where children are shivering before empty chimneys. There are thousands of weavers who ask for nothing better than to weave stuffs in order to replace the Whitechapel rugs with linen. And so in all branches of industry. How can we talk about a want of means of subsistence when 246 blasting furnaces and thousands of factories lie idle in Great Britain alone; and when there are, just now, thousands and thousands of unemployed in London alone; thousands of men who would consider themselves happy if they were permitted to transform (under the guidance of experienced men) the heavy clay of Middlesex into a rich soil, and to cover with rich cornfields and orchards the acres of meadow-land which now yield only a few pounds' worth of hay? But they are prevented from doing so by the owners of the land, of the weaving factory, and of the coal-mine, because capital finds it more advantageous to supply the Khedive with harems and the Russian Government with "strategic railways" and Krupp guns. Of course the maintenance of harems *pays;* it gives ten or fifteen per cent. on the capital, while the extraction of coal does not pay—that is, it brings three or five per cent.,—and that is a sufficient reason for limiting the production and permitting would-be economists to indulge in reproaches to the working classes as to their too rapid multiplication!

Here we have instances of a direct and conscious limitation of production, due to the circumstance that the requisites for production belong to the few, and that these few have the right of disposing of them at their will, without caring about the interests of the community. But there is also the indirect and unconscious limitation of production—that which results from squandering the produce of human labor in luxury, instead of applying it to a further increase of production.

The last even cannot be estimated in figures, but a walk through the rich shops of any city and a glance at the manner in which money is squandered now, can give an approximate idea of this indirect limitation. When a rich man spends a thousand pounds for his stables, he squanders five to six thousand days of human labor, which might be used, under a better social organization, for supplying with comfortable homes those who are compelled to live now in dens. And when a lady spends a hundred pounds for her dress, we cannot but say that she squanders, at least, two years of human labor, which, again under a better organization, might have supplied a hundred women with decent dresses, and much more if applied to a further improvement of the instruments of production. Preachers thunder against luxury, because it is shameful to squander money for feeding and sheltering hounds and horses, when thousands live in the East End on sixpence a day, and other thousands have not even their miserable sixpence every day. But the economist sees more than that in our modern luxury, when millions of days of labor are spent every year for the satisfaction of the stupid vanity of the rich, he says that so many millions of workers have been diverted from the manufacture of those useful instruments which would permit us to decuple and centuple our present production of means of subsistence and of requisites for comfort.

In short, if we take into account both the real and the potential increase of our wealth, and consider both the direct and indirect limitation of production, which are unavoidable under our present economical system, we must recognize that the supposed "pressure of population on the means of subsistence" is a mere fallacy, repeated, like many other fallacies, without even taking the trouble of submitting it to a moment's criticism. The causes of the present social disease must be sought elsewhere.

Let us take a civilized country. The forests have been cleared, the swamps drained. Thousands of roads and railways intersect it in all directions; the rivers have been rendered navigable, and the seaports are of easy access. Canals connect the seas. The rocks have been pierced by deep shafts; thousands of manufactures cover the land. Science has taught men how to use the energy of nature for the satisfaction for his needs. Cities have slowly grown in the long run of ages, and treasures of science and art are accumulated in these centres of civilization. But— who has made all these marvels?

The combined efforts of scores of generations have contributed towards the achievement of these results. The forests have been cleared centuries ago; millions of men have spent years and years of labor in draining the swamps, in tracing the roads, in building the railways. Other millions have built the cities and created the civilization we boast of. Thousands of inventors, mostly unknown, mostly dying in poverty and neglect, have elaborated the machinery in which man admires his genius. Thousands of writers, philosophers and men of science, supported by many thousands of compositors, printers, and other laborers whose name is legion, have contributed in elaborating and spreading knowledge, in dissipating errors, in creating the atmosphere of scientific thought, without which the marvels of our century never would have been brought to life. The genius of a Mayer and a Grove, the patient work of a Joule, surely have done more for giving a new start to modern industry than all the capitalists of the world; but these men of genius themselves are, in their turn, the children of industry; thousands of engines had to transform heat into mechanical force, and mechanical force into sound, light and electricity—and they had to do so years long, every day, under the eyes of humanity—before some of our contemporaries proclaimed the mechanical origin of heat and the correlation of physical forces, and before we ourselves became prepared to listen to them and understand their teachings, Who knows for how many decades we should continue to be ignorant of this theory which now revolutionizes industry, were it not for the inventive powers and skill of those unknown workers who have improved the steam-engine, who brought all its parts to perfection, so as to make steam more manageable than a horse, and to render the use of the engine nearly universal? But the same is true with regard to each smallest part of our machinery. In each machine, however simple, we may read a whole history—a long history of sleepless nights, of delusions and joys, of partial inventions and partial improvements which brought it to its present state. Nay, nearly each new machine is a synthesis, a result of thousands of partial inventions made, not only in one special department of machinery, but in all departments of the wide field of mechanics.

Our cities, connected by roads and brought into easy communication with all peopled parts of the globe, are the growth of centuries ; and each house in these cities, each factory, each shop, derives its value, its very *raison d'etre* from the fact that it is situated on a spot of the globe where thousands or millions have gathered together. Every smallest part of the immense whole which we call the wealth of civilized nation derives its value precisely from being a part of this whole. What would be the value of an immense London shop or storehouse were it not situated precisely in London, which has become the gathering spot for five millions of human beings? And what the value of our coal-pits, our manufactures, our ship buildin yards, were it not for the immense traffic which goes on across the seas, for the railways which transport mountains of merchandise, for the cities which number their inhabitants by millions? Who, is, then, the individual who has the right to step forward and, laying his hands on the smallest part of this immense whole, to say, "I have produced this; it belongs to me?" And how can we discriminate, in this immense interwoven whole, the part which the isolated individual may appropriate to himself with the slightest approach to justice? Houses and streets, canals and railways, machines and works of art, all these have been created by the combined efforts of generations past and present, of men living on these islands and men living thousands of miles away.

But it has happened in the long run of ages that everything which permits men further to increase their production, or even to continue it, has has been appropriated by the few. The land which derives its value precisely from its being necessary for an ever-increasing population belongs to the few, who may prevent the community from cultivating it. The coal-pits, which represent the labor of generations, and which also derive their value from the wants of the manufactures and railroads, from the immense trade carried on and the density of population (what is the value of coal-layers in Transbaikilia?) belong again to the few, who have even the right of stopping the extraction of coal if they choose to give another use to their capital. The lace-weaving machine, which represents in its present state of perfection, the work of three generations of Lancashire weavers, belongs again to the few; and if the grandsons of the very same weaver who invented the first lace-weaving machine claim their rights of bringing one of these machines into motion, they will be told 'Hands off! this machine does not belong to you!' The railroads, which mostly would be useless heaps of iron if Great Britain had not its present dense population, its industry, trade, and traffic, belong again to the few—to a few shareholders, who may even not know where the railway is situated which brings them a yearly income largely than that of a mediæval king; and if the children of those people who died by thousands in digging the tunnels would gather and go—a ragged and starving crowd—to ask bread or work from the shareholders, they would be met with bayonets and bullets.

Who is the sophist who will dare to say that such an organization is just? But what is unjust cannot be beneficial for mankind; and it is not. In consequence of this monstrous organization, the son of a workman, when he is able to work, finds no acre to till, no machine to set in motion, unless he agrees to sell his labor for a sum inferior to its real value. His father and grandfather have contributed in draining the field, or erecting the factory, to the full extent of their capacities—and nobody can do more than that—but he comes into the world more destitute than a savage. If he resorts to agriculture, he will be permitted to cultivate a plot of land, but on the condition that he gives up one quarter of his crop to the landlord. If he resorts to industry, he will be permitted to work, but on the condition that out of the thirty shillings he has produced, ten shillings or more will be pocketed by the owner of the machine. We cry against the feudal baron who did not permit anyone to settle on his land otherwise than on payment of one quarter of the crops to the lord of the manor; but we continue to do as they did—we extend their system. The forms have changed, but the essence has remained the same. And the workman is compelled to accept the feudal conditions which we call 'free contract,' because nowhere will he find better conditions. Everything has been appropriated by somebody; he must accept the bargain or starve.

Owing to this circumstance our production takes a wrong turn. It takes no care of the needs of the community; its only aim is to increase the benefits of the capitalist. Therefore—the continuous fluctuations of industry, the crisis periodically coming nearly every ten years, and throwing out of employment several hundred thousand men who are brought to complete misery, whose children grow up in the gutter, ready to become inmates of the prison and workhouse. The workmen being unable to purchase with their wages the riches they are producing, industry must search for markets elsewhere, amidst the middle clases of other nations. It must find markets, in the East, in Africa, anywhere; it must increase by trade, the number of its serfs in Eygpt, in India, in the Congo. But everywhere it finds competitors in other nations which rapidly enter into the same line of industrial development. And wars, continuous wars, must be fought for the supremacy on the world-market—wars for the possession of the East, wars for getting possession of the seas, wars for having the right of imposing heavy duties on foreign merchandise. The thunder of guns never ceases in Europe; whole generations are slaughtered; and we spend in armaments the third of the revenues of our States—a revenue raised, the poor know with what difficulties.

Education is the privilege of the few. Not because we can find no teachers, not because the workman's son and daughter are less able to receive instruction, but because one can receive no reasonable instruction when at the age of fifteen he descends into the mine, or goes selling newspapers in the streets. Society becomes divided into two hostile camps; and no freedom is possible under such conditions. While the radical asks for a further extension of liberty, the statesman answers him that a further increase of liberty would bring about an uprising of the paupers; and those political liberties which have cost so dear are replaced by coercion, by exceptional laws, by military rule.

And finally, the injustice of our repartition of wealth exercises the most deplorable effect on our morality. Our principles of morality say: "Love your neighbor as yourself;" but let a child follow this principle and take off his coat to give it to the shivering pauper, and his mother will tell him that he must never understand the moral principles in their right sense. If he lives according to them, he will go barefoot, without alleviating the misery round about him! Morality is good on the lips, not in deeds. Our preachers say, "Who works, prays," and everybody endeavors to make others work for himself. They say, "Never lie!" and politics is a big lie. And we accustom ourselves and our children to live under this double-faced morality, which is hypocrisy, and to conciliate our double-facedness by sophistry. Hypocrisy and sophistry become the very basis of our life. But society cannot live under such a morality. It cannot last so; it must, it will, be changed.

The question is thus no more a mere question of bread. It covers the whole field of human activity. But it has at its bottom a question of social economy, and we conclude: The means of production and of satisfaction of all needs of society, having been created by the common efforts of all, must be at the disposal of all. The private appropriation of requisites for production is neither just nor beneficial. All must be placed on the same footing as producers and consumers of wealth. That would be the only way for society to step out of the bad conditions which have been created by centuries of wars and oppression. That would be the only guarantee for further progress in a direction of equality and freedom, which always were the real though outspoken goal of humanity.

CHAPTER IV.

The Coming Anarchy.

The views taken in the preceding article as to the combination of efforts being the chief source of our wealth explain why most anarchists see in communism the only equitable solution as to the adequate remuneration of individual efforts. There was a time when a family engaged in agriculture, and supported by a few domestic trades, could consider the corn they raised and the plain woollen cloth they wove as productions of their own and nobody else's labor. Even then such a view was not quite correct; there were forests cleared and roads built by common efforts; and even then the family had continually to apply for communal help, as it is still the case in so many village communities. But now, under the extremely interwoven state of industry, of which each branch supports all others, such an individualistic view can be held no more. If the iron trade and the cotton industry of this country have reached so high a degree of development, they have done so owing to the parallel growth of thousands of other industries, great and small; to the extension of the railway system; to an increase of knowledge among both the skilled engineers and the mass of the workmen; to a certain training in organization slowly developed among British producers; and, above all, to the world-trade which has itself grown up, thanks to works executed thousands of miles away. The Italians who died from cholera in digging the Suez Canal, or from "tunnel-disease" in the St. Gothard Tunnel, have contributed as much towards the enrichment of this country as the British girl who is prematurely growing old in serving a machine at Manchester; and this girl as much as the engineer who made a labor-saving improvement in our machinery. How can we pretend to estimate the exact part of each of them in the riches accumulated around us?

We may admire the inventive genius or the organizing capacities of an iron lord; but we must recognize that all his genius and energy would not realize one-tenth of what they realize here if they were spent in dealing with Mongolian shepherds or Siberian peasants instead of British workmen, British engineers, and trustworthy managers. An English millionaire who succeeded in giving a powerful impulse to a branch of home industry was asked the other day what were, in his opinion, the real causes of his success? His answer was:—"I always sought out the right man for a given branch of the concern, and I left him full independence—maintaining, of course, for myself the general supervision." "Did you never fail to find such men?" was the next question. "Never." "But in the new branches which you introduced you wanted a number of new inventions." "No doubt; we spent thousands in buying patents." This little colloquy sums up, in my opinion, the real case of those industrial undertakings which are quoted by the advocates of "an adequate remuneration of individual efforts" in the shape of millions bestowed on the managers of prosperous industries. It shows in how far the efforts are really "individual." Leaving aside the thousand conditions which sometimes permit a man to show, and sometimes prevent him from showing, his capacities to their full extent, it might be asked in how far the same capacities could bring out the same results, if the very same employer could find no trustworthy managers and no skilled workmen, and if hundreds of inventions were not stimulated by the mechanical turn of mind of so many inhabitants of this country. British industry is the work of the British nation—nay, of Europe and India taken together—not of separate individuals.

While holding this synthetic view on production, the anarchist cannot consider, like the collectivists, that a remuneration which would be proportionate to the hours of labor spent by each person in the production of riches may be an ideal, or even an approach to an ideal. society. Without entering here into a discussion as to how far the exchange value of each merchandise is really measured now by the amount of labor necessary for its production—a separate study must be devoted to the subject—we must say that the collectivist ideal seems to us merely unrealizable in a society which would be brought to consider the necessaries for production as a common property. Such a society would be compelled to abandon the wage-system altogether. It appears impossible that the mitigated individualism of the collectivist school could co-exist with the partial communism implied by holding land and machinery in common—unless imposed by a powerful government, much more powerful than all those of our own times. The present wage-system has grown up from the appropriation of the necessaries for production by the few; it was a necessary condition for the growth of the present capitalist production; and it cannot outlive it, even if an attempt be made to pay the worker the full value of his produce, and money be substituted by hours of labor checks. Common possession of the necessaries for production implies the common enjoyment of the fruits of the common production; and we consider that an equitable organization of society can only arise when every wage-system is abandoned, and when everybody, contributing for the common well-being to the full extent of his capacities, shall enjoy also from the common stock of society to the fullest possible extent of his needs.

We maintain, moreover, not only that communism is a desirable state of society, but that the growing tendency of modern society is precisely towards communism—free communism—notwithstanding the seemingly contradictory growth of individualism. In the growth of individualism (especially during the last three centuries) we merely see the endeavors of the individual towards emancipating himself from the steadily growing powers of capital and state. But side by side with this growth we see also, throughout history up to our own times, the latent struggle of the producers of wealth for maintaining the partial communism of old, as well as for reintroducing communist principles in a new shape, as soon as favorable conditions permit it. As soon as the communes of the tenth, eleventh, and twelfth centuries were enabled to start their own independent life, they gave a wide extension to work in common, to trade in common, and to a partial consumption in common. All this has disappeared; but the rural commune fights a hard struggle to maintain its old features, and it succeeds in maintaining them in many places of Eastern Europe, Switzerland, and even France and Germany; while new organizations, based on the same principles, never fail to grow up as soon as it is possible. Notwithstanding the egotistic turn given to the public mind by the merchant-production of our century, the communist tendency is continually reasserting itself and trying to make its way into public life. The penny bridge disappears before the public bridge; so also the road which formerly had to be paid for its use. The same spirit pervades thousands of other institutions. Museums, free libraries, and free public schools; parks and pleasure grounds; paved and lighted streets, free for every body's use; water supplied to private dwellings, with a growing tendency towards disregarding the exact amount of it used by the individual; tramways and railways which have already begun to introduce the season ticket or the uniform tax, and will surely go much further on this line when they are no longer private property; all these are tokens showing in which direction further progress is to be expected.

It is in putting the wants of the individual *above* the valuation of the services he has rendered, or might render, to society; it is in considering society as a whole, so intimately connected that a service rendered to any individual is a service rendered to the whole society. The librarian of the British Museum does not ask the reader what have been his previous services to society, he simply gives him the books he requires; and for a uniform fee, a scientific society leaves its gardens and museums at the free disposal of each member. The crew of a life-boat do not ask whether the men of a distressed ship are entitled to be rescued at a risk of life; and the Prisoners' Aid Society do not inquire what the released prisoner is worth. Here are men in need of a service; they are *fellow* men, and no further rights are required. And if this very city, so egotistic to-day, be visited by a public calamity—let it be besieged, for example, like Paris in 1871, and experience during the siege a want of food—this very same city would be unanimous in proclaiming that the first needs to be satisfied are those of the children and old, no matter what services they may render or have rendered to society. And it would take care of the active defenders of the city, whatever the degrees of gallantry displayed by each of them. But, this tendency already existing, nobody will deny, I suppose, that, in proportion as humanity is relieved from its hard struggle for life, the same tendency will grow stronger. If our productive powers be fully applied for increasing the stock of the staple necessities for life; if a modification of the present conditions of property increased the number of producers by all those who are not producers of wealth now; and if manual labor reconquered its place of honor in society—all this decuplating our production and rendering labor easier and more attractive—the communist tendencies already existing would immediately enlarge their sphere of application.

Taking all that into account, and still more the practical aspects of the question as to how private property *might* become common property, most of the anarchists maintain that the very next step to be made by society, as soon as the present *regime* of property undergoes a modification, will be in a communist sense. We are communists. But our communism is not that of either the Phalanstere or the authoritarian school: it is anarchist communism, communism without government, free communism. It is a synthesis of the two chief aims prosecuted by humanity since the dawn of its history—economical freedom and political freedom.

I have already said that anarchy means no-government. We know well that the word "anarchy" is also used in the current language as synonymous with disorder. But that meaning of "anarchy," being a derived one, implies at least two suppositions. It implies, first, that wherever there is no government there is disorder; and it implies, moreover, that order, due to a strong government and a strong police, is always beneficial. Both implications, however, are anything but proved. There is plenty of order—we should say, of harmony—in many branches of human activity where the government, happily, does not interfere. As to the beneficial effects of order, the kind of order that reigned at Naples under the Bourbons surely was not preferable to some disorder started by Garibaldi; while the protestants of this country will probably say that the good deal of disorder made by Luther was preferable, at any rate, to the order which reigned under the Pope. As to the proverbial "order" which was once "restored at Warsaw," there are, I suppose, no two opinions about it. While all agree that harmony is always desirable, there is no such unanimity about order, and still less about the "order" which is supposed to reign in our modern societies; so that we have no objection whatever to the use of the word "anarchy" as a negation of what has been often described as order.

By taking for our watchword anarchy, in its sense of no-government, we intend to express a pronounced tendency of human society. In history we see that precisely those epochs when small parts of humanity broke down the power of their rulers and reassumed their freedom were epochs of the greatest progress, economical and intellectual. Be it the growth of the free cities, whose unrivalled monuments—free work of free associations of workers—still testify to the revival to the mind and of the well-being of the citizen; be it the great movement which gave birth to the Reformation—those epochs witnessed the greatest progress when the individual recovered some part of his freedom. And if we carefully watch the present development of civilized nations, we cannot fail to discover in it a marked and ever-growing movement towards limiting more and more the sphere of action of government, so as to leave more and more liberty to the initiative of the individual. After having tried all kinds of government, and endeavored to solve the insoluble problem of having a government "which might compel the individual to obedience, without escaping itself from obedience to collectivity," humanity is trying now to free itself from the bonds of any government whatever, and to respond to its needs of organization by the free understanding between individuals prosecuting the same common aims. Home rule even for the smallest territorial unit or a group, becomes a growing need; free agreement is becoming a substitute for law; and free co-operation a substitute for governmental guardianship. One after the other those functions which were considered as the functions of government during the last two centuries are disputed; society moves better the less it is governed. And the more we study the advance made in this direction, as well as the inadequacy of governments to fullfil the expectations laid in them, the more we are bound to conclude that humanity, by steadily limiting the functions of government, is marching towards reducing them finally to *nil*; and we already see a state of society where the liberty of the individual will be limited by no laws, no bonds—by nothing else but his own social habits and the necessity, which everyone feels, of finding co-operation, support, and sympathy among his neighbors.

Of course, the no-government ethics will meet with at least as many objections as the no-capital economics. Our minds have been so nurtured in prejudices as to the providential functions of government that anarchist ideas *must* be received with distrust. Our whole education, since childhood up to the grave, nurtures the belief in the necessity of a government and its beneficial effects. Systems of philosophy have been elaborated to support this view; history has been written from this standpoint; theories of law have been circulated and taught for the same purpose. All politics are based on the same principle, each politician saying to people he wants to support him: "Give me the governmental power; I will, I can, relieve you from the hardships of your present life." All our education is permeated with the same teachings. We may open any book of sociology, history, law, or ethics; everywhere we find government, its organization, its deeds, playing so prominent a part that we grow accustomed to suppose that the State and the political men are everything; that there is nothing behind the big statesmen. The same teachings are daily repeated in the press. Whole columns are filled up with minutest records of parliamentary debates, of movements of political persons; and, while reading these columns, we too often forget that there is an immense body of men—

mankind, in fact—growing and dying, living in happiness or sorrow, laboring and consuming, thinking and creating, besides those few men whose importance has been swollen up as to overshadow humanity.

And yet, if we revert from the printed matter to our real life, and cast a broad glance on society as it is, we are struck with the infinitesimal part played by government in our life. Millions of human beings live and die without having had anything to do with government. Every day millions of transactions are made without the slightest interference of government; and those who enter into agreements have not the slightest intention of breaking bargains. Nay, those agreements which are not protected by government (those of the exchange, or card debts) are perhaps better kept than any others. The simple habit of keeping his word, the desire of not losing confidence, are quite sufficient in the immense overwhelming majority of cases to enforce the keeping of agreements. Of course, it may be said that there is still the government which might enforce them if necessary. But not to speak of the numberless cases which even could not be brought before a court, everybody who has the slightest acquaintance with trade will undoubtedly confirm the assertion that, if there were not so strong a feeling of honor to keep agreements, trade itself would become utterly impossible. Even those merchants and manufacturers who feel not the slightest remorse when poisoning their customers with all kind of abominable drugs, duly labelled, even they also keep their commercial agreements. But, if such a relative morality as commercial honesty exists now, under the present conditions, when enrichment is the chief motive, the same feeling will further develop very fast as soon as robbing somebody of the fruits of his labor is no longer the economical basis of our life.

Another striking feature of our century tells in favor of the same no-government tendency. It is the steady enlargement of the field covered by private initiative, and the recent growth of large organizations resulting merely and simply from free agreement. The railway net of Europe—a confederation of so many scores of separate societies—and the direct transport of passengers and merchandise over so many lines which were built independently and federated together, without even so much as a central board of European railways, are a most striking instance of what is already done by mere agreement. If fifty years ago somebody had predicted that railways built by so many separate companies finally would constitute so perfect a net as they do to-day, he surely would have been treated as a fool. It would have been urged that so many companies, prosecuting their own interests, would never agree without an international board of railways, supported by an international convention of the European States, and endowed with governmental powers. But no such board was resorted to, and the agreement came nevertheless. The Dutch *Beurden* extending now their organizations over the rivers of Germany, and even to the shipping trade of the Baltic; the numberless amalgamated manufacturers' associations, and the *syndicats* of France, are so many instances in point. If it be argued that many of these organizations are organizations for exploitation, it would prove nothing, because, if men prosecuting their own egotistic, often very narrow, interests can agree together, better inspired men, compelled to be more closely connected with other groups, will necessarily agree still easier and still better.

But there also is no lack of free organizations for nobler pursuits. One of the noblest achievements of our century is undoubtedly the Lifeboat Association. Since its first humble start, which we all remember, it has saved no less than 32,000 human lives. It makes appeal to the noblest instincts of man; its activity is entirely dependent upon devotion to the common cause; while its internal organization is entirely based upon the independence of the local committees. The Hospitals Association and hundreds of like organizations, operating upon a large scale and covering each a wide field, may also be mentioned under this head. But, while we know everything about governments and their deeds what do we know about the results achieved by free co-operation? Thousands of volumes have been written to record the acts of governments; the most trifling amelioration due to law has been recorded; its good effects have been exaggerated, its bad effects passed by in silence. But where is the book recording what has been achieved by free co-operation of well-inspired men?—At the same time, hundreds of societies are constituted every day for the satisfaction of some of the infinitely varied needs of civilized men. We have societies for all possible kinds of studies—some of them embracing the whole field of natural science, others limited to a small special branch; societies for gymnastics, for shorthand-writing, for the study of a separate author, for games, and all kinds of sport, for forwarding the science of maintaining life, and for favoring the knowledge of how to destroy it; philosophical and industrial, artistic and anti-artistic; for serious work and for mere amusement—in short, there is not a single direction in which men would exercise their faculties without combining together for the prosecution of some common aim. Every day new societies are formed, while every year the old ones aggregate together into larger units, federate across the national frontiers, and co-operate in some common work.

The most striking feature of these numberless free growths is that they continually encroach upon what was formerly the domain of the State or the Municipality. A householder in a Swiss village on the banks of Lake Leman belongs now to, at least, a dozen different societies which supply him with what is considered elsewhere as a function of the municipal government. Free federation of independent communes for temporary or permanent purposes lies at the very bottom of Swiss life, and to these federations many a part of Switzerland is indebted for its roads and fountains, its rich vineyards, well-kept forests, and meadows which the foreigner admires. And beside these small societies, substituting themselves for the State within some limited sphere, do we not see other societies doing the same on a much wider scale? Each German *Burger* is proud of the German army, but few of them know how much it borrows of its force from the numberless private societies for military studies, exercise, and games; and how few are those who understand that their army would become an incoherent mass of men the day that each soldier was no longer inspired by the feelings which inspire him now? In this country, even the task of defending the territory—that is, the chief, the great function of the State—has been undertaken by an army of volunteers, and this army surely might stand against any army of slaves obeying a military despot. More than that: a private society for the defense of the coasts of England has been seriously spoken of. Let it only come into life, and surely it will be a more effective weapon for self-defense than the iron clads of the navy. One of the most remarkable societies, however, which has recently arisen is undoubtedly the Red Cross Society. To slaughter men on the battle fields, that remains the duty of the State; but these very States recognize themselves unable to take care of their own wounded, they abandon the task, to a great extent, to private initiative. What a deluge of mockeries would not have been cast over the poor "Utopist" who should have dared to say twenty-five years ago that the care of the wounded might be left to private societies! "Nobody would go in the dangerous places! all hospitals would gather where there was no need of them! national rivalries would result in the poor soldiers dying without any help, and so on,"—such would have been the outcry. The war of 1871 has shown how perspicacious those prophets are who never believe in human intelligence, devotion, and good sense.

These facts—so numerous and so customary that we pass by without even noticing them—are, in our opinion, one of the most prominent features of the second half of our century. The just mentioned organisms grew up so naturally; they so rapidly extended and so easily aggregated together; they are such unavoidable outgrowths of the multiplication of needs of the civilized man, and they so well replace State-interference, that we must recognize in them a growing factor of our life. Modern progress is really towards the free aggregation of free individuals so as to supplant government in all those functions which formerly were entrusted to it, and which it mostly performed so badly.

As to parliamentary rule, and representative government altogether they are rapidly falling into decay. The few philosophers who have already shown their defects have only timidly summed up the growing public discontent. It is becoming evident that it is merely stupid to elect a few men, and to entrust them with the task of making laws on all possible subjects, of which subjects most of them are utterly ignorant. It is becoming understood that majority rule is as effective as any other kind of rule; and humanity searches, and finds, new channels for resolving the pending questions. The Postal Union did not elect an international postal parliament in order to make laws for all postal organizations adherent to the Union. The railways of Europe did not elect an international railway parliament in order to regulate the march of the trains and the repartition of the income of international traffic; and the meteorological and geological societies of Europe did not elect either meteorological or geological parliaments for scheming polar stations, or for establishing a uniform subdivision of geological formations and a uniform coloration of geological maps. They proceeded by means of agreements. To agree together they resorted to congresses; but, while sending delegates to their congresses, they did not elect M. P.'s *bons a tout faire;* they did not say to them, "Vote about everything you like—we shall obey." They put questions and discussed them first themselves; then they sent delegates acquainted with special questions to be discussed at the congress, and they sent *delegates*—not rulers. Their delegates returned from the congress with no *laws* in their pockets, but with *proposals of agreements*. Such is the way assumed now (the very old way, too) for dealing with questions of public interest—not the way of law-making by means of a representative government. Representative government has accomplished its historical mission; it has given a mortal blow to court-rule; and by its debates it has awakened public interest in public questions. But to see in it the government of the future socialist society, is to commit a gross error. Each economical phase of life implies its own political phase; and it is impossible to touch the very bases of the present economical life—private property—without a corresponding change in the very bases of the political organization. Life already shows in which direction the change will be made. Not in increasing the powers of the State, but in resorting to free organization and free federation in all those branches which are now considered as attributions of the State.

The objections to the above may be easily foreseen. It will be said of course: "But what is to be done with those who do not keep their agreements? What with those who are not inclined to work? What with those who would prefer breaking the written laws of society, or, in the anarchist hypothesis, its unwritten customs? Anarchy may be good for a higher humanity, not for the men of our own times."

First of all there are two kinds of agreements; there is the free one which is entered upon by free consent, as a free choice between different courses equally open before each of the agreeing parties; and there is the enforced agreement, imposed by one party upon the other, and accepted by the latter from sheer necessity; in fact, it is no agreement at all; it is a mere submission to necessity. Unhappily, the great bulk of what are now described as agreements belong to the latter category. When a workman sells his labor to an employer, and knows perfectly well that some part of the value of his produce will be unjustly taken by the employer; when he sells it without even the slightest guarantee of being employed so much as six consecutive months, and he is compelled to do so because he and his family would otherwise starve next week—it is a sad mockery to call that a free contract. Modern economists may call it free, but the father of political economy—Adam Smith—was never guilty of such a misrepresentation. As long as three-quarters of humanity are compelled to enter into agreements of that description. force is, of course, necessary, both to enforce the supposed agreements and to maintain such a state of things. Force—and a good deal of force—is necessary for preventing the laborers from taking possession of what they consider unjustly appropriated by the few; and force is necessary for always bringing new "uncivilized nations under the same conditions. The Spencerian no-force party perfectly well understand that; and while they advocate no force for changing the existing conditions, they advocate still more force than is now used for maintaining them. As to anarchy, it is obviously as incompatible with plutocracy as with any kind of *cracy*.

But we do not see the necessity of force for enforcing agreements freely entered upon. We never heard of a penalty imposed on a man who belonged to the crew of a lifeboat and at a given moment preferred to abandon the association. All that his comrades would do with him, if he were guilty of a gross neglect, would be probably to refuse further to do anything with him. Nor did we hear of fines imposed on a contributor of Mr. Murray's Dictionary for a delay in his work, or of *gendarmes* driving the volunteers of Garibaldi to the battle-fields. Free agreements need not be enforced.

As to the so-often repeated objection that nobody would labor if he were not compelled to do so by sheer necessity, we heard enough of it before the emancipation of slaves in America, as well as before the emancipation of serfs in Russia; and we have had the opportunity of appreciating it at its just value. So we shall not try to convince those who can be convinced only by accomplished facts. As to those who reason, they ought to know that, if it really was so with some parts of humanity at its lowest stages—and yet, what do we know about it?—or if it is so with some small communities, or separate individuals, brought to sheer despair by unsuccesses in their struggle against unfavorable conditions, it is not so with the bulk of the civilized nations. With us, work is a habit, and idleness an artificial growth. Of course, when to be a manual worker means to be compelled to work all the life long for ten hours a day, and often more, at producing some part of something —a pin's head, for instance; when it means to be paid wages on which a family can live only on the condition of the strictest limitation of all its needs; when it means to be always under the menace of being thrown to-morrow out of employment—and we know how frequent are the industrial crises, and what a misery they imply; when it means, in a very great number of cases, premature death in a paupers' hospital, if not in the workhouse; when to be a manual worker signifies to wear all life long a stamp of inferiority in the eyes of those very people who live on the work of their "hands;" when it always means the renouncement of all those higher enjoyments that science and art give to man— oh, then there is no wonder that everybody—the manual worker as well —has but one dream: that of rising to a condition where others would work for him. When I see writers who boast that they are the workers, and write that the manual workers are an inferior race of lazy and improvident fellows, I am inclined to ask them, Who, then, has made all you see round about you: the houses you live in, the chairs, the carpets, the streets you enjoy, the clothes you wear? Who built the universities where you were taught, and who provided you with food during your school years? And what would become of your readiness to "work," if you were compelled to work in the above conditions all your life on a pin's head? No doubt, anyhow *you* would be reported as a lazy fellow! And I affirm that no intelligent man can be closely acquainted with the life of the European working classes without wondering, on the contrary, at their readiness to work, even under such abominable conditions.

Overwork is reluctant to human nature—not work. Overwork for supplying the few with luxury—not work for the well-being of all. Work, labor, is a physiological necessity, a necessity of spending accumulated bodily energy, a necessity which is health and life itself. If so many branches of useful work are so reluctantly done now, it is merely because they mean overwork, or they are improperly organized. But we know—old Franklin knew it—that four hours of useful work every day would be more than sufficient for supplying everybody with the comfort of a moderately well-to-do middle-class house, if we all gave ourselves to productive work, and if we did not waste our productive powers as we do waste them now. As to the childish question, repeated for fifty years (who would do disagreeable work?), frankly I regret that none of our *savants* has ever been brought to do it, be it for only one day in his life. If there is still work which is really disagreeable in itself, it is only because our scientific men have never cared to consider the means for rendering it less so; they always knew that there were plenty of starving men who would do it for a few pence a day.

As to the third—the chief—objection, which maintains the necessity of a government for punishing those who break the law of society, there is so much to say about it that it hardly can be touched incidentally. The more we study the question, the more we are brought to the conclusion that society itself is responsible for the anti-social deeds perpetrated in its midst; and that no punishment, no prison, and no hangman can diminish the numbers of like deeds; nothing short of a re-organization of society itself. Three-quarters of all the acts which are brought every year before our courts have their origin, either directly or indirectly, in the present disorganized state of society with regard to the production and distribution of wealth—not in the perversity of human nature. As to the relatively few anti-social deeds which result from anti-social inclinations of separate individuals, it is not by prisons, nor even by resorting to the hangman, that we can diminish their numbers. By our prisons, we merely multiply them and render them worse. By our detectives, our "price of blood," our executions, and our jails, we spread in society such a terrible flow of basest passions and habits, that he who would realize the effects of these institutions to their full extent, would be frightened by what society is doing under the pretext of maintaining morality. We *must* search for other remedies, and the remedies have been indicated long since.

Of course now, when a mother in search of food and shelter for her children must pass by shops filled up with the most refined delicacies of refined gluttony; when gorgeous and insolent luxury is displayed side by side with the most execrable misery; when the dog and the horse of a rich man are far better cared for than millions of children whose mothers earn a pitiful salary in the pit or the manufactory; when each "modest" evening dress of a lady represents eight months, or one year, of human labor; when enrichment on somebody's account is the avowed aim of the "upper classes," and no distinct boundary can be traced between honest and dishonest means of making money—then force is the only means for maintaining such a state of things; then an army of policemen, judges, and hangmen becomes a necessary institution.

But if all our children—all children are *our* children—received a sound instruction and education—and we have the means of doing so; if every family lived in a decent home—and they *could* under the present high pitch of our production; if every boy and girl were taught a handicraft at the same time as he or she receives a scientific instruction, and *not* to be a manual producer of wealth were considered as a token of inferiority; if men lived in closer contact with one another, and had continually to come into contact on those public affairs which now are invested in the few; and if, in consequence of a closer contact, we were brought to take as lively an interest in our neighbors' difficulties and pains as we formerly took in those of our kinsfolk—then we should not resort to policemen and judges, to prisons and executions. The antisocial deeds would be prevented in bud, not punished; the few contests which would arise would be easily settled by arbitrators; and no more force would be necessary to impose their decisions than is required now for enforcing the decisions of the family tribunals of China, or of the Valencia water-courts.

And here we are brought to consider a great question: What would become of morality in a society which would recognize no laws and proclaim the full freedom of the individual? Our answer is plain. Public morality is independent from, and anterior to, law and religion. Until now, the teachings of morality have been associated with religious teachings. But the influence which religious teachings formerly exercised on the mind has faded of late, and the sanction which morality derived from religion has no more the power it formerly had. Millions and millions grow in our cities who have lost the old faith. Is it a reason for throwing morality overboard, and for treating it with the same sarcasm as primitive cosmogony?

Obviously not. No society is possible without certain principles of morality generally recognized. If everybody grew accustomed to deceive his fellow-men; if we never could rely on each other's promise and words; if everybody treated his like as an enemy, against whom every means of warfare is justifiable—no society could exist. And we see, in fact, that notwithstanding the decay of religious beliefs, the principles of morality remain unshaken. We even see irreligious people trying to raise the current standard of morality. The fact is that moral principles are independent of religious beliefs; they are anterior to them. The primitive Tchuktchis have no religion; they have only superstitions and fear of the hostile forces of nature; and nevertheless we find with them the very same principles of morality which are taught by Christians and Buddhists, Mussulmans and Hebrews. Nay, some of their practices imply a much higher standard of tribal morality than that which appears in our civilized society. In fact, each new religion takes its moral principles from the only real stock of morality—the moral habits which grow with men as soon as they unite to live together in tribes, cities, or nations. No animal society is possible without resulting in a growth of certain moral habits of mutual support and even self-sacrifice for the common well-being. These habits are a necessary condition for the welfare of the species in its struggle for life—co-operation of individuals being a much more important factor in the struggle for the preservation of the species than the so-much-spoken-of physical struggle between individuals for the means of existence. The "fittest" in the organic world are those who grow accustomed to life in society; and life in society necessarily implies moral habits. As to mankind, it has, during its long existence, developed in its midst a nucleus of social habits, of moral habits, which cannot disappear as long as human societies exist. And, therefore, notwithstanding the influences to the contrary which are now at work in consequence of our present economical relations, the nucleus of our moral habits continues to exist. Law and religion only formulate them and endeavor to enforce them by their sanction.

Whatever the variety of theories of morality, all can be brought under three chief categories: the morality of religion; the utilitarian morality; and the theory of moral habits resulting from the very needs of life in society. Each religious morality sanctifies its prescriptions by making them originate from revelation; and it tries to impress its teachings on the mind by a promise of reward, or punishment, either in this or in a future life. The utilitarian morality maintains the idea of reward, but it finds it in man himself. It invites men to analyze their pleasures, to classify them, and to give preference to those which are most intense and most durable. We must recognize, however, that, although having exercised some influence, this system has been judged too artificial by the great mass of human beings. And finally—whatever its varieties—there is the third system of morality which sees in moral actions—in those actions which are most powerful in rendering men best fitted to life in society—a mere necessity of enjoying the joys of his brethren, of suffering when some of his brethren are suffering; a habit and a second nature, slowly elaborated and perfected by life in society. That is the morality of mankind; and that is also the morality of anarchy.

I could not better illustrate the difference between the three systems of morality than by repeating the following example. Suppose a child is drowning in a river, and three men stand on the bank of the river: the religious moralist, the utilitarian, and the plain man of the people. The religious man is supposed, first, to say to himself that to save the child would bring him happiness in this or another life, and then save the child; but if he does so, he is merely a good reckoner, no more. Then comes the utilitarian, who is supposed to reason thus: "The enjoyments of life may be of the higher and of the lower description. To save the child would assure me the higher enjoyment. Therefore, let me jump in the river." But, admitting that there ever was a man who reasoned in this way, again, he would be a mere reckoner, and society would do better not to rely very much upon him; who knows what a sophism might pass one day through his head! And here is the third man. He does not much calculate. But he has grown in the habit of always feeling the joys of those who surround him, and to feel happy when others are happy; of suffering, deeply suffering when others suffer. To act accordingly is his second nature. He hears the cry of the mother, he sees the child struggling for life, and he jumps in the river like a good dog, and saves the child, thanks to the energy of his feelings. And when the mother thanks him, he answers: "Why! I could not do otherwise than I did." That is the real morality. That is the morality of the masses of the people; the morality grown to a habit, which will exist, whatever the ethical theories made by philosophers, *and will steadily improve in proportion as the conditions of our social life are improved. Such a morality needs no laws for its maintenance.* It is a natural growth favored by the general sympathy which every advance towards a wider and higher morality finds in all fellow-men.

Such are, in a very brief summary, the leading principles of anarchy. Each of them hurts many a prejudice, and yet each of them results from an analysis of the very tendencies displayed by human society. Each of them is rich in consequences and implies a thorough revision of many a current opinion. And it is not a mere insight into a remote future. Already now, whatever, the sphere of action of the individual, he can act, either in accordance with anarchist principles or on an opposite line. And all that may be done in that direction will be done in the direction whereto further development goes. All that may be done in the opposite way will be an attempt to force humanity to go where it will *not* go.

PETER KROPOTKIN.

CHAPTER V.

AN ANARCHIST ON ANARCHY.

[From the Contemporary Review.]

To most Englishmen the word anarchy is so evil-sounding that ordinary readers of the Contemporary Review will probably turn from these pages with aversion, wondering how anybody could have the audacity to write them. With the crowd of commonplace chatterers we are already past praying for; no reproach is too bitter for us, no epithet too insulting. Public speakers on social and political subjects find that abuse of anarchists is an unfailing passport to popular favor. Every conceivable crime is laid to our charge, and opinion, too indolent to learn the truth, is easily persuaded that anarchy is but another name for wickedness and chaos. Overwhelmed with opprobrium and held up to hatred, we are treated on the principle that the surest way of hanging a dog is to give it a bad name.

There is nothing surprising in all this. The chorus of imprecations with which we are assailed is quite in the nature of things, for we speak in a tongue unhallowed by usage, and belong to none of the parties that dispute the possession of power. Like all innovators, whether they be violent or pacific, we bring not peace but a sword, and are in nowise astonished to be received as enemies.

Yet it is not with light hearts that we incur so much ill-will, nor are we satisfied with merely knowing that it is undeserved. To risk the loss of so precious an advantage as popular sympathy without first patiently searching out the truth and carefully considering our duty were an act of reckless folly. To a degree never dreamt of by men who are borne unresistingly on the great current of public opinion, are we bound to render to our conscience a reason for the faith that is in us, to strengthen our convictions by study of nature and mankind, and, above all, to compare them with that ideal justice which has been slowly elaborated by the untold generations of our race. This ideal is known to all, and is almost too trite to need repeating. It exists in the moral teaching of every people, civilized or savage; every religion has tried to adapt it to its dogmas and precepts, for it is the ideal of equality of rights and reciprocity of services. "We are all brethren," is a saying repeated from one end of the world to the other, and the principle of universal brotherhood expressed in this saying implies a complete solidarity of interests and efforts.

Accepted in its integrity by simple souls, does not this principle seem to imply as a necessary consequence the social state formulated by modern socialists: "To each according to his needs, from each according to his powers?" Well, we are simple souls, and we hold firmly to this ideal of human morality. Of a surety there is much dross mixed with the pure metal, and the personal and collective egoisms of families, cities, castes, peoples, and parties have wrought on this groundwork some startling variations. But we have not to do here with the ethics of selfish interests, it is enough to identify the central point of convergence towards which all partial ideas more or less tend. This focus of gravitation is justice. If humanity be not a vain dream, if all our impressions, all our thoughts, are not pure hallucinations, one capital fact dominates the history of man—that every kindred and people yearns after justice. The very life of humanity is but one long cry for that fraternal equity which still remains unattained. Listen to the words, uttered nearly three thousand years ago, of old Hesiod, answering beforehand all those who contend that the struggle for existence dooms us to eternal strife: "Let fishes, the wild beasts and birds, devour one another—but our law is justice."

Yet how vast is the distance that still separates us from the justice invoked by the poet in the very dawn of history! How great is the progress we have still to make before we may rightfully cease comparing ourselves with wild creatures fighting for a morsel of carrion! It is in vain that we pretend to be civilized, if civilization be that which Mr. Alfred R. Wallace has described as "the harmony of individual liberty with the collective will." It is really too easy to criticise contemporary society, its morals, its conventions, and its laws, and to show how much its practices fall short of the ideal justice formulated by thinkers and desired by peoples. To repeat stale censures is to risk being called mere declaimers, scatterers of voices in the market-place. And yet so long as the truth is not heard, is it not our duty to go on speaking it in season and out of season? A sincere man owes it to himself to expose the frightful barbarity which still prevails in the hidden depths of a society so outwardly well-ordered. Take, for instance, our great cities, the leaders of civilization, especially the most populous, and, in many respects, the first of all—that immense London, which gathers to herself the riches of the world, whose every warehouse is worth a king's ransom; where are to be found enough, and more than enough, of food and clothing for the needs of the teeming millions that throng her streets in greater numbers than the ants which swarm in the never-ending labyrinth of their subterranean galleries. And yet the wretched who cast longing and hungry eyes on those hoards of wealth may be counted by the hundred thousand; by the side of untold splendors, want is consuming the vitals of entire populations, and it is only at times that the fortunate for whom these treasures are amassed hear, as a muffled wailing, the bitter cry which arises eternally from those unseen depths. Below the London of fashion is a London accursed, a London whose only food are dirt-stained fragments, whose only garments are filthy rags, and whose only dwellings are fetid dens. Have the disinherited the consolation of hope? No; they are deprived of all. There are some among them who live and die in dampness and gloom without once raising their eyes to the sun.

What boots it to the wretched outcast, burning with fever or craving for bread, that the book of the Christians opens the doors of heaven more widely to him than to the rich! Besides his present misery all these promises of happiness, even if he heard them, would seem the bitterest irony. Does it not appear, moreover—judging by the society in which the majority of the preachers of the gospel most delight—that the words of Jesus are reversed, that the "Kingdom of God" is the guerdon of the fortunate of this world—a world where spiritual and temporal government are on the best of terms, and religion leads as surely to earthly power as to heavenly bliss? "Religion is a cause for preferment, irreligion a bar to it," as a famous commentator of the Bible, speaking to his sovereign, said it ought to be.

When ambition thus finds its account in piety, and hypocrites practice religion in order to give what they are pleased to call their conscience a higher mercantile value, is it surprising that the great army of the hopeless should forget their way to church? Do they deceive themselves in thinking that, despite official invitations, they would not always be well received in the "house of God?" Without speaking here of churches whose sittings are sold at a price, where you may enter only purse in hand, is it nothing to the poor to feel themselves arrested on the threshold by the cold looks of well-clad men and the tightened lips of elegant women? True, no wall bars the passage, but an obstacle still more formidable stops the way—the dark atmosphere of hatred and disgust which rises between the disinherited and the world's elect.

Yet the first word uttered by the minister when he stands up in in the pulpit is "brethren," a word which, by a characteristic differentiation, has come to mean no more than a sort of potential and theoretic fraternity without practical reality. Nevertheless, its primitive sense has not altogether perished, and if the outcast that hears it be not stupefied by hunger, if he be not one of those boneless beings who repeat idiotically all they hear, what bitter thoughts will be suggested by this word "brethren" coming from the lips of men who feel so little its force! The impressions of my childhood surge back into my mind. When I heard for the first time an earnest and eager voice beseech the "Father who is in heaven" to give us "our daily bread," it seemed to me that by a mysterious act a meal would descend from on high on all the tables of the world. I imagined that these words, repeated millions and milliards of times, were a cry of human brotherhood, and that each, in uttering them, thought of all. I deceived myself. With some the prayer is sincere; with the greater part it is but an empty sound, a gust of wind like that which passes through the reeds.

Governments at least talk not to the poor about fraternity; they do not torment them with so sorry a jest. It is true that in some countries the jargon of courts compares the sovereign to a father whose subjects are his children, and upon whom he pours the inexhaustible dews of his love; but this formula, which the hungry might abuse by asking for bread, is no longer taken seriously. So long as governments were looked upon as direct representatives of a heavenly sovereign, holding their powers by the grace of God, the comparison was legitimate; but there are very few now that make any claim to this *quasi*-divinity. Shorn of the sanctions of religion, they no longer hold themselves answerable for the general weal, contenting themselves instead with promising good administration, impartial justice, and strict economy in the administration of public affairs. Let history tell how these promises have been kept. Nobody can study contemporary politics without being struck by the truth of the words attributed alike to Oxenstjerna and Lord Chesterfield: "Go, my son, and see with how little wisdom the world is governed!" It is now a matter of common knowledge that power, whether its nature be monarchic, aristocratic, or democratic, whether it be based on the right of the sword, of inheritance, or of election, is wielded by men neither better nor worse than their fellows, but whose position exposes them to greater temptations to do evil. Raised above the crowd, whom they soon learn to despise, they end by considering themselves essentially superior beings; solicited by ambition in a thousand forms, by vanity, greed, and caprice, they are all the more easily corrupted that a rabble of interested flatterers is ever on the watch to profit by their vices. And possessing as they do a preponderant influence in all things, holding the powerful lever whereby is moved the immense mechanism of the State—functionaries, soldiers, and police—every one of their oversights, their faults, or their crimes repeats itself to infinity, and magnifies as it grows. It is only too true: a fit of impatience in a sovereign, a crooked look, an equivocal word, may plunge nations into mourning, and be fraught with disaster for mankind.

English readers, brought up to a knowledge of biblical lore, will remember the striking parable of the trees who wanted a king. The peaceful trees and the strong, those who love work and whom man blesses; the olive that makes oil, the fig-tree that grows good fruit, the vine that produces wine, "which cheereth God and man," refuse to reign; the bramble accepts, and of that noxious briar is born the flame which devours the cedars of Lebanon.

But these depositaries of power who are charged, whether by right divine or universal suffrage, with the august mission of dispensing justice, can they be considered as in any way more infallible, or even as impartial? Can it be said that the laws and their interpreters show towards all men the ideal equity as it exists in the popular conception? Are the judges blind when there come before them the wealthy and the poor—Shylock, with his murderous knife, and the unfortunate who has sold beforehand pounds of his flesh or ounces of his blood? Hold they always even scales between the king's son and the beggar's brat? That these magistrates should firmly believe in their own impartiality and think themselves incarnate right in human shape, is quite natural; every one puts on—sometimes without knowing it—the peculiar morality of his calling; yet judges, no more than priests, can withstand the influence of their surroundings. Their sense of what constitutes justice, derived from the average opinion of the age, is insensibly modified by the prejudices of their class. How honest soever they may be, they cannot forget that they belong to the rich and powerful, or to those, less fortunate, who are still on the look-out for preferment and honor. They are moreover blindly attached to precedent, and fancy that practices inherited from their forerunners must needs be right. Yet when we examine official justice without prejudice, how many iniquities do we find in legal procedures! Thus the English are scandalized—and rightly so—by the French fashion of examining prisoners, those sacred beings who, in strict probity, ought to be held innocent until they are proved guilty; while the French are disgusted, and not without reason, to see English justice, through the English government, publicly encourage treachery by offers of impunity and money to the betrayer, thereby deepening the degradation of the debased and provoking acts of shameful meanness which children in their schools, more moral than their elders, regard with unfeigned horror.

Nevertheless, law, like religion, plays only a secondary part in contemporary society. It is invoked but rarely to regulate the relations between the poor and the rich, the powerful and the weak. These relations are the outcome of economic laws and the evolution of a social system based on inequality of conditions.

Laissez faire! Let things alone! have said the judges of the camp. Careers are open; and although the field is covered with corpses, although the conqueror stamps on the bodies of the vanquished, although by supply and demand, and the combinations and monopolies in which they result, the greater part of society becomes enslaved to the few, let things alone—for thus has decreed fair play. It is by virtue of this beautiful system that a *parvenu*, without speaking of the great lord who receives counties as his heritage, is able to conquer with ready money thousands of acres, expel those who cultivate his domain, and replace men and their dwellings with wild animals and rare trees. It is thus that a tradesman, more cunning or intelligent, or, perhaps, more favored by luck than his fellows, is enabled to become master of an army of workers, and as often as not to starve them at his pleasure. In a word, commercial competition, under the paternal ægis of the law, lets the great majority of merchants—the fact is attested by numberless medical inquests—adulterate provisions and drink, sell pernicious substances as wholesome food, and kill by slow poisoning, without for one day neglecting their religious duties, their brothers in Jesus Christ. Let people say what they will, slavery, which abolitionists strove so gallantly to extirpate in America, prevails in another form in every civilized country; for entire populations, placed between the alternatives of death by starvation and toils which they detest, are constrained to choose the latter. And if we would deal frankly with the barbarous society to which we belong, we must acknowledge that murder, albeit disguised under a thousand insidious and scientific forms, still, as in the times of primitive savagery, terminates the majority of lives. The economist sees around him but one vast field of carnage, and with the coldness of the statistician he counts the slain as on the evening after a great battle. Judge by these figures. The mean mortality among the well-to-do is, at the utmost, one in sixty. Now the population of Europe being a third of a thousand millions, the average deaths, according to the rate of mortality among the fortunate, should not exceed five millions. They are three times five millions! What have we done with these ten million human beings killed before their time? If it be true that we have duties, one towards the other, are we not responsible for the servitude, the cold, the hunger, the miseries of every sort, which doom the unfortunate to untimely deaths? Race of Cains, what have we done with our brothers?

And what are the remedies proposed for the social ills which are consuming the very marrow of our bones? Can charity, as asserts many good souls—who are answered in chorus by a crowd of egotists—can charity by any possibility deal with so vast an evil? True, we know some devoted ones who seem to live only that they may do good. In England, above all, is this the case. Among the childless women who are constrained to lavish their love on their kind are to be found many of those admirable beings whose lives are passed in consoling the afflicted, visiting the sick, and ministering to the young. We cannot help being touched by the exquisite benevolence, the indefatigable solicitude shown by these ladies towards their unhappy fellow-creatures; but, taken even in their entirety, what economic value can be attached to these well-meant afforts? What sum represents the charities of a year in comparison with the gains which hucksters of money and hawkers of loans oftentimes make by the speculations of a single day? While ladies bountiful are giving a cup of tea to a pauper, or preparing a potion for the sick, a father or a brother, by a hardy stroke on the stock exchange or a successful transaction in produce, may reduce to ruin thousands of British workmen or Hindoo coolies. And how worthy of respect soever may be deeds of unostentatious charity, is it not a fact the bestowal of alms is generally a matter of personal caprice, and that their distribution is too often influenced rather by the political and religious sympathies of the giver than by the moral worth of the recipient? Even were help always given to those who most need it, charity would be none the less tainted with the capital vice, that it infallibly constitutes relations of inequality between the benefitted and the benefactor. The latter rejoices in the consciousness of having done a good thing, as if he were not simply discharging a debt; and the former asks bread as a favor, when he should demand work as a right, or, if helpless, human solidarity. Thus are created and developed hideous mendicity with its lies, its tricks, and its base, heart-breaking hypocrisy. How much nobler are the customs of some so-called "barbarous countries" where the hungry man simply stops by the side of those who eat, is welcomed by all, and then, when satisfied, with a friendly greeting withdraws—remaining in every respect the equal of his host, and fretting under no painful sense of obligation for favors received! But charity breeds patronage and platitudes—miserable fruits of a wretched system, yet the best which a society of capitalists has to offer us!

Hence we may say that, in letting those whom they govern—and the responsibility for whose fate they thereby accept—waste by want, sink under exposure, and deteriorate by vice, the leaders of modern society have committed moral bankruptcy. But where the masters have come short, free men may, perchance, succeed. The failure of governments is no reason why we should be discouraged; on the contrary, it shows us the danger of entrusting to others the guardianship of our rights, and makes us all the more firmly resolved to take our own cause into our own care. We are not among those whom the practice of social hypocricies, the long weariness of a crooked life, and the uncertainty of the future have reduced to the necessity of asking ourselves —without daring to answer it—the sad question: "Is life worth living?" Yes, to us life does seem worth living, but on condition that it has an end—not personal happiness, not a paradise, either in this world or the next—but the realization of a cherished wish, an ideal that belongs to us and springs from our innermost conscience. We are striving to draw nearer to that ideal equality which, century after century, has hovered before subject peoples like a heavenly dream. The little each of us can do offers an ample recompense for the perils of the combat. On these terms life is good, even a life of suffering and sacrifice—even though it may be cut short by premature death.

The first condition of equality, without which any other progress is merest mockery—the object of all socialists without exception—is that every man shall have bread. To talk of duty, of renunciation, of ethereal virtues to the famishing, is nothing less than cowardice. Dives has no right to preach morality to the beggar at his gates. If it were true that civilized lands did not produce food enough for all, it might be said that, by virtue of vital competition, bread should be reserved for the strong, and that the weak must content themselves with the crumbs that fall from the feasters' tables. In a family where love prevails things are not ordered in this way; on the contrary, the small and the ailing receive the fullest measure; yet it is evident that dearth may strengthen the hands of the violent and make the powerful monopolizers of bread. But are our modern societies really reduced to these straits? On the contrary, whatever may be the value of Malthus' forecast as to the distant future, it is an actual, incontestable fact that in the civilized countries of Europe and America the sum total of provisions produced, or received in exchange for manufactures, is more than enough for the sustenance of the people. Even in times of partial dearth the granaries and warehouses have but to open their doors that every one may have a sufficient share. Notwithstanding waste and prodigality, despite the enormous losses arising from moving about and "handling" in warehouses and shops, there is always enough to feed generously all the world. And yet there are some who die of hunger! And yet there are fathers who kill their children because when the little ones cry for bread they have none to give them.

Others may turn their eyes from these horrors; we socialists look them full in the face, and seek out their cause. That cause is the monopoly of the soil, the appropriation by a few of the land which belongs to all. We anarchists are not the only ones to say it: the cry for nationalization of the land is rising so high that all may hear it who do not wilfully close their ears. The idea spreads fast, for private property, in its present form, has had its day, and historians are everywhere testifying that the old Roman law is not synonymous with eternal justice. Without doubt it were vain to hope that holders of the soil, saturated, so to speak, with ideas of cast, of privilege and of inheritance, will voluntarily give back to all the bread-yielding furrows; the glory will not be theirs of joining as equals their fellow-citizens; but when public opinion is ripe—and day by day it grows—individuals will oppose in vain the general concourse of wills, and the axe will be applied to the upas tree's roots. Arable land will be held once more in common; but instead of being ploughed and sown almost at hazard by ignorant hands, as it has hitherto been, science will aid us in the choice of climate, of soils, of methods of culture, of fertilizers, and of machinery. Husbandry will be guided by the same prescience as mechanical combinations and chemical operations; but the fruits of his toil will not be lost to the laborer. Many so-called savage societies hold their land in common, and humble though in our eyes they may seem, they are our betters in this: want among them is unknown. Are we, then, too ambitious in desiring to attain a social state which shall add to the conquests of civilization the privileges of these primitive tribes? Through the education of our children we may to some extent fashion the future.

After we have bread for all, we shall require something more—equality of rights; but this point will soon be realized, for a man who needs not incline himself before his fellows to crave a pittance is already their equal. Equality of conditions, which is in no way incompatible with the infinite diversity of human character, we ardently desire and look upon as indispensable, for it offers us the only means whereby a true public morality can be developed. A man can be truly moral only when he is his own master. From the moment when he awakens to a comprehension of that which is equitable and good it is for him to direct his own movements, to seek in his conscience reasons for his actions, and to perform them simply without either fearing punishment or looking for reward. Nevertheless his will cannot fail to be strengthened when he sees other men, guided like himself by their own volition, following the same line of conduct. Mutual example will soon constitute a collective code of ethics to which all may conform without effort; but the moment that orders, enforced by legal penalties, replace the personal impulses of the conscience, there is an end to morality. Hence the saying of the apostle of the Gentiles, "the law makes sin." Even more, it is sin itself, because, instead of appealing to man's better part, to his bold initiative, it appeals to his worst—it rules by fear. It thus behooves every one to resist laws that he has not made, and to defend his personal rights, which are also the rights of others. People often speak of the antagonism between rights and duties. It is an empty phrase; there is no such antagonism. Whoso vindicates his own rights fulfills at the same time his duty towards his fellow-men. Privilege, not right, is the converse of duty.

Besides the possession of a man's own person, sound morality involves yet another condition—mutual good-will, which is likewise the outcome of equality. The time-honored words of Mahabarata are as true as ever: "The ignorant are not the friends of the wise; the man who has no cart is not the friend of him who has a cart. Friendship is the daughter of equality; it is never born of inequality." Without doubt it is given to some men, great by their thoughts, by sympathy, or by strength of will, to win the multitude; but if the attachment of their followers and admirers comes otherwise than of an enthusiastic affinity of idea to idea, or of heart to heart, it is speedily transformed either into fanaticism or servility. He who is hailed lord by the acclamations of the crowd must almost of necessity attribute to himself exceptional virtues, or a "grace of God," that marks him in his own estimation as a predestined being, and he usurps without hesitation or remorse privileges which he transmits as a heritage to his children. But, while in rank exalted, he is morally degraded, and his partisans and sycophants are more degraded still; they wait for the words of command which fall from the master's lips; when they hear in the depths of their conscience some faint note of dissent, it is stifled; they become practiced liars, they stoop to flattery, and lose the power of looking honest men in the face. Between him who commands and him who obeys, and whose degradation deepens from generation to generation, there is no possibility of friendship. The virtues are transformed; brotherly frankness is destroyed; independence becomes a crime; above is either pitying condescension or haughty contempt, below either envious admiration or hidden hate. Let each of us recall the past and ask ourselves in all sincerity this question: "Who are the men in whose society we have experienced the most pleasure? Are they personages who have 'honored' us with their conversation, or the humble with whom we have 'deigned' to associate? Are they not rather our equals, those whose looks neither implore nor command, and whom we may love with open hearts without afterthought or reserve?"

It is to live in condition of equality and escape from the falsehoods and hypocrisies of a society of superiors and inferiors, that so many men and women have formed themselves into close corporations and little worlds apart. America abounds in communities of this sort. But these societies, few of which prosper while many perish, are all ruled more or less by force; they carry within themselves the seeds of their own dissolution, and are reabsorbed by nature's law of gravitation into the world which they have left. Yet even were they perfection, if man enjoyed in them the highest happiness of which his nature is capable, they would be none the less obnoxious to the charge of selfish isolation, of raising a wall between themselves and the rest of their race; their pleasures are egotistical, and devotion to the cause of humanity would draw back the best of them into the great struggle.

As for us anarchists, never will we separate ourselves from the world to build a little church, hidden in some vast wilderness. Here is the fighting ground, and we remain in the ranks, ready to give our help wherever it may be most needed. We do not cherish premature hopes, but we know that our efforts will not be lost. Many of the ignorant, who either out of love of routine or simplicity of soul now anathematize us, will end by associating themselves with our cause. For every man whom circumstances permit to join us freely, hundreds are hindered by the hard necessities of life from openly avowing their opinions, but they listen from afar and cherish our words in the treasury of their hearts. We know that we are defending the cause of the poor, the disinherited, the suffering; we are seeking to restore to them the earth, personal rights, confidence in the future; and is it not natural that they should encourage us by look and gesture, even when they dare not come to us? In times of trouble, when the iron hand of might loosens its hold, and paralyzed rulers reel under the weight of their own power; when the "groups," freed for an instant from the pressure above, reform themselves according to their natural affinities, on which side will be the many? Though making no pretension to prophetic insight, may we not venture without temerity to say that the great multitude would join our ranks? Albeit they never weary of repeating that anarchism is merely the dream of a few visionaries, do not even our enemies, by the insults they heap upon us and the projects and machinations they impute to us, make an incessant propaganda in our favor? It is said that when the magicians of the middle ages wanted to raise the devil, they began their incantations by painting his image on a wall. For a long time past modern exorcists have adopted a similar method for conjuring anarchists.

Pending the great work of the coming time, and to the end that this work may be accomplished, it behooves us to utilize every opportunity for rede and deed. Meanwhile, although our object is to live without government and without law, we are obliged, in many things, to submit. On the other hand, how often are we enabled to disregard their behests and act on our own free will? Ours be it to let slip none of these occasions, and to accept tranquilly whatever personal consequences may result from doing that which we believe to be our duty. In no case will we strengthen authority by appeals or petitions, neither shall we sanction the law by demanding justice from the courts, nor by giving our votes and influence to any candidate whatsoever, become the authors of our own ill-fortune. It is also easy for us to accept nothing from power, to call no man "master," neither to be called "master" ourselves, to remain in the ranks as simple citizens and to maintain resolutely, and in every circumstance, our quality of equal among equals. Let our friends judge us by our deeds, and reject from among them those of us who falter.

There are unquestionably many kind-hearted men that, as yet, hold themselves aloof from us, and even view our efforts with a certain apprehension, who would nevertheless gladly lend us their help were they not repelled by fear of the violence which almost invariably accompanies revolution. And yet a close study of the present state of things would show them that the supposed period of tranquility in which we live is really an age of cruelty and violence. Not to speak of war and its crimes, from the guilt of which no civilized State is free, can it be denied that chief among the consequences of the existing social system are murder, maladies and death? Accustomed order is maintained by rude deeds and brute force, yet things that happen every day and every hour pass unperceived; we see in them a series of ordinary events no more phenomenal than times and seasons. It seems no less than impious to rebel against the cycle of violence and repression which comes to us hallowed by the sanction of ages. Far from desiring to replace an era of happiness and peace by an age of disorder and warfare, our sole aim is to put an end to the endless series of calamities which has hitherto been called, by common consent, "The progress of civilization." On the other hand, vengeances are the inevitable incidents of a period of violent changes. It is in the nature of things that they should be. Albeit deeds of violence, prompted by a spirit of hatred, bespeak a feeble moral development, these deeds become fatal and necessary whenever the relations between man and man are not the relations of perfect equity. The original form of justice, as understood by primitive peoples, was that of retaliation, and by thousands of rude tribes this system is still observed. Nothing seemed more just than to offset one wrong by a like wrong. Eye for eye! Tooth for tooth! If the blood of one man has been shed, another must die! This was the barbarous form of justice. In our civilized societies it is forbidden to individuals to take the law into their own hands. Governments, in their quality of social delegates, are charged, on behalf of the community, with the enforcement of justice, a sort of retaliation somewhat more enlightened than that of the savage. It is on this condition that the individual renounces the right of personal vengeance; but if he be deceived by the mandatories to whom he entrusts the vindication of his rights, if he perceives that his agents betray his cause and league themselves with his oppressors, that official justice aggravates his wrongs; in a word, if whole classes and populations are unfairly used, and have no hope of finding, in the society to which they belong, a redresser of abuses, is it not certain that they will resume their inherent right of vengeance and execute it without pity? Is not this indeed an ordinance of nature, a consequence of the physical law of shock and counter-shock? It were unphilosophic to be surprised by its existence. Oppression has always been answered by violence.

Nevertheless, if great human evolutions are always followed by sad outbreaks of personal hatreds, it is not to these bad passions that well-wishers of their kind appeal when they wish to arouse the motive virtues of enthusiasm, devotion and generosity. If changes had no other result than to punish oppressors, to make them suffer in their turn, to repay evil with evil, the transformation would be only in seeming. What boots it to him who truly loves humanity and desires the happiness of all, that the slave becomes master, that the master is reduced to servitude, that the whip changes hands, and that money passes from one pocket to another? It is not the rich and the powerful whom we devote to destruction, but the institutions which have favored the birth and growth of these malevolent beings. It is the medium which it behooves us to alter, and for this great work we must reserve all our strength; to waste it in personal vindications were merest puerility. "Vengeance is the pleasure of the gods," said the ancients; but it is not the pleasure of self-respecting mortals; for they know that to become their own avengers would be to lower themselves to the level of their former oppressors. If we would rise superior to our adversary, we must, after vanquishing him, make him bless his defeat. The revolutionary device. "For our liberty and for yours," must not be an empty word.

The people in all times have felt this; and after every temporary triumph the generosity of the victor has obliterated the menaces of the past. It is a constant fact that in all serious popular movements, made for an idea, hope of a better time, and above all, the sense of a new dignity, fills the soul with high and magnanimous sentiments. So soon as the police, both political and civil, cease their functions and the masses become masters of the streets, the moral atmosphere changes, each feels himself responsible for the prosperity and contentment of all; molestation of individuals is almost unheard of; even professional criminals pause in their sad career, for they too feel that something great is passing through the air. Ah! if revolutionaries, instead of obeying a vague idea, as they have almost always done, had formed a definite aim, a well-considered scheme of social conduct, if they had firmly willed the establishment of a new order of things, in which every citizen might be assured bread, work, instruction, and the free development of his being, there would have been no danger in opening all prison gates to their full width and saying to the unfortunates whom they shut in, "Go, brothers, and sin no more."

It is always to the nobler part of man that we should address ourselves when we want to do great deeds. A general fighting for a bad cause stimulates his soldiers with promises of booty, a benevolent man who cherishes a noble object encourages his companions by the example of his own devotion and self-sacrifice. For him faith in his idea is enough. As says the proverb of the Danish peasant: "His will is his paradise." What matters it that he is treated as a visionary. Even though his undertaking were only a chimera, he knows nothing more beautiful and sweet than the desire to act rightly and do good; in comparison with this, vulgar realities are for him but shadows, the apparitions of an instant.

But our ideal is not a chimera. This, public opinion well knows: for no question more preoccupies it than that of social transformation. Events are casting their shadows before. Among men who think is there one who in some fashion or another is not a socialist—that is to say, who has not his own little scheme for changes in economical relations? Even the orator who noisily denies that there is a social question affirms the contrary by a thousand propositions. And those who would lead us back to the middle ages, are they not also socialists? They think they have found in a past, restored after modern ideas, conditions of social justice which will establish forever the brotherhood of man. All are awaiting the birth of a new order of things; all ask themselves, some with misgiving, others with hope, what the morrow will bring forth. It will not come with empty hands. The century which has witnessed so many grand discoveries in the world of science cannot pass away without giving us still greater conquests. Industrial appliances, that by a single electric impulse make the same thought vibrate through five continents, have distanced by far our social morals, which are yet in many regards the outcome of reciprocally hostile interests. The axis is displaced; the world must *crack* that its equilibrium may be restored. In spirit revolution is ready; it is already thought it is already willed; it only remains to realize it, and this is not the most difficult part of the work. The governments of Europe will soon have reached the limits to the expansion of their power and find themselves face to face with their increasing populations. The superabundant activity which wastes itself in distant wars must then find employment at home unless in their folly the shepherds of the people should try to exhaust their energies by setting Europeans against Europeans, as they have so often done before. It is true that in this way they may retard the solution of the social problem, but it will arise again after each postponement, more formidable than before.

Let economists and rulers invent political constitutions or salaried organizations, whereby the workman may be made the friend of his master, the subject the brother of his potentate, we, "frightful anarchists" as we are, know only one way of establishing peace and goodwill among men—the suppression of privilege and the recognition of right. Our ideal, as we have said, is that of the fraternal equity for which all yearn, but almost always as a dream; with us it takes form and becomes a concrete reality. It pleases us not to live if the enjoyments of life are to be for us alone; we protest against our good fortune if we may not share it with others; it is sweeter for us to wander with the wretched and the outcast than to sit crowned with roses, at the banquets of the rich. We are weary of these inequalities which make us the enemies of each other; we would put an end to the furies which are ever bringing men into hostile collision, and all of which arise from the bondage of the weak to the strong under the form of slavery, serfage and service. After so much hatred we long to love each other, and for this reason are we enemies of private property and despisers of the law.

ELISÉE RECLUS.

CHAPTER VI.

DYER D. LUM ON ANARCHY.

[From the Alarm.]

I—WHAT IS ANARCHY.

The statesman, intent on schemes to compromise principles and tide over clamorous demands for justice, says it is disorder and spoliation. New taxes are then levied to defend the state, to repress incendiary talk, and protect privileged prerogatives. Or false and surface issues are prepared to distract attention, to embroil citizens in partisan quarrels, and furnsh new offices for the spoils-hunter. The people pay the bills and the statesman remains.

The priest, intent on saving souls, and setting less value on temporal things—for others—says it is abolition of marriage, atheism, and draws a frightful picture of a state wherein his voice would be derided, yet ever careful to bring no testimony to corroborate his dismal forebodings of social chaos.

The financier, intent on new schemes for manipulating public credit to personal ends, says it means "a dividing up"; that the lazy and worthless want to share with the industrious and honest the fruits of industry; and thousands believe it and never think to ask whether any one ever saw an anarchist who believed in this fancied "divvy."

The landlord, comfortably collecting toll for the use of land from those who have been placed upon this earth, says it is the destruction of the foundation and framework of society and removal of all incentive to progress and then proceeds to invest tolls received in fresh acres.

The merchant seeking by every means to obtain a monopoly of the market, says it is the negation of freedom, a gigantic despotism in which life would be burdened with prison rules and social intercourse regulated with clock-like regularity.

One and all incessantly dinning this into the public ear, their cry re-echoed by that social prostitute, the "able editor," in whose sheet their respective callings are advertised, the timid shrink from the word, women grow pale, and children learn to believe an anarchist is a first cousin to Old Nick. And, laughing in their sleeves over their success, the statesman lays pipe for a re-election, the priest pictures another world where corner lots have no speculative value, the financier busies himself in cutting coupons and computing interest, the landlord in figuring how soon he may safely raise rents, the merchant in converting "surplus values" into profits.

In the tenement house human beings are huddled like sheep in a pen; in the factories women and children crowd out husbands and fathers; in the potter's field trenches are continually opened and filled; in the cities vice and crime are spreading gaudy attractions for idle feet; in the country able bodied men vainly seek employment; men grow disheartened and sullen, women overworked and cross, girls and boys dejected and lost. Yet while rent and interest are collected and profits amassed society is safe and law and order secure, though

> Our fathers are praying for pauper pay,
> Our mothers with Death's kiss are white;
> Our sons are the rich man's serfs by day.
> And our daughters his slaves by night.

Yet anarchy will not down, but continues to gain adherents, and says to the statesman: Your surface issues are dead and party questions misguiding. We ask justice, and would stop the spoliation from which we have so long suffered. Producing all, we too often lack food and warmth and clothing. Where all are prosperous the state must be so too, and until we are state interests are of secondary importance to us.

It says to the priest: There can be no healthful organization of the moral forces while poverty sets at our hearths and vice beckons our youth to gayer scenes than home can afford. Give us freedom from unrequited toil and enforced destitution and our emotional natures will warm into unity from higher aspirations.

It says to the financier: Your function in society should not be determined by monopoly, but under equal opportunities. Your privileges are our restrictions; your charters our disfranchisement. We demand freedom to co-operate in financial as in other matters; to co-operate for mutual banking as well as for mutual insurance; and when you are shorn of privileges we may co-operate to base credit upon all wealth as well as on that you would dictate, for equal opportunities would destroy your prerogative to fashion and control a medium of exchange. Justice would reign and interest cease, because it could not be exacted.

It says to the landlord: Equal opportunities give you no monopoly of the soil. Again, monopoly has conferred a chartered right and men are disinherited. Destroy this chartered privilege and strong arms will labor with joy and find in mutual credit new avenues to invade the province of nature. Co-operation would enlarge production, extend consumption, and equalize distribution. Overproduction and underconsumption would become myths, and demand would seek supply with unfailing regularity without other guarantee than absence of restrictoin.

It says to the merchant: Exchange is a social function, and, in the absence of the monopolies of money and land, labor, free from artificial restriction, free to co-operate in mutual banking to organize credit based on all products, thus free to connect use with possession of soil, free from the enforced payment of interest for monopoly money. free from enforced payment of rent for production, would through co-operation organize exchanges and leave you free to whistle for profits.

To them all it says: Gentlemen, we ask no privilege, we propose no restriction; nor, on the other hand, will we permit it. We have no new shackles to propose, we seek emancipation from shackles. We ask no legislative sanction, for co-operation asks only for a free field and no favors; neither will we permit their interference.

It asserts that in freedom of the social unit lies the freedom of the social state.

It asserts that in freedom to the capitalization of all acquired wealth lies social advancement and the death of interest.

It asserts that in freedom to possess and utilize soil lies social happiness and progress and the death of rent.

It asserts that in freedom to co-operate the labor exchange will displace the penny-pinching tradesmen and prove the death of profits.

It asserts that in freedom from restriction co-operation will result, and in free co-operation capital will seek labor as well as provide guarantees for security.

It asserts that order can only exist where liberty prevails, and that progress leads and never follows order.

It asserts, finally, that this emancipation will inaugurate liberty, equality, fraternity.

II.—WHAT ANARCHY OFFERS.

The world of activity is one of inducements. Why should I do thus or so? Because my highest interests are concerned. To follow a given course, to advocate certain measures, there must be sufficient inducement therein to satisfy my mind that such is for my interest to do so. We propose no change in human nature, we take it as we find it, and ask: Does anarchism offer any inducements superior to those of the present system? Can self-interest see any advantage in the change? It is a question of comparison, of weighing of advantages and disadvantages. Self-interest shall be umpire.

Let us see what are the inducements now offered, what are the prizes in the lottery of life, and the chances of winning them. We find men placed upon earth dependent upon labor for enjoyment of life. In our zone nature withholds her gifts and makes them the reward of exertion. Every faculty of individuality is thus aroused to exertion and self-reliance developed. We do not pluck and eat, but labor and develop natural resources, and hence provide. Herein lies the cause of progress, of civilization. Natural conditions must be accepted and our activity governed in accordance therewith.

But at the first glance we see that our efforts are limited by artificial regulations. Nature has placed us upon the earth, but we are denied its use for productive purposes. We find the source of all production resting in land, and on every lot we find the placard: "Taken." Nature's gift has been monopolized, and artificial conditions are first to be surmounted before access can be had to the use of soil. Held, not for use, but for sale, it assumes a speculative value. Have you a lot, a homestead left to you? This speculative value extends over to it, increases your taxes, places a fine upon all improvements, and where such are made requires increased exertions to meet new exactions. Society says that you have no natural right to the soil. The right to produce must be bought. You must first accumulate through production before you can have access to the source of production, hence you must crave employment. You must realize sufficient profits from the sale of time or products before you can purchase the right to produce for yourself. Therefore, you work for others, and from the values you create there is diverted one part to the owner of land, from whom you purchase the right to remain on earth, under the form of rent, and another portion to the employer as inducement for giving you employment, instead of starving, under the form of profits. After these requirements are met you receive wages. And were we studying political economy instead of glancing at some of its salient points, it would be seen that this applies as well to the farmer as to the laborer.

The laborer's wages are paid in the form of money, the current medium of exchange. Advancement lies in saving, in economy, in postponement of marriage, in accumulating money by which privilege may be purchased or capital secured. Possession of land is not enough; there must be joined to it ability to use. But labor saved is only wealth till turned to reproductive use, when it becomes capital. But here, again, artificial conditions are introduced. Society in its wisdom having privileged the landlord, now grants prerogatives to the capitalist. It limits the medium of exchange to a particular form of wealth. All credit must flow through a specified sluice. A, B, and C seek through co-operation to escape from the necessity of working for others. A has wealth saved in a house; B has wealth saved in machinery; C has wealth saved in products; all having equal exchangeable value. But their wealth had cannot be capitalized into wealth used, save by purchasing monopoly money. As a basis for mutual credit it is valueless; as a basis for sale or mortgage it can command money, be capitalized. Thus by this privilege conferred upon one form of wealth to constitute the sole medium of exchange and basis for credit another toll is laid upon industry in the form of interest.

All these artificial complications by which the surplus value of production is diverted from the producer into the coffers of the, so to speak, complicators of normal social relations require the support of the source of interference, hence taxation claims its share before the residual sum is dealt out as wages. Therefore it is that, as under slavery and serfdom, the producer works for as little as may be necessary to support him. The competition of labor for privilege to live keeps the minimum of wages at the line of cost of subsistence, while taxation, profits, and rent have no determinable limit. Labor, lying under all these superimposed burdens, paying all these exactions, is necessarily remunerated by this iron law of wages. Anarchism must offer emancipation from this enforced subjection of labor to land and capital, and, logically, in proclaiming emancipation it must proclaim freedom to the oppressed—liberty!

Emancipation from the thralldom of man to land; the individual right to possession and use, carrying with it the right to co-operate for guaranteeing security and protection. Emancipation from the thralldom of man to capital, the individual right to utilize all wealth, and the right through co-operation to organize mutual credit with the same facility we are now graciously permitted in mutual insurance.

Emancipation from bondage to rent would base all titles upon occupancy and use; would open avenues of escape to the toiler, and in nowise limit the farmer's capacity to produce, nor his ability to enjoy the reward thereof. In increased production, application to labor would be lightened, the necessity for struggle lessened, an inflation of wealth would ensue, distribution be more equitably adjusted, and natural right to a footing on earth receive social sanction and, through co-operation, social guarantee.

Emancipation from bondage to interest would join means to possession of the source of production. Co-operative effort would offer sanction to co-operative credit, and in freedom to capitalize all products interest would be abolished in the same sense as petroleum "abolished" candles.

Labor, free from the exactions of speculative rent, and released from necessity to buy a monopolized medium of exchange, would offer as inducements to exertion:

Opportunity to freely enjoy the fruits of industry without paying toll.

Opportunity to the endless increase of wants and means to wrest from nature their supply.

Opportunity to the use of all wealth had in the extension of productive activity.

Opportunity to freely co-operate to secure:
1. Protection and security from invasion of these natural rights. 2. Insurance against depredation and risks. 3. A medium of exchange based upon wealth saved, having social sanction, discharging social functions, and serving social ends. 4. The organization of labor exchanges from which profits would have fled to join rent and interest. 5. The organization of all forms of activity, and thus release from enforced taxation.

In short, where capital seeks labor where supply waits upon demand, where order follows progress, where authority dissolves under the genial glow of liberty, and necessity for wage-labor disappears.

The present system offers government to defend privilege. Anarchist-socialism offers co-operation to extend opportunities. The one, in making co-operation compulsory and fostering privilege, sets a premium upon greed and culminates in tyranny. The other, in removing privilege, places a premium upon voluntary co-operation, and tends to eliminate greed.

III.—WHO SHOULD BE ANARCHISTS?

First, we might ask: Why should there be any? Are not our cities filled with evidences of ceaseless traffic? Is not capital ever on the alert for investment in profitable enterprises? Are not our western towns rivaling each other in " booms " in real estate, thus testifying to increasing revival of business? Is not the army of the unemployed steadily diminishing, and demand for labor increasing? Are not our public documents teeming with statistical columns showing national prosperity? The building trades find employment in building new and grander palaces; in their decoration and furnishing an army of skilled employes find remunerative labor; in the clothing and adornment of their inmates thousands are fed and clothed. On every hand new church spires arise, as if to serve as exclamation points to the astonishment which the voice of anarchy arouses.

Festive revelries were never more frequent; people marry and are given in marriage, and display to reporters the bridal gifts; luxury is creating new demands upon industry; salaries of officials and popular preachers are raised, and pews sell at a higher premium; in fact, everything goes as merry as a marriage bell were it not for the discordant note of frequent strikes.

Ah! Here is a depth which statistical compilations of productions and exports does not reach, it seems. Let us peer beneath the veneering of " national prosperity," and see if the structure be sound or wormeaten. Let us see if the gilded rays of boulevard prosperity radiates into tenement-denizened streets and " nigger alley "; whether the magic wand of the speculative genie of the business boom has transformed these humble homes.

Alas! to ask is to answer; the toiler still delves on in his weary tread-mill round, and finds advancing age but brings added cares and disquietudes. To him the business boom and national prosperity are only visible when seen recapitulated in the eloquent words which flow from the " able editor's " prostitute pen.

In his thinking moments the artisan dreams of a co-operative society in which freemen will combine to wrest from nature her hidden wealth, in which liberty to labor will no longer be restricted as a boon to crave, in which with manly independence, he may look forward to the calmer enjoyment of the fruits of industry in old age. Nor stands he alone. The farmer wonders if his mortgage will ever be paid. The tradesman asks whether life has no other aim than the constant necessity of counting pennies. The clerk thinks that there cannot be room at the top for all, and what if he should miss his hold on the ladder?

Through all grades of society unrest prevails, because in all success depends upon ability or craft to climb over the fallen forms of your associates; to rise out of the slough by using them as stepping-stones, though every upward step plunges them deeper into the abyss.

Modern society, monarchical, parliamentary, and republican alike, cries with one voice: Law and order first and foremost, liberty and progress secondary and resultant. Anarchy says: Not so; law must not deny liberty, order must not precede progress; they are causes, not results. It proclaims progress first, to which order must adapt itself; liberty at all times, over which law has no control.

It whispers to the artisan, the laborer, the miner, the factory hand, the farmer, the tradesman, the clerk, to all whose hearts have not been seared by the blighting hand of successful greed: Your happiness lies in freedom from artificial restrictions, not in strife for privilege.

Look over the broad fields teeming with golden grain and then at the numberless acres held by speculators to extort from human necessity an onerous toll as prerequisite condition to their use to further increase production. Look over the crowded human bee-hives where the toilers jostle each other and then at the vacant lots surrounding them, serving but as receptacles for broken crockery. Ask yourselves by what title deed has the landlord disinherited you from nature's estate? Has God set his seal to it? Is nature's sign-manual there? Have you surrendered your natural claim to a footing on earth? Whence, then, the privilege to him and the restriction upon you? There is but one answer: The law so ordains!

You dream of co-operation, but when you essay it you find rent and interest as firmly seated astride your shoulders as was the Old Man of the Sea upon Sinbad. Not only are you denied possession of the source of production—land—but monopoly also steps in to dictate upon what conditions you may have the means of production by conferring the privilege of capital on a certain form of wealth only. Your buildings, your machinery, your products, your possessions, the reward of honest industry, may be used, but not capitalized: they cannot be made the basis of credit except in the terms of the monopoly money furnished for the purpose of selling to you permission to utilize your own credit. To the question: Why is this so? again there is but one answer: The law so ordains!

Instead of praying: From rent and interest, good Lord, deliver us! strike down that which breathes vitality into their grasping tentacles, crush it, throttle it, damn it like freemen, and assert your right to co-operate in producing wealth without making terms with the land-robber, and to co-operate to furnish mutual credit without paying toll to the credit robber.

Anarchy is freedom from artificial regulation and restriction; and in freedom, the farmer, as well as the artisan and all the classes into which society is now divided, will find that wider scope to activity will bring increased comfort; and in freedom to use of land and to organize credit, rent, interest, and profits will disappear together like bats before the dawning light; and in co-operation find full security for wealth attained and opportunity for its application.

In anarchy labor and capital would be merged into one, for capital would be without prerogatives and dependent upon labor, and owned by it. The laborer would find that to produce was to enjoy and the nightmare of destitution banished. The artisan would find in co-operation that nature alone remained to be exploited. The tradesman would find that production offered greater inducement than exchange, unless he accepted a position of competence and ease in the labor exchange which would supplant isolated stores. The clerk, no longer with his horizon bounded by a ribbon counter, would have full scope to display his talents in any direction. The farmer, above all, free from irksome care to meet interest, to dread foreclosure from enforced taxation, with his family growing up around him, and rendered secure by a common title and mutual inter-dependence, or seeking in insurance indemnity for depredation, would find in anarchy release from useless drudgery and his labor crowned with plentiness and peace.

The only question then likely to arise would be: Who would not be an anarchist?

IV.—CO-OPERATION.

Now that questions of forms of faith in theology and government have ceased to divide men into hostile factions, that political as well as religious toleration has become firmly rooted as a social virtue, economic questions rise into greater importance. Here again we find the old struggle of past centuries under new standards; again liberty is arrayed against authority on other fields. Co-operation in religion has passed out of the field of strife and been declared victorious; our creed is no longer dealt to us. Co-operation in government has won its place in the world's history; our rulers no longer claim divine right to govern. The scaffolding of past centuries has brought mankind to the completion of the social structure. Reason and intelligence on the one hand and necessity and discord on the other are instructing them in its aims and preparing them for the application of the requisite means It is the dream of the toiler, the hope of the thoughtful, and the goal of the progressive humanitarian.

How shall we substitute co-operation? Efforts have been many, satisfactory results few. Unforseen obstacles are met to be overcome;

artificial environments limit freedom of action; chartered privileges impede progress; restrictions hamper and clog activity.

Co-operation in the distribution of products sacrifices the producer to the consumer. Buying at the lowest competition price, and following current trade principles, it would swell profits for the benefit of customers. If it tends to lessen prices the consumer, so far as he is a producer, but gives from one hand what the other hand gains. An English writer indulges in the following criticism on the system:

> The co-operative wholesale society is a gigantic middleman. In its workshops it pays the lowest of competition wages. In the language of one of the workers in one of the shoe factories: "The workmen have to work for what they can get; they know there is no true co-operation." In its transactions with other producers it pays the lowest of competition prices. The profits made out of the retail prices are distributed among the members; labor is depressed. In short, it is as far from displaying a single feature of real co-operation as any private trader is who uses the weapons of competition and capitalism for his personal ends, regardless of the interests of others.

Even where success attends the enterprise it can hardly rank as even ameliorative. The few, the stockholders, the customers alone are its beneficiaries; the great mass are left, and further, so far as co-operation lifts a few out of the social slough it is at the expense of less fortunate fellow-creatures, who find their own fate more irrevocably fixed in becoming stepping-stones upon which the few mount to privileged enjoyment. Co-operation to eliminate the middleman and retaining rent and interest is but a sorry makeshift for the bright ideal our dreams had presaged.

Anarachy presents a wider and grander view of co-operation than that involved in joint stock or profit-sharing concerns—a view which requires no elaborate scaffolding to erect nor exercise of legislative authority to preserve. It seeks no charter, for it asks no privileges; it seeks no aid, for it contains within itself capacity to provide for all needs. All it asks is a free field—the removal of restrictions which limit its scope and deny it full exercise. And as it finds these restrictions in legislative sanction given to privileges, in chartered rights bestowed upon some, it demands their abrogation.

It claims for co-operation of freemen ability to discharge any social function, and as production and exchange are the principal directions in which modern activity manifests itself it imperatively demands as means of industrial emancipation that neither shall be endowed with privilege, that the source of production and the means of exchange cannot be subject to letters patent.

With freedom of access to land, to hold for occupancy and use, resting upon this common title, common needs will draw occupants and users to co-operate to secure what is beyond the power of the individual to obtain. The common title would produce independence, mutual reliance and organization, and precisely as privilege was eliminated fraternity of spirit and common aims would naturally arise. Co-operation would not have to be invented, it would be evolved; common needs would require common efforts, and whenever union would present benefits unattainable to divided efforts that moment steps toward co-operative unity would be taken.

But freedom of land is not enough. Capital, clad in the legalized armor of monopoly, holding in its power the medium of exchange and thus imposing a tax upon its use as a means to further production, can well afford to laugh at the puny effort to co-operate and make it also tributary to its gains. Again anarchism says to secure perfect co-operation there must be freedom in financial as well as in other matters. The privilege bestowed upon gold, by bestowing upon it as if by divine right a royal crown over other products of labor, has made it the despot of exchange. Anarchy declares that it has no natural right to the exclusive discharge of this social function over any or all other products; that so far from facilitating exchange it fastens upon industry the clog of interest, causing all other wealth to pay tribute to it and at the same time regulating values by a speculative standard. Anarchy asserts that in the overthrow of this old superstition, exploded everywhere else save in financial matters, men will be thrown upon their own resources to organize mutual credit; that in co-operaton a medium of exchange can be issued based upon any and all forms of wealth as security, and that in this ability to capitalize products for purposes of production of increased wealth there will be no monopoly to command interest for use. Anarchy, therefore, sees in emancipation from the monopoly of land and credit the opportunity for complete and perfect co-operation. Not a governmental scheme by which our functions are prescribed but a free alliance to achieve common ends; not necessarily a unity in one national association, but co-operation for local or national ends, just as the need arises, confident that under equal opportunities that which best discharges its social function will best commend itself for support.

The great trouble is that we have so long been nursed that we are not yet fully aware of our own capacities. So much have we been dominated by the state that we have not encouraged self-reliance. If, however, freedom is preferable to restrictions co-operation can only be secured by the joint efforts of free individuals, and just so far as the social units are emancipated from restriction so far will society reflect that liberty; just so far as the individuals are happy, prosperous, and moral, so far only will society be happy, prosperous, and moral. Social virtues are results, not causes.

Liberty, therefore, is the basis upon which true co-operation rests. To remove the shackles from individual activity in order that co-operative activity may have natural genesis is the mission of anarchy. It looks to the state only to abolish privilege; it looks to the freeman for the co-operative unit. It lays its foundation at the bottom, rather than beginning at the top to build downward.

In co-operation it sees that which will supplant the state, which will open avenues to every faculty, provide supply for every demand, and furnish to all the fullest and freest scope for the development of individuality, without the necessity of pleading a "baby act" to invoke guidance or desire to compel others to follow our co-operative lead and example.

CHAPTER VII.

ANARCHY.

[From C. L. James' "Tract for the Times."]

Anarchy, from the Greek *a* or *an* (not) and *arche* (the first, the chief) or *archon* (a magistrate), means that state of society in which there is no government. It is, therefore, very improperly applied to that state in which there are two or more governments contending for the supremacy. What anarchists desire is the permanent abolition of all government. It is contended, and is doubtless true, that this would involve the abolition of all property, understanding by property, not the mere right of using or possessing anything (which is inseparable from man's life on earth), but the right to keep anything, even without using it, and to impose a tax on whoever does use it, which is derived from government and law, and not from nature. Hence anarchists are often called, though I think tautologically, anarchistic socialists, or anarchist-communists.

* * * * *

By the State socialists, it is proposed that the government should assume the regulation of all industries, becoming the sole capitalist and landlord, employing the *proletariate*, or actual laborers, with a view to their own benefit. Now, since State socialism is the natural end of democracy or *ochlocracy*, and since modern governments (the result of an alliance between the serfs and the *bourgeois* against the feudal nobility) are, in the main, domocratic, it need not surprise us to find that our economic system is, to a great extent, State socialistic, as has been said. The post office, the tariff, the laws about child labor and female labor, the regulation of savings banks and other loan offices, the State ownership of the railroads, telegraphs, etc., which exist in so many countries, are evidently arrangements of this type. And when we hear it proposed with applause that the government shall take possession of the land it is evident how popular this remedy for prevailing wrongs is becoming in America. We often hear it pronounced impracticable. But the remark needs qualification. Impracticable for good, it may, I fear, be a "coming slavery" much too feasible for ill. Surely the State socialists forget to give us their reasons for thinking that the government would make a better landlord or capitalist than any other. It cannot, surely, be the manner in which governments originate that makes them think so; nor the simplicity of governmental machinery and the directness of its methods; and if it is the character of the individuals composing the administration, they must estimate the wisdom and virtue of professional politicians at a figure which argues very little actual acquaintance with this class of our fellow citizens. The truth is that their faith in government is a superstition, our inheritance from days when kings were gods. The remarks of Lord Macauley on this point always seemed to me extremely pertinent. "It scarcely ever happens that any private man or body of men will invest property in a canal, a tunnel or a bridge, but from an expectation that the outlay will be profitable to them. No work of this sort can be profitable to private speculators unless the public be willing to pay for the use of it. The public will not pay of their own accord for what yields no profit or convenience to them. There is thus a direct and obvious connection between the motive which induces individuals to undertake such a work, and the utility of the work. Can we find any such connection in the case of a public work executed by a government? If it is useful, are the individuals who rule the country richer? If it is useless, are they poorer? A public man may be solicitous about his credit. But * * * the fame of public works is a much less certain test of their utility than the amount of toll collected at them. In a corrupt age, there will be direct embezzlement. In the purest age, there will be abundance of jobbing. * * * * In a bad age, the fate of the public is to be robbed outright. In a good age, it is merely to have the dearest and worst of everything. * * We firmly believe that five hundred thousand pounds subscribed by individuals for railroads or canals would produce more advantage to the public than five millions voted by parliament for the same purpose. There are certain old saws about the master's eye and everybody's business in which we place very great faith." These observations are fully borne out by the actual result of State socialistic experiments. In Russia, the land still belongs to the village, and is annually divided among the people by an elective magistrate. And Russia is the only country left in Europe which is periodically scourged by famine. In France, after the revolution of 1848, the government set up workshops known as *ateliers,* which failed to pay their expenses. In our own country, examples crowd on the memory like shrieking ghosts. The post office, in the more settled portions of America, is only protected against the competition of individuals by penal laws. In the wilder portions, it produces more frauds than any other part of our public institutions, which is saying a great deal. In all, it is the well-known sanctuary of office brokerage and corruption. With the best patronized system of schools in the world, we have, for all the purposes of education, very nearly the worst. The protective tariff, having destroyed our most thriving industries, such as that of shipbuilding, has reduced the laborers in all others to "starvation wages," as we are every day informed. The subsidies and lands granted by the government of the nation, states and towns, to railroad and other corporations, have reduced the agricultural class to a condition not materially different from that of the serfs in the middle ages. From experience of the State socialistic tendency on a small scale, we may infer how it would work upon a great. It would at once create a swarming army of officeholders, that is, so many more non-producers, for the rest of us to support. It would create a corresponding multitude of office-seekers, as if we had not far too many of them already. It would entail on all branches of business and trade the slowness, clumsiness, inefficiency and corruption which always characterize officialism. It would reduce the standard of labor to the capacity of the least intelligent, industrious and successful workman. It would either require a system of impressed labor, like that of the Egyptian fellahs, or convert a large portion of the people into State-supported paupers, desiring only "bread and shows." It would paralyze invention, progress and improvement. It would discourage manufactures, continence and luxury, and promote overpopulation with that slovenly kind of agriculture in which each family lives on the produce of its own garden patch. Of course, famines would be frequent. And finally, we should *not* all be equal, even in our misery. The new officeholding aristocracy would find means to feather their nests after all. The *pons asinorum* of the subject is that people do not take the trouble to govern for nothing, nor for the meager wages of republican legislators. Ambition, the love of power, is what calls government into being; in other words, under no form of government can the people really be the masters. That the evil consequences of State socialism, predicted here, as they are also by the *bourgeois* economists, would *not* follow from anarchistic socialism, will be demonstrated in due course.

I am ready now to maintain my thesis—that government can be abolished, and that there is no necessity for it to be restored. That it can be abolished is perhaps too readily admitted by most people. We hear the assertion continually repeated that it has been overthrown and restored many times; but the truth is that government in general never was overthrown since it was first established. A government has frequently been overthrown, but always by some hostile, foreign or revolutionary government; and a struggle of two or more rival governments, such as sometimes followed, is not anarchy, though it has often been so incorrectly called by historians and publicists. To appreciate the feasibility of abolishing government, we must consider the social changes which have taken place since it was instituted. All government rests, as we have said, on armed force, and all governments originated among savages, except those of new countries, like America, which were imported by the colonists. Now savages have certain propensities predisposing them to establish government, which civilized men have not, at least, in the same degree. They are very warlike, often living on human flesh, by the slave trade or by pillage; while, as wealth increases, war becomes increasingly inconvenient and undesirable. They are very patriotic after a narrow fashion, devoted to the tribe, eager to revenge a family or national wrong, and destitute of any sense of duty toward foreigners. They have an idolatrous reverence both for the personal qualities of a ruler and for all kinds of precedent, custom and authority. The evolutionary philosopher will see in these traits the instincts of a gregarious and imitative animal, which loses power as man becomes a rational and commercial animal, an individualist toward his relations and neighbors; among strangers, a citizen of the world. Accordingly, with the progress of civilization, the sphere of government and the reverence for its authority tend to spontaneously contract. It is true, as a writer in the *Encyclopædia Britannica* has recently pointed out, that the mere number of laws of the State socialistic type, by which modern governments encroach on individual freedom, has, of late, materially increased. But the magnitude of those relations which governments, as a rule, have, at least partially, ceased to regulate, such as religion, contract, foreign trade, speech, literature, bequest, marriage, far exceeds that of their encroachments. And, besides, the State socialistic arrangements of modern times are, at least ostensibly, in the interest of freedom. They are quack remedies for *bourgeois* tyranny. It by no means follows, therefore, that government, if abolished now, would be reproduced, because savages, who were without it, instituted it. The argument is a familiar fallacy; a case of undistributed middle. A somewhat similar criticism applies to the argument from the restoration of government after the quasi-anarchistic revolutions of modern times. If such events prove anything, they prove, not only that some sort of government, but much the same kind which previously existed, must be restored. But it was the *bourgeois* class which, in every case, effected the restoration. Nothing, therefore, can be inferred as to what will happen when the reign of the *bourgeois* terminates, either by its inherent tendencies to decay or by a forcible revolution. The reign of the *bourgeois* rests, as we have said, on gunpowder. It cannot survive the use by the proletariate of a weapon requiring no capital, and against which gunpowder would be as impotent as armor and castles against gunpowder. Such a weapon is dynamite, using that word by a synecdoche to denote all the cheap and rapid agents of destruction described in Herr Most's now famous pamphlet. In a war with such weapons, the rich man's capital, instead of his tower of strength, would be his vulnerable point. And the same machinery of destruction is destined to remove the prime reason for the existence of government by putting an end to international wars. That war, which has become much less deadly since the invention of long-range weapons, will cease when the weapons become too deadly to let sane combatants get together at all, is a commonplace; though, like the others which we have cited, it is applied only by anarchists.

Thus we come to our last thesis, that after the abolition of government, crime, instead of increasing, will be more promptly, humanely and inexorably dealt with than at present; to which we may add that all the social functions, as if relieved of an incubus, will work at increased pressure and with the energy of a new life. There are almost innumerable illustrations of the truth that repression has no tendency to prevent crime, but that freedom has; that liberty, as Proudhon said, is not the daughter, but the mother of order.

* * * * *

Anarchy, being universal liberty, would exercise on the human faculties an effect the reverse of that general paralysis induced by State socialism, which is universal restraint and regulation. Its practical effect, if it were peaceably, or even forcibly, established to-morrow, would be about as follows: The useless class would at once be driven to work, and the free land would give them abundant opportunities. The farmer, relieved from his mortgages and taxes, would call on the country merchant for some unaccustomed luxury, as a meerschaum pipe. The answer, at first, would probably be, "We have none. Since law has been abolished, we are afraid of our lives and our property." But the farmer insists, and the merchant at last succeeds in finding a meerschaum, which he exchanges for the farmer's produce. Within four-and-twenty hours a score of other farmers come in inquiring for similar luxuries. The merchant writes to his wholesale house, to report that trade is sensibly reviving. He gets about the same answer which he gave the farmer. "Since law is abolished, we are afraid to import." But, in a few days, similar communications come in from all parts of the country. The wholesale house determines to engage an importing agent; and business resumes with double its accustomed energy. Rent, which seems so great an evil to Mr. George, would be no evil if only actual cultivators received it. Of course, those engaged in trade and transportation could expect no profit beyond the wages of superintendence. *But their success to getting that, would depend absolutely upon the value of their services to the public; while, at present, the profits of the capitalist depend, too commonly, not on the value of his work, but on its noxiousness*—that is, on his skill in making a "corner," manipulating a legislature, procuring a prohibitory tariff, or in some other way hindering, instead of facilitating production and trade. The hours of labor would be reduced to two or three a day. Increased consumption might raise them, but new machinery would cut them down again. Anarchy, to be short, is but the *laissez faire* of the economists, pushed to its logical result. It requires no one to work who would rather be idle. It forbids no man to hoard who wants to—if he can stand guard over his own treasure, or get some one else at his own cost, to do so for him. It forbids no one to worship the Virgin—or Mumbo Jumbo, if he likes it better. If one man chooses to get a fine house, while another is content with beer enough and a lodging in a cellar, the anarchist is willing that one man should have his house, and the other his beer. Anarchy allows every one to assume authority so far as others are willing to accept it. Anarchy does not even forbid any one to be a *slave* who likes provided his slavery lasts only as long as both slave and master are content. Similarly, it is willing that men and women should contract to live together, for a year, a day, a month, an hour, or as they can agree, *provided* each expects to take the natural consequences of his or her own wisdom or folly, relieved only by such voluntary compassion as he or she can excite among the more experienced. It has faith enough in women to believe that their absolute freedom would destroy prostitution. It would also remove all the evils which attend on marriage. The Malthusian dilemma would solve itself. We have heard of free trade, free religion, free rum, free love. *Anarchy is free everything*. It leaves free to commit even arson or murder, those who choose to run the risk of being lynched, or confined as dangerous lunatics. It sees that competition, if really free, might do as much good as it does harm. *It antagonizes no natural instinct*. Like other systems of philosophy, it recognizes this truth, that all natural instincts have a normal limit—benevolence and ideality just as much as alimentiveness and destructiveness—but it also sees that natural selection reduces them all to this limit; and that with this benificent process arbitrary regulation can only interfere; albeit natural selection finally governs after all. Anarchy is Liberty; Liberty is Justice; Justice is Virtue. And it is not the nature of Virtue to hurt any one. "Length of days are in her right hand, and in her left riches and honor; her ways are the ways of pleasantness, and all her paths are PEACE."

CHAPTER VIII.

THE SOCIAL REVOLUTION.

"The theory of politics, which has possessed the minds of men, and which they have expressed the best they could in their laws and their resolutions, consider persons and property as the two objects for whose protection government exists. Of persons, all have equal rights, in virtue of being identical in nature. This interest, of course, with its whole power demands a democracy. Whilst the rights of all as persons are equal, in virtue of their access to reason, their rights in property are very unequal. One man owns his clothes, and another owns country. This accident, depending primarily on the skill and virtue of the parties, of which there is every degree, and, secondarily, on patrimony falls unequally, and its rights, of course, are unequal. Personal rights, universally the same, demand a government framed on the ratio of the census: property demands a government framed on the ratio of owners and the owning. * * *·

"Every actual State is corrupt. Good men must not obey the laws too well. What satire on government can *equal* the severity of censure conveyed in the word *politic*, which now for ages has signified *cunning*, intimating that the State is a trick?—*Ralph Waldo Emerson*.

"The achievements of liberty are the epochs of history. Villanage, serfdom, and chattel slavery—the past system of labor have forever disappeared. The laborers of the civilized world have gained the right to starve." The existing wage-system though it began to supersede other labor systems in the fifteenth century has by the recent discovery of steam and electricity applied to machinery been developed enormously. Production *en masse* has supplanted the feeble powers of hand labor until the powers of production *and distribution* have increased during the past decade a thousand fold. But the poverty of the producers remains not only unchanged but intensified. Millions of human beings die yearly of cold, hunger or exposure. The workers are forced to subsist upon their wages, and when unable to procure employment become objects of capitalist charity. Therein the wage-system differs from those systems which preceded it. Villanage, serfage, and chattel slavery secured the laborer his daily bread. The master class were impelled by pecuniary interest to provide for the existence of their laborers. The person of the laborer was held as property and his sickness or death entailed a pecuniary loss upon the owner. Hence, as property they were cared for, provided for not by themselves, but by their owners. The wage-system changed the relationship by making the laborer a "free" man, dependent upon his wage for subsistence. It also forced him to compete with his fellow-laborer for the chance to earn wages—a competition that constantly tended to reduce wages to a bare subsistence. The competition among the capitalist class—employers—for control of markets also tended constantly to reduce wages to the subsistence point. Out of this double competition,—from above and below—arose the combinations, pools, trusts, syndicates etc, of capital which has for its object first,—control of markets by regulating prices, and secondly protection against demands of laborers for better pay and shorter hours. So likewise, the laborers formed combinations, unions, etc., their object being to dull the edge of competition among themselves for opportunities to work and earn wages, and secondly to check the demands of employers for large profits through reduced wages and increased working hours. On these lines the capital and labor conflict is always waged sometimes openly, at other times covertly, but never ceasing. These antagonisms, inherent to the wage system creates the class struggle, and throws race in conflict with race, and nations are by their necessities driven to retard the progress of their fellows. Each machine, each device added to the processes of production and distribution to simplify its methods or increase its power only serves to intensify the class struggle by sharpening competition. Monopoly, the first of competition, is the triumph on the economic battle-field of the best armed, equipped and officered army. The workers of the whole world constitute the rank and file, and the captains of industry reap the honors and rewards. The wage-system has now reached that development where vast numbers of homeless outcasts in every country, (estimated in the United States alone at more than a million persons) are driven to steal, beg or starve.

Under the pressure of enforced poverty, the workers engage in strikes, boycotts and riots. But the vast herd of the proletariat being unorganized, suffer on, mutely, patiently. The bourgeois (capitalist) class are compelled to employ force to suppress the demands of the laborers for work, or better pay, etc. Thus to-day, in every civilized country, the wage-system is propped and maintained by bayonets. Never before in the world's history was society divided into classes upon the question of economic freedom. The contentions of the past arose out of interest affecting the ruling class alone, such as foreign or civil war, forms of government, religious worship, etc. But, now, there is the one question—economic liberty—arraying upon one side the privileged class and their hired retainers, while upon the other side gathers the countless host of the disinherited—the wage-workers.

The labor question, growing out of the wage-system of labor is, therefore, a social, not a political or local or national question, but international and affecting the whole human race.

The capitalist or wage-system cannot provide for or take care of the mendicants it creates. Having reached its full growth, that is to say, having concentrated all the means of existence into the hands of a few who monopolize the wealth created by all, it stands as a barrier across the pathway of progress and liberty. It cannot be made to serve or minister to the wants and aspirations of the people. Its tension is now drawn taut and will snap in twain. Buttressed, walled and cemented with law—statute law—and government; with organized armies of armed officials; with prisons and poor-houses innumerable it defies the people, and dares them to touch any of its vested rights. The hostile attitude of the classes, the growing distrust of the people toward their rulers, the contempt of the rulers for the people, is the characteristic of society in every country to-day. The capitalist system is the essence of force, coercion, authority. No amelioration, no lightening of the people's burden is possible under it. For the peoples'—the workers,—complaints it has but one answer—obey! The capitalist system therefore will inevitably, irresistibly drive the people into revolt as the last and only recourse to relief from oppression. The people will then trample the law under foot, they will destroy government. Coercive control will cease and anarchy—the right to voluntarily associate—prevail.

Some circumstance, apparently accidental, will precipitate the social revolt of the people. The miseries which they had endured by reason of enforced poverty will compel them to give heed to the necessities of their existence, their primary needs and immediate wants, and as the social revolution will have been forced upon them by the fact that they could not attain their natural development in the form of society which they overthrew in order to make room for liberty and the rights of man, their first act will, of necessity, be the application of communistic principles. They will expropriate all wealth; they will take possession of all foundries, workshops, factories, mines, etc., for in no other way could they be able to continue to produce what they require on a basis of equality, and be, at the same time, independent of any authority. The great warehouses and stores and granaries, filled with what their labor had produced, with their enormous quantities of food, clothing, etc., for man's nourishment and protection, will be made to minister freely to the wants of all. So likewise, the laborers of the agricultural regions, exploited by landlords and despoiled by money-lenders, will, in their turn, take possession of the soil which they till, but from which they did not enjoy the fruits of their toil. Thus there will be no fear for the morrow and every man will sit beneath his vine and fig tree, with none to molest or make him afraid. A new race of men and women will be evolved from the new civilization, whose progress and advancement, now no longer weighed down with the sorrows and cares of poverty, will bound forward into the light of intelligence, the happiness of peace, and the manhood of Liberty, Fraternity, Equality.

Anarchy means without rulers, governors, dictators. Anarchy is the negation of force, of coercion, of authority. Nevertheless, there is a studied and persistent effort made by those who are interested in perpetuating society as it is, and who assume to mold or lead public opinion, to impress the uninformed with the idea that anarchy means force, chaos, disorder. But the readers of these pages will have their minds disabused of any such error. Anarchy is the opposite of the present disorder called " law and order "—the reverse of legality and its offspring, privilege. The revolutionists of the coming time are not therefore necessarily anarchists. Far from it. The great mass of humanity who engage in the revolt against the present social system do not know of or understand the philosophy or science of anarchism. The revolting masses will act from impulse, resentment and fear, unconscious of the final result. The transition, revolutionary period, separating the old from the new society, will doubtless be a scene of overwhelming disorder, war, brute force, carnage and destruction. The social revolt will cease when the wage system is overthrown, and anarchism will begin only when the revolution ends—when peace, based on liberty, prevails. This is anarchism. Anarchy is therefore a state of society at peace with itself and all the world.

APPENDIX.

APPENDIX.

The Philosophy of Anarchism.

It will be comprehended by the thoughtful reader, who has perused these pages thus far, that the popular conception of anarchism is a mistaken one. An insane anger against personal tyrants, and a vague desire to destroy and kill, are not the characteristics of the philosophy known as anarchy, as a majority of the people up to this time have been led to believe.

The philosophy of anarchism is included in the one word "Liberty;" yet it is comprehensive enough to include all things else. No barriers whatever to human progression, to thought, or investigation, are placed by anarchism; nothing is considered so true or so certain, that future discoveries may not prove it false; therefore, it has but one infallible, unchangeable motto, "Freedom." Freedom to discover any truth, freedom to develop, to live naturally and fully. Other schools of thought are composed of crystallized ideas—principles that are caught and impaled between the planks of long platforms, and considered too sacred to be disturbed by a close investigation. In all other "issues" there is always a limit; some imaginary line beyond which the searching mind dare not penetrate, lest some pet idea melt into a myth. Science has been merciless and without reverence, because it is compelled to be: the discoveries and conclusions of one day are exploded by the discoveries and conclusions of the next. But anarchism is the usher of science—the master of ceremonies to all forms of truth. It would remove all barriers between the human being and natural development. From the natural resources of the earth, all artificial restrictions, that the body might be nurtured, and from universal truth, all bars of prejudice and superstition, that the mind may develop harmoniously.

It is then the complete opposite of ideas of force and violence. Force, in invading the rights of individuals, is entirely repudiated; legalized, national force as well as the irresponsible force of the individual. "How then," perhaps the inquirer, even at this stage, may ask, "do you reconcile your advocacy of a violent revolution with so peaceful a philosophy?"

That force will be used in the coming change, whether we advocate it or not, is quite evident to students of history; that there is a reconcilable reason for our advising people to be ready for it, is shown in the constant use of force that is necessary to maintain the present so-called "order," but actual disorder. Every institution which now works injustice to human kind is possible only through the violence or threats of violence that are continually exerted. Well-filled armories and well-drilled regiments are the pillars of class rule, and monopoly rests on the strength of courts and constabulary.

Force (legalized) invades the personal liberty of man, seizes upon the natural elements, and intervenes between man and natural laws; from this exercise of force through governments flows nearly all the misery, poverty, crime and confusion existing in society. So, we perceive, there are actual, material barriers blockading the way. These must be removed. If we could hope they would melt away, or be voted or prayed into nothingness, we would be content to wait and vote and pray. But they are like great frowning rocks towering between us and a land of freedom, while the dark chasms of a hard-fought past yawn behind us. Crumbling they may be with their own weight and the decay of time, but to quietly stand under till they fall is to be buried in the crash. There is something to be done in a case like this —the rocks must be removed. Passivity while slavery is stealing over us is criminal. For the moment we must forget that we are anarchists—when the work is accomplished we may forget we were revolutionists.

And what of the glowing beyond that is so bright that the Gradgrinds say it is a dream? It is no dream, it is the real, stripped of brain-distortions materialized into thrones and scaffolds, mitres and guns. It is nature acting on her own interior laws as in all her other associations. It is a return to first principles; for were not the land, the water, the light all free before governments took shape and form? In this free state we will again forget to think of these things as "property." It is real, for we, as a race, are growing up to it. The idea of less restriction and more liberty, and a confiding trust that nature is equal to her work, is permeating all modern thought. From the dark years—not so long by—when it was generally believed that man's soul was totally depraved and every human impulse bad; when every action, every thought, and every emotion was controlled and restricted; when the human frame, diseased, was bled, dosed, suffocated and kept as far from nature's remedies as possible; when the mind was seized upon and distorted before it had time to evolve a natural thought—from those days to these latter years the progress of this idea has been swift and steady. It is becoming more and more apparent that in every way we are "governed best where we are governed least."

Still unsatisfied perhaps, the inquirer seeks for details, for ways and means, and whys and wherefores. How will we go on like human beings eating and sleeping, working and loving, exchanging and dealing, without government. So used have we become to "organized authority" in every department of life that ordinarily we cannot conceive of the most common-place avocations being carried on without their interference and "protection." But anarchism is not therefore compelled to outline a complete organization of a free society. To do so with any assumption of authority would be to place another barrier in the way of coming generations. The best thought of to-day may become the useless vagary of to-morrow, and to crystallize it into a creed is to make it an unwieldy obstacle as well. Still we may prophesy and conjecture, and while we believe no great principle is compromised if we say "let the coming freemen take care of themselves," we may judge from our present knowledge of human characteristics and the action of natural law something of what future societary arrangements will be. "We can judge of the future only by the past." We can believe it is only necessary to remove the barriers, to abolish the powers that force man into unnatural channels, to recognize no "organized authority," and believe that new systems will spring spontaneously from the spirit of the times, and the conditions surrounding the social units—yet we may have logical conceptions of societary arrangements, and the wisdom to give them to inquirers.

We judge from experience that man is a gregarious animal, and instinctively affiliates with his kind—co-operates, unites in groups, works to better advantage, combined with his fellow workmen than when alone. This would point to the formation of co-operative communities, of which our present trades-unions are embryonic patterns. Each branch of industry will no doubt have its own organization, regulations, leaders, etc.; it will institute methods of direct communication with every member of that industrial branch in the world, and establish equitable relations with all other branches. There would probably be conventions of industry which delegates would attend, and where they would transact such business as was necessary, adjourn and from that moment be delegates no longer, but simply members of a group. To remain permanent members of a continuous congress would be to establish a power that is certain sooner or later to be abused.

No great central power, like a congress consisting of men who know nothing of their constituents' trades, interests, rights or duties, would be over the various organizations or groups; nor would they employ sheriffs, policemen, courts or jailors to enforce the conclusions arrived at while in session. The members of groups might profit by the knowledge gained through mutual interchange of thought afforded by conventions if they choose, but they will not be compelled to do so by any outside force.

Vested rights, privileges, charters, title deeds, upheld by all the paraphernalia of government—the visible symbol of power—such as prisons, scaffolds and armies will have no existence. There can be no privileges bought or sold, and the transaction kept sacred at the point of the bayonet. Every man will stand on an equal footing with his brother in the race of life, and neither chains of economic thralldom nor mental drags of superstition shall handicap the one to the advantage of the other.

Property will lose a certain attribute which sanctifies it now. The absolute ownership of it—"the right to use or abuse" will be abolished—and possession, use, will be the only title. It will be seen how impossible it would be for one person to "own" a million acres of land, without a title deed backed by a government ready to protect that title at all hazards, even to the loss of thousands of lives. He could not use the million acres himself, nor could he wrest from its depths the possible resources it contains. The accidental discovery of a coal field or a gas well could not as now make one man enormously rich in a moment, the arbiter and master of several hundred lives, who, robbed of their own rightful inheritance, are entirely dependent on the will of the lucky man. There will be no law, of course, to prevent his hiring men to work for him, but as every man will have an equal chance at mother earth, the probabilities are that they will have too much business of their own to be hired.

The division of labor now developing in the field of production already illustrates the benefits of co-operative efforts, and it is quite evident that future production will be carried on in this line. Communities and groups will form, and in the interests of those concerned will make their regulations. All organization will be voluntary, with the sacred right forever reserved to each individual "to think and to rebel." "But this will create chaos and eternal confusion!" the objector will say. Why should it? It has been seen even under present systems that liberty of action is a great civilizer. One learns by observation that it is not the restraints thrown around the individual by laws and religious creeds, that make him "good." Often the removal of these very restrictions renders him surprisingly manful and upright, feeling that he is not *forced* into a path he would tread naturally, if let alone. It was thought not long ago by nearly all, that to destroy the belief in an everlasting hell would be to break the bonds which held in check millions of wicked people ready to plunge into every species of evil, like a torrent raging onward to its own destruction. There is a benighted old journal still existing in these latter days which teaches that "hell and the scaffold are the civilizers of the people." The dear good old lady with one of the kindest hearts in the world, who said, "If I didn't believe in the everlasting punishment of eternal fires, I would do all sorts of wicked things, steal, lie, murder, dissipate," should become its editor.

The belief in a literal place of torment has nearly melted away; and instead of the direful results predicted, we have a higher and truer standard of manhood and womanhood. People do not care to go to the bad when they find they can as well as not. Individuals are unconscious of their own motives in doing good. While acting out their natures according to their surroundings and conditions, they still believe they are being kept in the right path by some outside power, some restraint thrown around them by church or state. So the objector believes that with the right to rebel and secede sacred to him, he would forever *be* rebelling and seceding, thereby creating constant confusion and turmoil. Is it probable that he would, merely for the reason that he *could* do so? Men are to a great extent creatures of habit, and grow to love associations; under reasonably good conditions, he would remain where he commences; and if he did not, who has any natural right to force him into relations distasteful to him? Under the present order of affairs, persons do unite with societies and remain good, disinterested members for life where the right to retire is always conceded. The final outcome, many disciples of anarchism believe will be communism—the common possession of the resources of life and the productions of united labor. No anarchist is compromised by this statement, who does not reason out the future outlook in this way; the many of us who do, are responsible only for our own opinions on the subject.

Many expedients will be tried by which a just return may be awarded the worker for his exertions. The time check or labor certificate, which will be honored at the store-houses hour for hour, will no doubt have its day. But the elaborate and complicated system of bookkeeping this would necessitate, the impossibility of balancing one man's hour against another's with accuracy, and the difficulty in determining how much more one man owed to natural resources, conditions, and the studies and achievements of past generations, than did another, would, we believe, prevent this system from obtaining a thorough and permanent establishment. The mutual banking system outlined by W. B. Greene may be in operation in the future free society. Another system, more simple, to the writer appears the most acceptable and likely to prevail, Members of the groups will carry cards, showing their standing in their respective societies, and if honest producers, they will be honored in any other group they may visit, and given whatever is necessary to their welfare and comfort.

But, after all, as we grow more enlightened under this "larger liberty," we will grow to care less and less for that exact distribution of material wealth, which, in our greed-nurtured senses, seems *now* so impossible to think upon carelessly. The men and women of loftier intellects, in the present, think not so much of the riches to be gained by their efforts as of the good they can do. There is an innate spring of healthy action in every human being who has not been crushed and pinched by poverty and drudgery from before his birth, that impels him onward and upward. He cannot be idle, if he would; it is as natural for him to develop, expand, and use the powers within him when not repressed, as it is for the rose to bloom in the sunlight and fling its fragrance on the passing breeze. The grandest works of the past were never performed for the sake of money. Who can measure the worth of a Shakespeare, an Angelo or Beethoven in dollars and cents? Agassiz said "he had no time to make money," there were higher and better objects in life than that. And so will it be when humanity is once relieved from the pressing fear of starvation, want, and slavery, it will be concerned, less and less, about the ownership of vast accumulations of wealth. Such possessions would be but an annoyance and trouble. When two or three or four hours a day of easy, of healthful labor will produce all the comforts and luxuries one can use, and the opportunity to labor is never denied, people will become indifferent as to who owns the wealth they do not need. Wealth will be below par, and it will be found that men and women will not accept it for pay, or be bribed by it to do what they would not willingly and naturally do without it. Some higher incentive must, and will, supersede the greed for gold. The involuntary aspiration born in man to make the most of one's self, to be loved and appreciated by one's fellow-beings, to "make the world better for having lived in it," will urge him on to nobler deeds than ever the sordid and selfish incentive of material gain has done.

If, in the present chaotic and shameful struggle for existence, when organized society offers a premium on greed, cruelty, and deceit, men can be found who stand aloof and almost alone in their determination to work for good rather than gold, who suffer want and persecution rather than desert principle, who can bravely walk to the scaffold for the good they can do humanity, what may we expect from men when freed from the grinding *necessity* of selling the better part of themselves for bread? The terrible conditions under which labor is performed, the awful alternative if one does not prostitute talent and morals in the service of mammon; the power acquired with the wealth obtained by ever so unjust means, combine to make the conception of free and voluntary labor almost an impossible one. And yet, there are examples of this principle even now. In a well-bred family each person has certain duties, which are performed cheerfully, and are not measured out and paid for according to some pre-determined standard; when the united members sit down to the well-filled table, they do not scramble to get the most, while the weakest do without, or gather greedily around them more food than they could possibly consume. Each patiently and politely awaits his turn to be served, and leaves what he does not want; he is certain that when again hungry plenty of good food will be provided.

Again, the utter impossibility of awarding to each an exact return for the amount of labor performed will render absolute communism a necessity sooner or later. The land and all it contains, without which labor cannot be exerted, belong to no one man, but to all alike. The inventions and discoveries of the past are the common inheritance of the coming generations; and when a man takes the tree that nature furnished free, and fashions it into a useful article, or a machine perfected and bequeathed to him by many past and succeeding generations, who is to determine what proportion is his and his alone? Primitive man would have been a week fashioning a rude resemblance to the article with his clumsy tools, where the modern worker has occupied an hour. The finished article is of far more real value than the rude one made long ago, and yet the primitive man toiled the longest and hardest. Who can determine with exact justice what is each one's due?

There must come a time when we will cease trying. The earth is so bountiful, so generous; man's brain is so active, his hands so restless, that wealth will spring like magic, ready for the use of the world's inhabitants. We will become as much ashamed to quarrel over its possession as we are now to squabble over the food spread before us on a loaded table.

"But all this," the objector urges, "is very beautiful in the far-off future, when we become angels. It would not do now to abolish governments and legal restraints; people are not prepared for it."

This is a question. We have seen, in reading history, that wherever an old-time restriction has been removed the people have *not* abused their newer liberty. Once it was considered necessary to compel men to save their souls, with the aid of governmental scaffolds, racks and stakes. Until the foundation of the present republic, it was considered absolutely essential that governments should second the efforts of the church in forcing people to attend the means of grace; and yet it is found that the standard of morals among the masses is raised since they are left free to pray as they see fit, or not at all, if they prefer it. It was believed the chattel slaves would not work if the overseer and whip were removed; they are so much more a source of profit now that ex-slave owners would not return to the old system if they could.

So many of the able writers quoted in this book have shown that the unjust institutions which work so much misery and suffering to the masses have their root in governments, and owe their whole existence to the power derived from government, we cannot help but believe that were every law, every title deed, every court, and every police officer or soldier abolished to-morrow with one sweep, the people would be better off than now. The actual, material things that man needs would still exist; his strength and skill would remain and his instinctive social inclinations retain their force. Freed from the systems that made him wretched before, he is not likely to make himself more wretched for lack of them. Much more is contained in the thought that conditions make man what he is, and not the laws and penalties made for his guidance, than is supposed by careless observation. We have laws, jails, courts, armies, guns and armories enough to make saints of us all, if *they* were the true preventives of crime; but we know they do not prevent crime; that wickedness and depravity exist in spite of them, nay, increase as the struggle between classes grows fiercer, wealth greater and more powerful, and poverty more gaunt and desperate. As an illustration of this truth, notice the statistics of Warden McClaughrey, given before the Union League Club of Chicago, a club consisting of millionaires. He stated that 500,000 criminals in the United States, according to the best obtainable statistics, *are under 21 years of age!*

What an army of outcasts! Does any one believe that these young persons deserted peaceful and virtuous walks of life, blessed with love, home and friends, voluntarily? Or, were they not crowded to the prison doors by the wretched surroundings the present civilization forces upon them? Prisons the guardians of the people's morals? The above showing damns forever this idea!

Have we not good reason to believe that the entire abolition of a centralized power, with all its facilities for granting privileges, for protecting monopolies and aiding robbers in stealing the people's inheritance, would result in great good to humanity, bad as it is become through long ages of injustice?

Oh, Liberty! No wonder the vision of thy realization is too bright to be deemed more than a fleeting dream! The weary toiler who now never thinks of rest, dare not look upon the picture, the sensuous idler scorns it. But how possible after all! Nature has denied us not one element towards its realization—man himself lacks not one faculty towards its appreciation and enjoyment. To know that little children will no more drudge and wither away in factories and mines; that women will not slowly coin their heart's blood over their needle, while starvation eternally stares in at the door, that strong men will not waste their lives in abject slavery or unwilling vagabondage, and that constant fear of cold and hunger and homelessness that so petrifies and stupifies the heart and soul will be banished forever; that women will be freed from the black clinging trail of the serpent winding through all ages, the selling of herself for bread or splendor; that genius will, no longer crushed in the narrow, suffering limits of neglect and poverty, rise to heights unknown before---is it not worth working, living and dying for? Ah, no, friends, anarchy is not buried---it is *not dead*. * * *

A. R. Parsons' Appeal to the People of America.

Fellow Citizens: As all the world knows, I have been convicted and sentenced to die for the crime of murder, the most heinous offense that can be committed. Under the forms of law, two courts, viz., the criminal and supreme courts of the State of Illinois, have sentenced me to death as an accessory before the fact, to the murder of officer Degan on May 4, 1886. Nevertheless I am innocent of the crime charged, and to a candid and unprejudiced world I submit the proof.

In the decision affirming the sentence of death upon me, the supreme court of the State of Illinois says: "It is undisputed that the bomb was thrown that caused the death of Degan. It is conceded that no one of the defendants threw the bomb with his own hands. Plaintiffs in error are charged with being accessories before the fact."

If I did not throw the bomb myself, it becomes necessary to prove that I aided, encouraged and advised the person who did throw it. Is that fact proven? The supreme court says it is. The record says it is not. I appeal to the American people to judge between them.

The supreme court quotes articles from *The Alarm*, the paper edited by me, and from my speeches, running back three years before the Haymarket tragedy of May 4, 1886. Upon said articles and speeches the court affirms the sentence of death as an accessory. The court says: "The articles in *The Alarm* were most of them written by the defendant Parsons, and some of them by the defendant Spies," and then proceeds to quote these articles. I refer to the record to prove that, of all the articles quoted, only one was shown to have been written by me. I wrote, of course, a great many articles for *The Alarm*, but the record will show that only one of the many quoted by the supreme court to prove my guilt as an accessory was written by me, and this article appeared in *The Alarm* December 6, 1884, one year and a half before the Haymarket meeting.

As to Mr. Spies, the record will show that during the three years I was editor of *The Alarm*, he did not write for the paper half a dozen articles. For proof as to this I appeal to the record.

The Alarm was a labor paper, and, as is well known, a labor paper is conducted as a medium through which working people can make known their grievances. *The Alarm* was no exception to this rule. I not only did not write "most of the articles," but wrote comparatively few of them. This the record will also show.

In referring to my Haymarket speech the court says: "To the men then listening to him he had addressed the incendiary appeals that had been appearing in *The Alarm* for two years." The court then quotes the "incendiary" article which I did write, and which is as follows: "One dynamite bomb properly placed will destroy a regiment of soldiers; a weapon easily made and carried with perfect safety in the pockets of one's clothing."

The record will show by referring to *The Alarm* that this is a garbled extract taken from a statement made by General Phillip Sheridan in his annual report to congress. It was simply a reiteration of General Sheridan's statement that dynamite was easily made, perfectly safe to handle. and a very destructive weapon of warfare. The article in full as it appeared in *The Alarm* is as follows:

"Dynamite. The protection of the poor against the armies of the rich. In submitting his annual report November 10, 1884, General Phillip Sheridan, commander of the United States army, says: 'This nation is growing so rapidly that there are signs of other troubles which I hope will not occur, and which will probably not come upon us if both capital and labor will only be conservative. Still it should be remembered destructive explosives are easily made, and that banks, United States sub-treasuries, public buildings, and large mercantile houses can be readily demolished, and the commerce of entire cities destroyed by an infuriated people with means carried with perfect safety to themselves in the pockets of their clothing.'"

The editorial comment upon the above, as it appeared in *The Alarm*, is as follows: "A hint to the wise is sufficient. Of course General Sheridan is too modest to tell us that he himself and army will be powerless in the coming revolution between the propertied and propertyless classes. Only in foreign wars can the usual weapons of warfare be used to any advantage. One dynamite bomb properly placed will destroy a regiment of soldiers; a weapon easily made and carried with perfect safety in the pockets of one's clothing. The first regiment may as well disband, for if it should ever level its guns upon the workingmen of Chicago it can be totally annihilated."

Again the court says: "He (Parsons) had said to them (referring to the people assembled at the Haymarket) Saturday, April 24, 1886, just ten days before May 4, in the last issue of *The Alarm* that had appeared: 'Workingmen, to arms! War to the palace, peace to the cottage, and death to luxurious idleness! The wage system is the only cause of the world's misery. It is supported by the rich classes, and to destroy it they must be either made to work or die. One pound of dynamite is better than a bushel of ballots! Make your demand for eight hours with weapons in your hands to meet the capitalist bloodhounds—police and militia—in a proper manner.'"

The record will show that this article was not written by me, but was published as a news item. By referring to the columns of *The Alarm* the following editorial comment appears attached to the above article, viz.: "The above handbill was sent to us from Indianapolis, Ind., as having been posted all over that city last week. Our correspondent says that the police tore them down wherever they found them."

The court, continuing, says: "At the close of another article in the same issue he said; 'The social war has come, and whoever is not with us is against us.'" Assistant State's Attorney Walker read this article to the jury, and at its conclusion stated that it bore my initials and was my article. It is a matter within the knowledge of everyone then present, that I interrupted him and called his attention to the fact that the article did not bear my initials and that I was not its author. Mr. Walker corrected his mistake to the jury.

Now these are the three articles quoted by the supreme court as proof of my guilt as an accessory in a conspiracy to murder officer Degan. The record will prove what I say. Now as to my speeches. All of them, with one exception, purporting to be my utterances at the Haymarket are given from the excited imagination and perverted memories of newspaper reporters. Mr. English, who alone took shorthand notes and swore to their correctness, reports me as saying: "It is time to raise a note of warning. There is nothing in the eight-hour movement to excite the capitalist. Don't you know that the military are under arms, and a Gatling gun is ready to mow you down? Was this Germany, or Russia, or Spain? [A voice: 'It looks like it.'] Whenever you make a demand for eight hours' pay, or increase of pay, the militia and deputy sheriffs and the Pinkerton men are called out, and you are shot and clubbed and murdered in the streets. I am not here for the purpose of inciting anybody, but to speak out—to tell the facts as they exist, even though it shall cost me my life before morning."

Mr. English, continuing, said: "There is another part of it [the speech] right here. 'It behooves you, as you love your wife and children, if you don't want to see them perish with hunger, killed, or cut down like dogs on the street—Americans, in the interest of your liberty and independence, to arm, arm yourselves!'"

This, be it remembered, is a garbled extract, and it is a matter of record that reporter English testified that he was instructed by the proprietor of his paper to report only the inflammatory portions of the speeches made at that meeting. Mayor Harrison, who was present and heard this speech, testified before the jury that it was simply "a violent political harangue," and did not call for his interference as a peace officer.

The speech delivered by me at the Haymarket, and which I repeated before the jury, is a matter of record and undisputed; and I challenge anyone to show therein that I incited anyone to acts of violence. The extract reported by Mr. English, when taken in connection with what preceded and what followed, can not be construed by the wildest imagination as incitement to violence.

Extracts from three other speeches alleged to have been delivered by me more than one year prior to May 4, 1886, are given. Two of these speeches were reported from the memory of the Pinkerton detective, Johnson. These are the speeches quoted by the court as proof of my guilt as accessory to the murder of Degan. Where, then is the connection between these speeches and the murder of Degan? I am bold to declare that such connection is imperceptible to the eye of a fair and unprejudiced mind. But the honorable body, the supreme court of Illinois, has condemned me to death for speeches I never made and articles I never wrote. In the affirmation of the death sentence the court has "assumed," "supposed," "guessed," "surmised" and "presumed" that I said and did "so and so." This the record fully proves.

The court says: "Spies, Schwab, Parsons and Engel were responsible for the articles written and published by them as above shown. Spies, Schwab, Fielden, Parsons and Engel were responsible for the speeches made by them respectively, and there is evidence in the record tending to show that the death of Degan occurred during the prosecution of a conspiracy planned by the members of the International groups who read these articles and heard those speeches."

Now I defy any one to show from the record the proof that I wrote more than one of the many articles alleged to have been written by me. Yet the supreme court says that I wrote and am responsible for all of them. Again, concerning the alleged speeches, they were reported by the Pinkerton detective, Johnson, who was, as the record shows, employed by Lyman J. Gage, vice-president of the First National Bank, as the agent of the Citizens' Association, an organization composed of the millionaire employers of Chicago. I submit to a candid world if this hired spy would not make false reports to earn his blood money. Thus it is for speeches I did not make and articles I did not write I am sentenced to die because the court "assumes" that these articles influenced some unknown and still unidentified person to throw the bomb that killed Degan. Is this law? Is this justice?

The supreme court in affirming the sentence of death upon me, proceeds to give further reasons, as follows:

"Two circumstances are to be noted: First, it can hardly be said that Parsons was absent from the Haymarket meeting when he went into Zepf's hall. It has already been stated that the latter place was only a few steps north of the speakers' wagon, and in sight from it. We do not think that the defendant Parsons could escape his share of the responsibility for the explosion at the Haymarket because he stepped into a neighboring saloon and looked at the explosion through a window. While he was speaking, men stood around him with arms in their hands. Many of these were members of the armed sections of the International groups. Among them were men who belonged to the International Rifles, an organization in which he himself was an officer, and with which he had been drilling in preparation for the events then transpiring."

The records of the trial will show that not one of the foregoing allegations is true. The facts are these: Zepf's hall is on the northeast corner of Lake and Desplaines streets, just one block north of the speakers' wagon. The court says: "It was only a few steps north of the speakers' wagon." The court says further that, "it can hardly be said that Parsons was absent from the Haymarket meeting, when he was at Zepf's hall." If this is correct logic, then I was at two different places a block apart at the same instant. Truly, the day of miracles has not yet passed. Again, the record will show that I did not "step into a neighboring saloon and look at the explosion through a window." It will show that I went to Zepf's hall, one block distant, and across Lake street, accompanied by my wife and another lady, and my two children (a girl of five and a boy of seven years of age,) they having sat upon a wagon about ten feet from the speakers' wagon throughout my speech; that it looked like rain; that we had started home, and went into Zepf's hall to wait for the meeting to adjourn, and walk home in company with a lot of friends who lived in that direction. Zepf's building is on the corner, and opens on the street with a triangular door six feet wide. Myself and ladies and children were just inside the door. Here, while waiting for our friends and looking toward the meeting, I had a fair view of the explosion. All this the record will show.

It would seem that, according to circumstances, a block is at one time "a few steps," or a "few steps" is "more than a block," as the case may suit. The logical as well as the imaginative faculties of the supreme court are further illustrated in a most striking manner by the credence of the court to the "yarn" of a reporter, who testifies that Spies had described to him the "czar" bomb and the men who were to use them, as follows:

"He spoke of a body of tall, strong men in their organization who could throw bombs weighing five pounds 150 paces. He stated that the bombs in question were to be used in case of conflict with the police or militia."

The court gives this sort of testimony as proof of the existence of a conspiracy to murder Degan. Wonderful credulity! To throw a five-pound bomb 150 paces or yards is to throw it 450 feet or one-quarter of a mile. Gulliver, in his travels among the Brobdingnagian race, tells of the giants he met, and we have also heard of the giants of Patagonia, but we did not know until now that they were Lilliputians as compared with the "Anarchist Swedes" of Chicago. The court proceeds to say: "While he (Parsons) was speaking, men stood around him with arms in their hands." The record, as quoted by the court, shows that only one man flourished a pistol, not a number of men. Again, the court says: "Most of the men were members of the armed sections of the International groups," thus making it appear that many of these men (when there was only one who was even alleged to have exhibited a pistol) were armed.

The court says: "Among them were men who belonged to the

International Rifles, an armed organization, in which he himself was an officer, and in which he had been drilling in preparation for the events then transpiring."

Now, I challenge the supreme court or any other honorable gentlemen to prove from the record that there ever existed such an organization as that armed section of the American group known as the "International Rifles." It can not be done. The record shows that some members of the American group did organize the "International Rifles," which never met but four or five times, was never armed with rifles or any other weapons, and disbanded nearly one year before May 4, 1886.

The Pinkerton man, Johnson, says that dynamite bombs were exhibited in the presence of the International Rifles. It will take corroborative testimony before the American people will credit the statements of such a man engaged for such a purpose, and it is well known that supreme courts have decided that testimony of detectives should be taken with great caution.

I appeal to the American people in their love of justice and fair play. I submit that the record does not show my guilt of the crime of murder, but, on the contrary, it proves my innocence.

Against me in this trial all the rules of law and evidence have been reversed in that I have been held as guilty until I proved my innocence.

I have been tried ostensibly for murder, but in reality for anarchism. I have been proven guilty of being an anarchist, and condemned to die for that reason. The state's attorney said in his statement before court and jury in the beginning of the trial: "These defendants were picked out and indicted by the grand jury, they are no more guilty than the thousands who follow them. They are picked out because they are leaders. Convict them, and our society is safe." And in their last appeal to the jury the prosecution said: "Anarchy is on trial. Hang these eight men and save our institutions. These are the leaders. Make examples of them." This is a matter of record.

So far as I have had time to examine the record I find the same fabrications and perversion of testimony against all my comrades as exists against myself. I therefore again appeal to the American people to avert the crime of judicial murder, and this appeal I have faith will not be in vain.

My ancestors partook of all the hardships incident to the establishment of this republic. They fought, bled, and some of them died, that the Declaration of Independence might live and the American flag might wave in triumph over those who claim the "divine right of kings to rule." Shall that flag now, after a century's triumph, trail in the mire of oppression, and protect the perpetration of outrages and oppressions that put the older despotisms of Europe to shame?

Knowing myself innocent of crime I came forward and gave myself up for trial. I felt that it was my duty to take my chances with the rest of my comrades. I sought a fair and impartial trial before a jury of my peers, and knew that before any fair-minded jury I could with little difficulty be cleared. I preferred to be tried and take the chances of an acquittal with my friends to being hunted as a felon. Have I had a fair trial?

The lovers of justice and fair play are assiduously engaged in an effort to thwart the consummation of judicial murder by the commutation of sentence to prison. I speak for myself alone when I say that for this I thank them and appreciate their efforts, but I am an innocent man. I have violated no law; I have committed no offense against anyone's rights. I am simply the victim of the malice of those whose anger has been aroused by the power, strength and independence of the labor organizations of America. I am a sacrifice to those who say: "These men may be innocent. No mattter. They are anarchists. We must hang them anyway."

My counsel informs me that every effort will be made to take this case before the highest tribunal in the land and that there is a strong hope of a hearing there. But I am also reliably informed that from three to five years will elapse before the supreme court of the United States can hear and adjudge the case. Since surrendering myself to the authorities I have been locked up in close confinement twenty-one hours of every twenty-four for six days, and from Saturday afternoon until Monday morning (thirty eight hours) each week in a noisome cell, without a ray of sunshine or a breath of pure air. To be compelled to bear this for five, or even three years, would be to suffer a lingering death, and it is only a matter of serious consideration with me, whether I ought to accept the verdict as it stands, rather than die by inches under such conditions. I am prepared to die. I am ready, if need be, to lay down my life for my rights and the rights of my fellowmen. But I object to being killed on false and unproven accusations. Therefore I cannot countenance or accept the effort of those who would endeavor to procure a commutation of my sentence to imprisonment in the penitentiary. Neither do I approve of any further appeals to the courts of law. I believe them to be all alike—the agency of the privileged class to perpetuate their power, to oppress and plunder the toiling masses. As between capital and its legal rights and labor and its natural rights, the courts of law must side with the capitalist class. To appeal to them is vain. It is the appeal of the wage slave to his capitalistic master for liberty. The answer is curses, blows, imprisonment, and death.

If I had never been an anarchist before, my experience with courts and the laws of the governing classes would make an anarchist of me now. What is anarchism? It is a state of society without any central or governing power. Upon this subject the court in its affirmation of the death sentence defines the object of the International Working Peoples' association as follows:

"It is designed to bring about a social revolution. Social revolution meant the destruction of the right of private ownership of property, or the right of the individual to own property. It meant the bringing about of a state of society in which all property should be held in common."

If this definition is right then it is very similar to that advocated by Jesus Christ, for proof of which refer to the fourth and fifth chapters of the Acts of the Apostles; also Matthew xxi., 10 to 14; and Mark xi, 15 to 19.

No, I am not guilty; I have not been proven guilty. I leave it to you to decide from the record itself as to my guilt or innocence. I can not, therefore, accept a commutation to imprisonment. I appeal not for mercy, but for justice. As for me, the utterance of Patrick Henry is so apropos that I cannot do better than let him speak:

"Is life so dear and peace so sweet as to be purchased at the price of chains and slavery? Forbid it, Almighty God! I know not what course others may pursue, but as for me, give me liberty, or give me death. A. R. PARSONS.

CHICAGO, ILL., Sept. 21, 1887. [Prison cell No. 29].

PARSONS' OPEN LETTER TO GOVERNOR OGLESBY.

To His Excellency Richard J. Oglesby, Governor of the State of Illinois—DEAR SIR: I am aware that petitions are being signed by hundreds of thousands of persons addressed to you, beseeching you to interpose your prerogative and commute the sentences of myself and comrades from death to imprisonment in the penitentiary. You are, I am told, a good constitutional lawyer and a sincere man. I therefore beg of you to examine the record of the trial, and then conscientiously decide for yourself as to my guilt or innocence. I know that as a just man you will decide in accordance with the facts, the truth, and the justice of this case. But I write to reiterate the declaration made in my published appeal to the people of America, September 21, 1887. I am guilty or I am innocent of the charge for which I have been condemned to die. If guilty, then I prefer death rather than to go "like the quarry slave at night scourged to his dungeon." If innocent, then I am entitled to and will accept nothing less than liberty. The records of the trial made in Judge Gary's court prove my innocence of the crime of murder. But there exists a conspiracy to judicially murder myself and imprisoned companions in the name and by virtue of the authority of the State. History records every despotic, arbitrary deed of the peoples' rulers as having been done in the name of the people, even to the destruction of the liberties of the people.

I am a helpless prisoner and completely in the power of the authorities, but I strongly protest against being taken from my cell and carried to the penitentiary as a felon. Therefore in the name of the people, whose liberty is being destroyed; in the name of peace and justice, I protest against the consummation of this judicial murder; this proposed strangulation of freedom on American soil. I speak for myself, I know not what course others may pursue, but for myself I reject the petition for my imprisonment. I am innocent, and I say to you that under no circumstances will I accept a commutation to imprisonment. In the name of the American people I demand my right, my lawful, constitutional, natural, inalienable right to liberty. Respectfully yours,

ALBERT R. PARSONS.

Prison Cell 29, Chicago, Ill., October 13, 1887.

LAW VS. LIBERTY.

[The Alarm, Dec. 3, 1887.]

"Anarchy is license," exclaim the law-abiding citizens.

"If this is true, then what in the name of liberty is law?" retort the anarchists.

What is law? It is a command, an order, and the State enforces compliance.

What is the State? The legislative, judicial and executive powers are what constitute the State. The law is manufactured, "made" to order by the legislators, and then expounded and applied by the judges, and then enforced or executed by the police, militia, army, and navy.

Law being a command or order to do or refrain from doing something, it is, therefore, not liberty, but license, and consequently despotic. Law—statute law—is designed to force or compel some person or persons to respect and support the privileges it confers upon some other person or persons. Law—statute law—is license, because it establishes the inequality of rights and duties, and maintains the inequality of conditions and opportunities. "Equal rights under the law," is a misnomer, since the only function of statute law is the creation of privileges and inequalities. Law—statute law—is the instrumentality by means of which people are made to serve and obey, to work and suffer for other peoples' benefit. Law—statue law—is the denial of a person's natural, inalienable rights by other persons. There are two kinds of law—natural and artificial. The artificial or manufactured law also manufactures police, militia, and prisons. Law—statute law—is "the coward's weapon, the tool of the thief." Cowardly, because man would not or could not otherwise degrade, enslave, and murder his fellow man. Rascally, because without it man would not and could not dominate and exploit his fellow man. Therefore, "equal rights under the law" means no more nor less than the rascality necessary to take an advantage and the cowardly brutality necessary to keep it. This is law; its sole and only purpose.

Life and liberty insures happiness; privilege destroys both. Law is privilege, is license. Life is denied to all those who are denied the equal right to the free use of the means of existence—capital. Only by the use of the means of subsistence is life possibly maintained; and only by the equal right to its free use is liberty possible. Happiness is the child, and its parents are life and liberty. The slave has life. The freeman possesses both liberty and life. The dependence of one person upon another for permission to work and eat is the foundation upon which the wage-slave system of industry is built. Capital is a law-protected institution. It is privileged property. There is no such thing in nature's law as privilege, chartered rights. This moloch devours nine-tenths of the human race, who feed its ravenous jaws with their own flesh and blood. This beast, "the property beast," is what is otherwise known as law and government. Law—statute law—is license, because its sole and only function is to deny the producer the possession and enjoyment of his product.

Law does not and cannot, in fact, create anything but privileges. Rights exist inherently. Labor, and labor alone, does or can create wealth, and the wealth-creators are poor by virtue of and solely on account of law. Law takes wealth from the producer and bestows it upon the non-producer; it curses industry with poverty and blesses idleness with wealth. Law is the mainspring of everlasting contention among men. It creates classes, produces masters and slaves; it is the source of ignorance, disease, crime, war, of every moral, social and physical evil. Law creates and perpetuates poverty: first, by depriving the producers and keeping them poor, and, secondly, by preventing the unlimited application of wealth-creating forces in steam, electricity and machinery.

Law—statute law—is an insult to our natures, a repression upon human capacity, and the degradation of social effort. Do away with all compulsory statutes; abolish all legislative enactments based upon authority, as a conspiracy against man's ability to co-operate. Liberty calls out individuality, co-operative activity, and offers scope for the highest development of our powers. Cease treating men and women as children. Remove the crutches and society will spontaneously respond to every new demand, and men and women will walk freely and co-operate to secure all that is needful.

ALBERT R. PARSONS.

VIEWS OF GENERAL PARSONS.

NORFOLK, Va., Sept. 16.—Gen. W. H. Parsons, the eldest brother of A. R. Parsons, the condemned anarchist, was interviewed to-day by your correspondent at Newport News, where he holds the position of inspector of customs and is much respected for his scholarly attainments and his high-toned deportment. The general has been much averse to being interviewed and until the present has declined to converse with reporters on the subject of his brother's sentence. On being asked to give a brief outline of the life of A. R. Parsons he said:

"A. R. Parsons was born in Montgomery, Ala., June 20, 1848, and is, therefore, just 39 years of age. He is of pilgrim-father parentage, his ancestors—five brothers—landing together in 1632 on Narragansett Bay and their descendents of that name, according to John Mason of Virginia, who cites the authority of Berknap's "History of New England," were proverbial for good scholarship and honorable characer. Gen. Samuel Parsons, from whom Albert's father was named, was a major-general of the revolutionary war, and his grand-uncle of the same name lost an arm in the battle of Bunker Hill. Theophilus Parsons, the judicial author, was the pivot of the law, not only of New England but of American jurisprudence in his day. It has been the boast of all of that name in all lands and states that no one who bore it was ever convicted or justly charged with a felonious offense.

"Albert R. Parsons, the accused anarchist, is not an exception. He is a political offender, and not a criminal. We assert this, because the incidents of his biography, upon which you interrogate me, will demonstrate this. His father moved to Alabama in 1830. A. R. Parsons was left an orphan at 4 years of age and joined my family in Tyler, Tex., where I was at that time conducting the Tyler *Telegraph* as owner and editor. At 12 years of age he entered the Galveston *News* office and became a member of the family of its founder and proprietor, the venerable Willard Richardson, to learn the art preservative of all arts, of which profession and the Typographical Union he is now a member of high standing as well as a journalist of ripe experience, and was at the period of his arrest as accessory to the tragedy of May 4, 1886."

"Will you give his career during and since the war?"

"When the war broke out he was only 13 years old, but he joined a confederate infantry company called the Lone Star Grays. He was with them over a year and assisted in the capture of Gen. Twiggs. He joined an artillery company at Sabine Pass under his brother, Capt. Richard Parsons, who died at his post, of yellow fever. A. R. Parsons then attached himself to his elder brother's brigade—my own—on the west bank of the Mississippi, in Arkansas, and became a cavalry scout, graduating after four years service at 17 years of age.

"He edited the Waco *Spectator* in 1868. His marriage to a Mexican lady of youth, beauty and genius occurred in Austin, Texas, in 1871, and is a matter of record in that city, where miscegnation is a crime. Her Spanish and Aztec blood were then never questioned. She speaks the former language fluently, and was raised an orphan by her uncle, a Mexican ranchero, and lived with him in Johnson county, Texas, until the date of her marriage. By her A. R. Parsons has two children, a boy and girl, aged 8 and 7 respectively, the latter a rare beauty and inheriting the vivacity of her mother. In 1870 he was elected secretary of the Texas senate, and the following year was appointed a deputy United States internal revenue collector. He held this office until he went to Chicago in 1873, when he resumed his trade as a compositor on the *Times*.

"In 1876 he joined the socialists. During the labor troubles of the following year he was held by the chief of police for a speech he had made to 20,000 laboring men at the Market Square, but was released the same night. He has been a compositor on the *Inter Ocean* and the *Daily News*. For three years he filled the position of president of the trade and labor association. He has been nominated for alderman three times, for congress twice, and once each for sheriff and county clerk. At the national convention of the socialistic labor party, held at Allegheny, Pa., in 1879, he was nominated as the candidate for president of the United States. At the time of his voluntary surrender to the court he was editor of the *Alarm*."

"Will you give his disposition and any proof of his aversion to violence or any words cautioning others against inflicting injury to persons or property?"

"A. R. Parsons is a philosophical anarchist and claims the gift of prophecy. He has never counseled revolution, but has prophesied revolution. In the prophetic words addressed to Mr. T. V. Powderly from the Chicago bastile, July 4, 1886, he said:

"'Whether we live or whether we die the social revolution is inevitable. The boundaries of human freedom must be enlarged and widened. The seventeenth century was a struggle for religious liberty; the eighteenth for political equality. and in the nineteenth century mankind is demanding economic or industrial freedom. The fruition of this struggle means the social revolution. We see it coming; we predict it; we hail it with joy. Are we criminals for that?'"

"As I am myself an old time, original Jeffersonian democrat, believing that all power where not expressly delegated to the state, is inherently in the people and not in corporations, and that the ballot is the sole and final arbiter of any existing grievances, I frequently expostulated with him on the idea involved in the word anarchy. His invariable reply to me, with the bars between us and the shadow of the scaffold impending above him, was:

"'I am not a revolutionist, for all revolutions are not made by agitators and prophets. They are the creatures of wrongs inflicted by the privileged few and their tools and agencies, the law-maker, the courts, and the executive force whether a pliant proletarian guard called police, or the new organized reserves of the police, known as our militia. I do not seek to make revolution. We simply see it coming; we predict it. Am I a criminal for that? Who dreamed among the masses of events of 1861-5? I now prophesy the downfall of wage slavery or the wage-slavery system and its replacement by the principle of co-operation and association between labor and capital. As I witnessed the overthrow of chattel slavery and now recognize the divinity which shaped that stupendous result, so I see that hand in the events, by no means circumscribed, now impending over my native land as well as over Europe—the emancipation of my own class. Every government, including our own as now organized, is a conspiracy to enslave labor whether of the hand or brain. Coercion is the basis of this conspiracy, and hence we would overthrow all existing law which fosters and maintains it. Labor will fight, but will only fight in self-defense. The universal depression and suffering and pauperism in Europe, as well as America, is the source of discontent and unrest and is fomenting a political cyclone.'"

"To these views frequently expressed when pressed for his purpose, I would interpose the plea that the people would yet administer the corrective for existing evils through the machinery of the ballot, as this was a free representative government, and we could not improve upon its form as a medium for the expression of the popular will. To this he would invariably reply, 'the people will attempt to apply the corrective through the ballot and will measurably succeed so far as form is concerned; but,' he would add, 'the vested wrongs of the privileged class, although in the hands of a very meager minority, will never be relinquished without coercion, as witness our late civil war. This meager minority will rebel against the voice and vote of the majority of the people constitutionally expressed. They have the example of a wealthy few in Rome who organized a mercenary praetorian guard of 10,000 policemen to overawe the unarmed populace of the capital and held in their pay the rival legions recruited from the plebian classes. Here is where and when the future revolution will be inaugurated. This plutocracy will rebel against the democratic and republican masses and recruit their mercenary police and praetorian guards from the very ranks of the men who will spoliate on both classes.'"

"That is anarchy as taught and understood by A. R. Parsons. I often pressed him for an exposition of the term anarchism as meant and believed by him. He invariably replied in substance that the meaning of philosophical anarchism was the very antipodes of anarchy as defined and understood by capitalism; that Webster's dictionary gave two meanings—one, without rulers or governors; and the other, disorder and confusion. The latter he defined as capitalistic anarchy, such as was now witnessed, he said, in all parts of the world, in all conditions of society below the privileged classes which had already absorbed and monopolized all the opportunities of life and the means of existence, except merely to exist.

"To be without rulers and governors invested with authority to dictate to others against their will and interests, he would say, 'is philosophical anarchism, and the state of society which the church is constantly prognostigating will usher in the millenial period when all governments will be abolished and the principles of Christ, as taught by him of the brotherhood of man and the supreme fatherhood of the Creator, will be established. Man is the agency through whom this result will be achieved, as God works alone by such agencies; and, as without the shedding of blood there is no remission of sins, I believe that the anarchism of the millenium, when there will be but one invisible ruler and all human governments overthrown, will be ushered in by the most stupenduous and bloody revolution in the annals of time. Is it criminal to report the prophecy of the seers and inspired men of the sacred oracles? Am I to be executed for predicting that the period when no ruler or law save the spirit of the Nazarine teacher of good-will on earth and peace to all men as the fruit of the golden rule of the then common brotherhood of man is soon to be inaugurated? Then incarcerate the incumbents of our pulpits, and again, as of yore, stone the prophets; for so stone they the prophets, even among his chosen people, when sent to warn them of judgment to come.'"

"What was his action at the meeting at which the bomb was thrown?"

"There is no pretence that A. R. Parsons or that any one of the defendants threw or even knew of the throwing of the fatal bomb. They are all condemned as supposed, although not proven, accessories, for there can be no accessories without a principal, and there was not even an attempt to prove who the principal was. He yet remains unknown, the circumstantial evidence much more strongly pointing to an agent of the stock exchanges through Pinkerton's mercenaries to break up the eight-hour movement by charging the offence on the leaders of that movement in Chicago than to these defendants. The New York *Times* advised that very course to involve the leaders and thus break down the eight-hour movement which was then sustained by 335,000 men. A. R. Parsons rehearsed on the trial his Haymarket speech, and it is of record. It was a strong statistical, philosophical argument. At its conclusion Capt. Black, counsel for the defense asked: 'When you were referring in your speech to Jay Gould or to the southwestern system do you remember any interruption from the crowd or any response?' to which A. R. replied: 'Yes, I omitted that in rehearsing my speech before the court just concluded. Some one said: "Hang Him! hang Gould!" My response to that was that it was not a conflict between individuals, but for a change of system, and that socialism designed to remove the cause which produced the pauper and the millionaire, but did not aim at the life of individuals.'"

"Reporter English of the Chicago *Tribune* and several other reporters present corroborated this statement. In fact is was originally drawn out of the reporters present before A. R. Parsons took the stand. It was proven by ten witnesses that A. R. Parsons was in Zepf's hall, at the corner of Randolph and Desplaines streets when the shell exploded, and yet he is condemned to death for having incited some one to throw the fatal bomb. It was proven that Lingg was two and a half miles away on Clybourn avenue at that hour; that Schwab was speaking elsewhere, seven miles distant; that Engel was with his family at home; that Neebe was not even present, and knew nothing of the meeting; that Parsons had finished and left the ground with his family, and that the only two of the eight present were Fielden and Spies, and they were on the speakers' stand when attacked and ordered to disperse by 200 armed policemen."

"Is it true he voluntarily surrendered?"

"It is true that conscious of his innocence, A. R. Parsons voluntarily came into open court on the first day of the trial and took his seat with the accused defendants at a time when the inflamed prejudices of the police rendered it doubtful if justice could be rendered with the entire machinery of the law in their hands. This act tended largely to disarm the hostility of disinterested men who believed in fair play, and that justice should be done though the heavens fall."

"Will the case, in your judgment, be called to the United States supreme court, and on what grounds?"

"It will; first, because under the sixth amendment of the federal constitution it is provided that in all criminal prosecutions the accused shall enjoy the right to a trial by an impartial jury of the state and district where the crime shall have been committed. The fifteenth amendment provides that no state shall deprive any person of life, liberty, or property without due process of law. If these men are executed the state of Illinois, through its courts, will have executed seven men without the due process provided and guaranteed by the constitution, which is the supreme law and which accords to the accused a trial by an impartial jury. It was proved on the trial that the special bailiff, Henry L. Ryce, who was appointed to serve the special venire, said to Otis S. Favor, a reputable merchant in Chicago, that he was managing the case against the accused and knew what he was about, and that the accused would hang as certain as death. 'I am calling such men as the defendants will have to challenge and so waste their challenges,' he said. This was made a special ground for a new trial, although Judge Gary had refused the defendants the privilege to introduce Mr. Otis Favor to prove that the bailiff acknowledged with a chuckle that he was packing the jury so that it would not be impartial. Juryman Adams admitted before the trial that if he was on the jury he would hang all of them. This was proved. Juror Denker stated to two credible witnesses before the trial that the whole d——d crowd ought to be hanged. Several of the jurors, who can be named, as they are all of record, admitted that they were prejudiced so that it would take strong evidence to overcome their already predetermined judgment of their guilt. On this statement of record the fourteenth amendment can be invoked and a writ of error must issue overruling the action of a state court, which has doomed seven men to death, having denied them an impartial trial, as required by the fourteenth amendment of the constitution. Their death would be judicial murder. Such would be the sentence of mankind and the verdict of history.

"2. There is a precedent from Missouri where a writ of error was for review by the United States supreme court on the ground that the evidence was obtained by unlawful search and seizure, and a violation of the sanctity of letters unlawfully seized. A letter to Mr. Spies, written a year before the trial, was seized, after breaking open his private editorial desk, and was permitted to be read on the trial by Judge Gary, the purpose of which was to show he had received—not answered—a letter from Herr Most about medicine that was good for the relief of the Hocking valley strikers of 1885. Evidence obtained by a violation of such safeguards to the citizen is a violation of all rights guaranteed by the constitution. Of course, where courts are now constituted to protect vested wrongs in many cases, as witness Justice Field's decisions in California in favor of the Chinese and in protection of Senator Stanford against the Pacific commission, there is no way to estimate the result of even an application for a writ of error in this case. It may be that blood is what is wanted and blood they must have, and thus verify the saying that 'whom the gods would destroy they first make mad.'"

"What is your own history and political status?"

"I have held positions of honor under three governors and two presidents. I was on the supreme court bench, a member of the United States centennial commission, was state senator, was in the Charleston convention of 1860, and commanded an active cavalry brigade in the confederate service throughout the war. I am a Jeffersonian democrat and believe the ballot will yet redeem the nation."— *Correspondence Daily News.*

LETTER TO GEORGE FRANCIS TRAIN.

PRISON CELL 29, CHICAGO, ILL., Oct. 14, 1887.

Citizen Geo. Francis Train, Champion of Free Speech, Free Press and Public Assemblage:

Despotism of America's money-mongers again demonstrated. They deny the right of the people to assemble to hear you speak to them. Free speech! They will not allow the people to buy or read the *Psycho-Anarchist*. Free press! They interdict the right of the people to assemble and petition for redress of grievances. Right of assembly!

United States constitution nullified by Supreme court's decision. Revolution!

The people clubbed, arrested, imprisoned, shot and hung in violation of law and constitution at behest of America's monopolists.

Free speech, free press, and right to assemble cost seven years' bloody revolution of 1776. But degenerate Americans style those who maintain the Declaration of Independence as anarchists. Jefferson, Adams, Hancock, Washington, Franklin, Paine, Henry and other revolutionary sires they ridicule as "fools," "cranks," etc. America's plutocrats of 1887 sneer at these things.

Police censorship over press, speech and assemblage! Russia, Spain, Italy, France—abashed! Working-womens' union prohibited by Chicago police from singing the "Marseilles" at social entertainments!

Tyrants forge missing link. Chain complete. America joins "International Brotherhood of Man." Proletariat of every clime and tongue, from Moscow, Berlin, Vienna, Madrid, London and Paris to Chicago, join refrain and sing the

MARSEILLES.

Ye sons of Toil, awake to glory;
  Hark! hark, what myriads bid you rise!
Your children, wives, and grandsires hoary
  Behold their tears and hear their cries!
  Behold their tears and hear their cries!
Shall hateful tyrants, mischief breeding!
  With hireling hosts, a ruffian band,
  Affright and desolate the land,
While peace and liberty lie bleeding?

CHORUS.

To arms, to arms, ye brave!
  The avenging sword unsheath!
March on, march on, all hearts resolved,
  On liberty or death!

With luxury and pride surrounded,
  The vile insatiate despots dare,
Their thirst of power and gold unbounded,
  To meet and vend the light and air,
  To meet and vend the light and air;
Like beasts of burden would they load us,
  Like gods would bid their slaves adore:
  But man is man, and who is more?
Then shall they longer lash and goad us?
            —CHORUS.

Oh! Liberty, can man resign thee
  Once having felt thy gen'rous flame?
Can dungeons, bolts, or bars confine thee?
  Or whips thy noble spirit tame?
  Or whips thy noble spirit tame?
Too long the world has wept, bewailing
  That falsehood's dagger tyrants wield:
  But freedom is our sword and shield,
And all their arts are unavailing.
            —CHORUS.

Onward! Citizen Train! Freedom *shall* not perish! Let the welkin ring, and from land to land labor's innumerable hosts proclaim—"Liberty! Fraternity! Equality!" *Salut!*

                            A. R. PARSONS,
                                  Proletar.

ARREST OF MRS. PARSONS AND CHILDREN.

Under the deep shadow of that awful tragedy, enacted on the eleventh day of November, many shameful deeds passed almost unnoticed; the gloom, so dense that the close of the century will scarcely see it lightened, veiled the blackness of injustices that would have appalled the hearts of the people if thrown up against the light of freedom in brighter days. Now, it is well that they be brought forth for investigation; the judgment of the people must be given on proceedings done in the name of "law and order," in this so-called free country.

It will be remembered that in the extras of Friday Nov. 11th a casual notice of the arrest of Mrs. Parsons "for persistent disobedience of orders," and that of a lady friend for haranging the people" was given. The officers were reported as being "very courteous and gentle," and the ladies "were given arm-chairs in the registry office merely to keep them away from the crowd and prevent trouble."

This is the true story: On Thursday evening after Governor Oglesby's tardy decision had been given, Mrs. Parsons accompanied by Mr. Holmes and myself, went to the jail to plead for a last sad interview. She was denied an entrance, but was told by the deputy-sheriff in charge that she would be admitted at half-past eight the following morning. At that time she, with her children and myself was promptly as near to the gates as the police would permit. Every street for two blocks away leading towards the jail was crossed by a rope and guarded by a line of police armed with Winchester rifles. At the first corner Mrs. Parsons quietly made known her errand. The lieutenant said she could not get in there, but that she should pass on to the next corner, and the officer there would perhaps let her through.

She did so with the same result. Another captain told her she must get an order from the sheriff; on inquiring where he could be found, she was told to go on to another corner where a message might be sent to him. At this corner no one knew anything about it and again we were sent on; and so, for more than an hour we were urged along in a veritable game of "Pussy wants a corner" that would have been rediculous had it not been so tragical. Sometimes it was a deputy sheriff who was to be found at a certain corner, sometimes it was the peculiarity of location that promised an entrance beyond the death-line; but it was always "not this corner but some other corner." Not once did an officer say, "you positively cannot see your husband. You are forbidden to enter his prison and bid him farewell," but always offered the inducement that if she passed quietly along, at some indefinite point she would be admitted.

Meanwhile the precious moments were flying; sweet little Lulu's face was blue with cold, and her beautiful eyes were swimming with tears. Manly little Albert, too, was shivering in the raw atmosphere, as he patiently followed his grief stricken mother from one warlike street to another.

Then Mrs. Parsons besought the officers only to take the children in for their father's last blessing and farewell; for one last interview that his memory might never be effaced from their young and impressible minds; one last look that the image of that noble father might dwell forever in their heart of hearts; one moment in which to listen to the last dear words that his loving and prophetic soul might dictate to the darling children left to live after him. In vain. The one humble prayer the brave woman ever voiced to the authorities in power, was denied her. They heeded her not except to hurry her along.

The last sad moments of her dear one's life were wasting so steadily, so relentlessly. Who can picture her agony? Who can wonder at her desperate protest against the "regulations of the law" which were killing her husband and forbidding her approach. She determinedly crossed the death line and told them "to kill her as they were murdering her husband." No, they were not so merciful. They dragged her outside, inveigled her around to a quieter corner, with the promise of "seeing about it," and there ordered her, her two children and myself into a patrol wagon awaiting us. What had the innocent children done?

Pleaded dumbly with soft, tearful eyes for their father. What was my crime? faithfulness to a sorrowing sister.

Once when some one asked me if I could not "prevail on that woman to keep quiet and go home," I had answered:

"I have no such influence over her and would not exert it if I had. Do you wonder that she is nearly distracted with grief at being driven from pillar to post like this, when in one short hour her husband will be dead? She has not seen him for five days, and now they deny her the sacred right of a last good bye; why the worst despotisms in Europe are not so bad as that."

At this a burly brutal-looking detective in citizen's clothes said:

"See here young woman! you shut up or we will send you off in the wagon!"

"Must I not even say this much, in a free country?" I asked in surprise.

"No, you can't," he growled, with a fierce frown.

And this, I suppose, constituted "my harangue to the people on the streets."

And so, into the patrol we were hustled, a heart-broken wife and mother, two innocent tearful children, and the one friend near her. The "polite" officers did not perhaps go out of their way to be brutal or rough, but were about as "courteous" as so many wooden men moving about like machines. Far from being given arm chairs in a comfortable office, we were locked up in dark, dirty stone cells— Mrs. Parsons and her children in one, myself in another.

And there—shame be it to America that I have it to relate! there we were stripped to the skin and searched! even the children, crying with fright, were undressed and carefully searched.

No excuse could be offered that we were ignorant foreigners and did not understand the laws of the country, and that the safety of American institutions depended on our being totally unarmed; for the blood of revolutionary forefathers coursed in our veins, while the matron and officers who gave the order (if there be any merit in being born in one country rather than another) had not been here long enough to speak our language correctly.

The woman ran her fingers through my hair, through the hems of my skirts, the gathers of my undergarments, even to my stockings; I asked her "what she expected to find."

"I don't know," she simpered, "this is my duty."

She clanged the doors behind her finally and we were left alone. We could hear each other's voices but could not see one another. And in those gloomy, underground cells we passed those terrible, anxious hours of Friday Nov. 11, 1887.

God knows her lot would have been bitter enough in her own comfortable home, with loving, sympathizing friends at her side to support her in that awful time. But who dare dwell upon the reality—the picture of that devoted wife in such a place at such an hour?

At a few minutes past twelve the matron came and said coldly "It is all over," and left us.

Not a soul came and asked the bereaved women if they could help her to even a cup of cold water. And I, the one friend near her, could only sit shivering with my face pressed to the cruel iron bars, listening to her low, despairing moans, as helpless as herself.

Every friend who called to inquire after our whereabouts and welfare was sent away without any information and we were not told that anyone had been to see us.

Mr. Holmes came as early as he received word that we had been arrested, and was not only denied any information, but was roughly ordered away and threatened with arrest himself "if he hung around there."

At three o'clock Capt. Schaack came down and asked how long we had been there, hypocritically expressed sorrow that we had been locked up, and opened our prison doors. They had done their worst and Mrs. Parsons was permitted to go to her desolated home.

And thus it was that while organized authority was judicially murdering the husband and strangling "the voice of the people," the wife and children were locked up in a dungeon, that no unpleasant scene might mar the smoothness of the proceedings. Where is there a parallel in history? Only in the state where dying men are forbidden to speak a few last words can such a scene be possible.

LIZZIE M. HOLMES.

Last Hours of Life.

The news of Governor Ogelsby's refusal to commute the death sentence except as to Fielden and Schwab was received by all the prisoners with perfect composure.

The deputy sheriff who was with Parsons for three hours on the night of Nov. 10, undertook, when he was relieved at one o'clock A. M. to tell what the condemned man had said, but when he began to realize the enormity of the task, he cut his narrative short by saying: "He was very cheerful and hopeful." Such was indeed the case. Parsons was never in better humor than he was that night. He seemed to forget entirely that he would have to die within twelve hours, so interested did he become in his own harangue to the death watch. He talked about socialism, about anarchy, the Haymarket, and his wife and children. It was not until he had reached this subject that he manifested any sorrow or regret, and the more he talked about it the more sorrowful he became. He said his wife was a brave woman, a true wife and a good mother.

During the early part of the night his rapt soul poured itself forth in song. He sang the old yet beautiful ballad:

ANNIE LAURIE.

Maxwelton's braes are bonny,
Where early fa's the dew,
And 'twas there that Annie Laurie

> Gave me her promise true;
> Gave me her promise true,
> Which ne'er forgot will be,
> And for bonnie Annie Laurie,
> I'd lay me down and dee.
>
> Her brow is like the snawdrift;
> Her throat is like the swan;
> Her face it is the fairest,
> That e'er the sun shone on:
> That e'er the sun shone on,
> And dark blue is her e'e,
> And for bonnie Annie Laurie,
> I'd lay me down and dee.
>
> Like dew on th' gowan lying,
> Is the fa' o' her fairy feet,
> And like winds in summer sighing,
> Her voice is low and sweet:
> Her voice is low and sweet,
> And she's a' the world to me,
> And for bonnie Annie Laurie,
> I'd lay me down and dee.

As the clear tenor voice rang through the gloomy corridors the other prisoners raised themselves on their elbows and listened. Doubtless to many the beautiful lines recalled tender memories of other days.

Early the morning of the 11th all the doomed men were awake. Parsons ate fried oysters and seemed to enjoy them. After breakfasting, he recited Marc Cook's beautiful poem, entitled "Waiting," with smiling features:

> Tell me, O sounding sea! I pray,
>   Eternally undulating,
> Where is the good ship that sailed away
> Once on a long-gone summer's day—
>   Sailed and left me waiting.
>
> No braver ship was ever seen,
>   As over the sunlit waters
> She glided on with stately mien
> Of a fair, white-vested ocean queen—
>   A queen among Neptune's daughters.
>
> Her sails were white as the wings of a dove—
>   Alas, for the fate she was daring!
> Gayly she rode the waves above,
> Gayly, as if all conscious of
>   The precious freight she was bearing.
>
> And never before sailed ship from shore
>   With a cargo half so precious;
> Youth, hope and love my good ship bore,
> And all the fair visions that come no more
>   In sadder days to refresh us.
>
> Yes, hope and love, the dreams of fame,
>   Youths sweet self-satisfaction,
> Ambition, which kindles the blood to flame,
> The lusty longing to win a name
>   On life's broad field of action:

All these my good ship bore away—
  With such rare treasures freighted
She sailed on that long-flown summer's day:
How long it is no tongue can say—
  Yet still have I waited   waited!

And ever this barren shore have I paced
  With eyes still wearily straining,
Gazing out on the water's waste,
Where naught remains of the faith that I placed
  In the blue waves, uncomplaining.

And so, through the long and desolate years,
  Have I watched for my ship's returning;
Watched and waited mid doubts and fears,
Waited and watched, when the scalding tears
  Adown my cheeks were burning.

The seasons have gone and rolled away,
  Each with its burden freighted,
But whether December or whether May,
In flush of the morn or twilight gray,
  Still have I waited - waited!

The busy world to the New has turned,
  Its pulses palpitating;
Again have life's bitter lessons been learned,
And hands have labored and hearts have burned,
  While I for my ship have been waiting.

But now I am weary and hope is flown
  And the sea's sad undulating
Breaks on my ear like a dismal moan;
My ship has gone down in the waters unknown,
  And vain has been all my waiting.

After awhile spent in conversation, the question of his funeral arising, he again drew upon his retentive memory and expressed his inmost thoughts in these beautiful lines, from the same author as the preceding:

A FAREWELL.

Come not to my grave with your mournings,
  With your lamentations and tears,
  With your sad forebodings and fears;
    When my lips are dumb,
    Do not come.

Bring no long train of carriages,
  No hearse crowned with waving plumes,
  Which the gaunt glory of death illumes;
    But with hands on my breast
    Let me rest.

Insult not my dust with your pity,
  Ye who're left on this desolate shore
  Still to suffer and lose and deplore
    'Tis I should, as I do,
    Pity you.

For me no more are the hardships,
  The bitterness, heartaches, and strife,
  The sadness and sorrow of life,
    But the glory divine
    This is mine.

> Poor creatures! Afraid of the darkness,
> Who groan at the anguish to come?
> How silent I go to my home;
> Cease your sorrowful bell;
> I am well!

During the reading of the death warrant his face was a study. His eyes were unnaturally brilliant, but whatever emotion he felt was firmly checked by the indomitable spirit which had hitherto sustained him. He toyed carelessly with his mustache and let his eyes rest easily upon the objects about him. As the men moved forward Parsons turned to the Jenkins' of the press, who were scrutinizing every action and said sarcastically: "Won't you come inside?"

When the halter was placed about his neck he never faltered. He stood erect, looking earnestly yet reproachfully at the people before him. The nooses were quickly adjusted, the caps pulled down, and a hasty movement made for the traps. Then from beneath the hoods came these words:

Spies: "There will be a time when our silence will be more powerful than the voices you strangle to-day!"

Fischer: "Hurrah for anarchy—"

Engel: "Hurrah for anarchy!"

Fischer: "This is the happiest moment of my life!"

Parsons: "Will I be allowed to speak, O men of America? Let me speak, Sheriff Matson! Let the voice of the people be heard! O——"
But the signal had been given, and the officers of the state performed their mission by strangling both speakers and speech.

Last Letter to an Old Comrade.

Cook County Jail, Nov. 11, 1887.—My Dear Comrade Lum: Eight (8) o'clock A.M. The guard has just awakened me. I have washed face and drank cup of coffee. The doctor asked if I wanted stimulants. I said no. The dear "boys," Engel, Fischer and Spies, saluted me with firm voices.

Please see Sheriff Matson and take charge of my papers and letters. Among them find MS. letters from Gen. W. H. Parsons' book—return it to Norfolk, Va. Please have my book on "Anarchism: Its Philosophy and Scientific Basis" put into good shape, etc.

Later.—Well, my dear old comrade, the fatal hour draws near. Cæsar kept me awake till late at night with the noise (music) of hammer and saw, erecting his throne, my scaffold. Refinement! Civilization! Matson (sheriff) tells me he refused to agree to let Cæsar (state) secrete my body, and he has just got my wife's address from me to send her my remains. Magnanimous Cæsar! Alas, good-bye! Hail the social revolution! Salutations to all.   A. R. Parsons.

TO THE PUBLIC!

The Following Books and Pamphlets Will be Sent, Post-paid, on Receipt of Price.

The Haymarket Speech of Albert R. Parsons,
Delivered at the Haymarket on May 4th, 1886, and repeated by him before the jury. Paper ... $0 10

The Facts Concerning the Eight Condemned Leaders.
By Leon Lewis. Mr. Lewis is a writer of national reputation, and sets forth the facts concerning the great trial in a spirited and trenchant manner. Paper ... 10

A Concise History of the Trial,
Taken from the Official Records. The only authentic history of the great trial ever written. By Dyer D. Lum. Paper ... 35

The Accused The Accusers.
Famous Speeches of the Eight Anarchists, delivered before Judge Gary on October 7th, 8th, and 9th, 1886. Paper ... 25

August Spies Autobiography.
Containing portraits of August Spies and Nina Van Zandt Spies, with notes and explanations. Paper, 25c. Cloth ... 65

Was it a Fair Trial?
By Gen. M. M. Trumbull. (Enlarged edition of Gen. Trumbull's Pamphlet now being prepared.) Paper ... 10

Anarchy.
By C. L. James. Historical and Scientific. Paper ... 20

Letters to Young People,
By Prince Kropotkin. Paper ... 05

French and German Socialism.
Prof. R. T. Ely. Paper 25c. Cloth ... 75

Manifesto of the Communists.
By Karl Marx. Important to Investigators ... 10

Law and Authority.
By Prince Kropotkin ... 05

Anarchy and the Anarchists.
A Sermon by Rev. J. C. Kimball, of Hartford, Conn. Paper ... 10

Our Boarders.
A pamphlet, by Lizzie M. Swank, is soon to be issued. Those who have read the writings of this well-known and talented woman will appreciate the treat in store for them. In this forthcoming work will be contained many of her miscellaneous articles ... --

Conventional Lies of Our Civilization.
A Scathing Criticism of Modern Society; by Max Nordau ... --

Women in the Past, Present and Future.
By August Bebel ... --

Cabinet Photographs of Albert R. Parsons as
"The Carpenter in Waukesha."

This photograph represents Mr. Parsons as he appeared while working as a carpenter, at Waukesha, Wis., where he sojourned seven weeks after his escape from Chicago. In this figure, in slouch hat, workman's apron and bare arms, it is difficult to recognize the features of the Ex-Editor of the Alarm. The eyes only are his.

SINGLE PHOTOGRAPHS, (POST-PAID), - - - - 25 Cents.

Song, "ANNIE LAURIE."

Arranged in Sheets, with Music, and Portrait of Albert R. Parsons.

Cabinet Photographs of
"Our Martyrs."

EACH, - - - - - - - 25 Cents.

Group Photographs of the
"Five Martyrs."

Both bust and full length Pictures, tastefully arranged. These are genuine photographs, and not lithographs.

PRICES RANGING FROM 50 Cents to $1.00;

Address - **MRS. A. R. PARSONS,** - Room 35.

169 Washington Street, CHICAGO.

"THE ALARM,"
FOUNDED BY ALBERT R. PARSONS.
A JOURNAL OF ANARCHISM.

DYER D. LUM, - - Editor.

SPECIAL CONTRIBUTORS.

LIZZIE M. SWANK, Illinois.	GERTRUDE B. KELLY, New York.
GEORGIA REPLOGLE, California.	JOHN F. KELLY, New York.
C. L. JAMES, Wisconsin.	GEO. SCHUMM, Minnesota.
JOS. LABADIE, Michigan.	ALBERT CURRLIN, Missouri.
G. C. CLEMENS, Kansas.	W. C. OWEN, Oregon.

☞ Every reader interested in Social Questions, all who are seeking information regarding Anarchy, what it is, what it proposes, what answers it gives to popular objections, and how it would treat mooted problems, - will find in THE ALARM its philosophical and practical sides discussed by able writers.

For One Year, - - $1.50.   For Six Months, - 75 Cents.

Address all letters to DYER D. LUM,

Room 23, 169 Washington Street, CHICAGO, ILL.

NOTICE.

The absorbing interest centering in the lives, the work, and heroic death of the five martyrs to liberty makes a further review of them not only desirable, but necessary. With this end in view, the posthumous papers of Albert R. Parsons will soon be published in book form at a low price. This book will contain the autobiography of the American anarchist; an account of his numerous missionary journeyings, with letters to his wife and friends while engaged in spreading socialistic truths among the miners of Ohio and Pennsylvania, the farmers and townsmen of the west, and the workmen of the cities; extracts from his published articles; reminiscences and anecdotes, and a faithful and graphic account of his escape from Chicago on the night of May 4, 1886, his wanderings, his life in Waukesha, and his adventurous return to Chicago for trial with his fellow-comrades. The whole will make a book of no common interest, and will be read by thousands whose hearts beat in sympathy with the cause of Universal Progress.

www.ingramcontent.com/pod-product-compliance
Lightning Source LLC
Chambersburg PA
CBHW080437110426
42743CB00016B/3197